T0213533

Introduction to Software Design with Java

Martin P. Robillard

Introduction to Software Design with Java

Second Edition

 Springer

Martin P. Robillard
School of Computer Science
McGill University
Montreal, QC, Canada

ISBN 978-3-030-97898-3   ISBN 978-3-030-97899-0   (eBook)
https://doi.org/10.1007/978-3-030-97899-0

Cover Photograph: © 2017 Circlecreativestudio/iStock

This Springer imprint is published by the registered company Springer Nature Switzerland AG
The registered company address is: Gewerbestrasse 11, 6330 Cham, Switzerland

Preface

This book is inspired by well over a decade of teaching software design at McGill University. At first, my focus was to explain the software design know-how available from high-quality references. Soon, however, I realized that the main challenge of teaching software design lay elsewhere. Communicating *how* to apply a design technique or use a programming language mechanism was relatively easy. The real struggle was to convey in which *context* we want to use a certain design technique, and *why*. To do this, I needed to explain what is going on in a software developer's head. Over time, my lectures came to be more about exploring the space of alternative design decisions one can make in a given context.

The goal of this book is to help readers learn software design by discovering the *experience* of the design process. I share my knowledge and experience of software design through a narrative that introduces each element of design know-how in context, and explores alternative solutions in that context. The narrative is supported by hundreds of code fragments and design diagrams.

My hope is that this book can serve as an effective resource and guide for learning software design. However, I do not believe that it is possible to develop significant design skills solely by reading a book. In my own learning process, I have benefited hugely from reading other people's code, regularly writing code, and relentlessly refactoring existing code to experiment with alternative design solutions. For this reason, this book emphasizes coding and experimentation as a necessary complement to reading the text. To support this aspect of the learning process, I provide a companion website with practice problems, and two sample applications that capture numerous design decisions. An orientation through these sample applications is provided in *Code Exploration* insets throughout the chapters.

As its title indicates, this book provides an introduction to software design using the Java programming language. The code used throughout the book, as well as the sample applications, are in Java (version 8). My use of the Java language, however, is a means to communicate design ideas, and not the topic of the book. I aimed to cover design concepts and techniques that are applicable in a host of technologies. Many concepts (such as encapsulation), will be relevant in any technology. Others (such as inheritance) will be paradigm-specific, but usable in multiple programming languages. For both general and paradigm-specific information, it should be possible to adapt the examples to other programming languages. In a few cases, the material needs to address a Java-specific mechanism with implications on design (for example, cloning). In such cases, I make sure to present the mechanism as one implementation of a more general idea.

This book is targeted at readers who have a minimum of programming experience and want to move from writing small programs and scripts to tackling the development of larger systems. This audience naturally includes students in university-level computer science and software engineering programs. However, I kept the prerequisites to specialized computing concepts to a minimum, so that the content is also accessible to programmers without a primary training in computing. In a similar vein, understanding the code fragments requires only a minimum knowledge of Java, such as would be taught in an introductory programming course. Information about Java that is crucial to understand the text is provided in an appendix, more advanced features are introduced and explained as necessary, and I make a minimum of references to specific elements of the language's class library. My hope is thus that the book can be useful to anyone who wants to write clean, well-designed software.

Organization of the Book

The first chapter is a general introduction to software design. The subsequent chapters provide a progressive coverage of design concepts and techniques presented as a continuous narrative anchored in specific design problems. In addition to the main content, the book includes different features to orient readers and help use the book as a launchpad for further exploration and learning.

- **Chapter Overview:** At the beginning of each chapter, a callout lists the concepts, principles, patterns, and antipatterns covered in the chapter.
- **Design Context:** Following the overview, a paragraph titled *Design Context* introduces the design contexts that are used as running examples in the chapter. It is thus not necessary to read all previous chapters to understand the code discussed in a given chapter.
- **Diagrams:** Each chapter includes numerous diagrams that illustrate design ideas. Although they are provided to illustrate the ideas in the text, the diagrams are also realistic illustrations of diagrams that can be used in practice as part of design discussions.
- **Code Fragments:** Each chapter includes many code fragments. The code generally follows the conventions presented in Appendix B, with occasional concessions made to make the code more compact. A complete version of the code fragments can be downloaded from the companion website (see below).
- **Insights:** In each chapter, the main numbered sections are followed by an unnumbered section titled *Insights*. This section forms an actionable summary of the key information and advice provided in the chapter. It is meant as a catalog of applicable design knowledge, and assumes the material in the chapter has been mostly assimilated. The insights are in bullet points to be easily perused.

- **Code Exploration:** At various points in the text, insets titled *Code Exploration* provide a discussion of software design in practice. To facilitate good flow and avoid getting lost in details, the design contexts discussed in the main chapters are kept as simple as possible. As a result, some interesting aspects of the software design experience do get lost in the simplification. The code exploration activity is the opportunity to consider how some of the topics presented in the chapter manifest themselves in reality. The *Code Exploration* insets points to specific parts of the code of the sample applications. In concert with reading the text of a *Code Exploration* inset, I recommend reviewing the code referenced and trying to understand it as much as possible. The sample applications are described in Appendix C. They include JetUML, the application used to create all the diagrams in the book.
- **Further Reading:** The *Further Reading* section provides pointers to references that complement the material presented in the chapter.
- **Companion Website** Additional resources for this book are available in the repository `https://github.com/prmr/DesignBook`. The material in the repository includes a complete and commented version of the code that appears in the chapter content, as well as practice exercises and their solutions.
- **Sample Applications** The two Java applications described in Appendix C were developed following many of the principles and techniques described in the book, and are provided as an accessible basis for additional study and exploration.

Acknowledgments

I am most grateful to Mathieu Nassif, who carried out a detailed technical review of the entire manuscript of the first edition, providing me with hundreds of corrections, suggestions, and interesting points for discussion. I warmly thank Jin Guo for reviewing most of the chapters and testing some of the material in her own teaching, and Alexa Hernandez, Kaylee Kutschera, Brigitte Pientka, and Clark Verbrugge for feedback on various parts of the manuscript. I am also thankful to Ralf Gerstner, the executive editor in charge of computer science at Springer, for believing in the project from the start and for seeing it through with his usual diligence and professionalism.

As this is the second edition, I am also very grateful to my readers and to the instructors who have adopted the book to support their teaching. The enthusiasm many have expressed has been a major source of motivation for me to continue this project. The feedback I received, and the numerous interesting discussions I had about the content, were an invaluable contribution to this revised text.

Martin P. Robillard
April 2019
December 2021

Contents

Chapter 1
Introduction

In 1988, a fascinating little piece of code hits the limelight. That year, one of the winners of the annual International Obfuscated C Code Contest features a program that writes out to the terminal console the text of an eighteenth-century poem titled *The Twelve Days of Christmas*. Figure 1.1 shows the first three verses of the text, as they appear on the output console when executing the code. This poem is particular in that its text has a regular structure. Text with such a structure is amenable to being constructed by software in a way that goes beyond printing hard-coded data. With a poem like *The Twelve Days of Christmas*, there was thus opportunity for creating a clear and compact solution for displaying a poem on the console. However, as promised by the name of the contest where it was featured, the program is anything but clear. If fact, its inner workings are unfathomable. Figure 1.2 reproduces the complete code of the program.

```
On the first day of Christmas my true love gave to me
a partridge in a pear tree.

On the second day of Christmas my true love gave to me
two turtle doves
and a partridge in a pear tree.

On the third day of Christmas my true love gave to me
three French hens, two turtle doves
and a partridge in a pear tree.
...
```

Fig. 1.1 Partial output of *The Twelve Days of Christmas* program of Figure 1.2

This quirky piece of computer science trivia illustrates the impact of a lack of self-evident structure in software. Here, we have a programming problem with trivial requirements: the functionality of interest requires no input and produces a sin-

© Springer Nature Switzerland AG 2022
M. P. Robillard, *Introduction to Software Design with Java*,
https://doi.org/10.1007/978-3-030-97899-0_1

```
main(t,_,a ) char* a;{return!0<t?t<3?main(-79,-13,a+main(-87,
1-_,main(-86, 0,a+1 )+a)):1,t<_?main( t+1, _, a ):3,main(-94,
-27+t, a )&&t == 2 ?_<13 ? main ( 2, _+1,"%s %d %d\n" ):9:16:
t<0?t<-72?main( _, t,"@n'+,#'/*{}w+/w#cdnr/+,{}r/*de}+,/*{*+\
,/w{%+,/w#q#n+,/#{l,+,/n{n+,/+#n+,/#;#q#n+,/+k#;*+,/'r :'d*'\
3,}}{w+K w'K:'+}e#';dq#'l q#'+d'K#!/+k#;q#'r}eKK#}w'r}eKK{nl]\
'/#;#q#n'){)#}w'){){nl]'/+#n';d}rw' i;# ){nl]!/n{n#'; r{#w'r\
 nc{nl]'/#{l,+'K {rw' iK{;[[nl]'/w#q#n'wk nw' iwk{KK{nl]!/w{\
%'l##w#' i; :{nl]'/*{q#'ld;r'}{nlwb!/*de}'c ;;{nl'-{}rw]'/+,\
}##'*}#nc,',#nw]'/+kd'+e}+;#'rdq#w! nr'/ ') }+}{rl#'{n' ')# \
}'+}##(!!/"):t<-50?_==*a?putchar(31[a]):main(-65,_,a+1):main
((*a == '/')+t, _,a+1):0<t?main ( 2, 2 , "%s"):*a=='/'||main
(0,main(-61,*a,"!ek;dc i@bK'(q)-[w]*%n+r3#l,{}:\nuwloca-O;m\
 .vpbks,fxntdCeghiry"),a+1);}
```

Fig. 1.2 Source code of the 1988 *The Twelve Days of Christmas* C program by Ian Phillips. This code compiles and executing it will produce the output illustrated in Figure 1.1. © 1988, Landon Curt Noll and Larry Bassel. Reproduced with permission.

gle, unchangeable output. Yet, the code to support this functionality cannot be understood by a normal human being. But what is the problem, if the code works?

Software needs to change, and for software to change, at least one person must be involved at some point. Software needs to change for a variety of reasons, from fixing bugs to adapting the code to an evolving world. For example, many of the gifts referred to in the poem are European birds (e.g., partridge, turtle doves, French hens). Contemporary software development best practices include the *localization* of software applications, namely, the option to tailor a software application to account for region-specific characteristics. It would thus be nice to adapt the code of the application to replace the name of European birds to some that readers could relate to based on their own region (for example, to replace *partridge* with *turkey* for North American users). To modify a piece of code, however, one must understand its structure, and this structure must, to a certain extent, accommodate the change. In the case of *The Twelve Days of Christmas*, any ambition to ever change the code is hopeless.

The example of *The Twelve Days of Christmas* is facetious for sake of illustration. Because this code was obfuscated on purpose, it would be comforting if we could discount it as irrelevant. Unfortunately, because writing messy code is often the path of least resistance in the complex social, technological, and economic reality of software development, badly designed code is not hard to find. For example, in a famous high-profile case where automotive software was determined by the courts to be responsible for a fatal accident, the experts who reviewed the software likened its structure to that of a bowl of spaghetti. Whether code is cryptic purposefully or accidentally, the result is similar: it is hard to understand and change without introducing errors.

To explore the contrast, let us design a version of the program where the structure is evident. Consistently with the rest of the code in this book, the program is in Java. First, we can tackle the issue of producing the first line of a verse:

```java
static String[] DAYS = {"first", "second", ..., "twelfth"};

static String firstLine(int day) {
  return "On the " + DAYS[day] +
    " day of Christmas my true love gave to me:\n";
}
```

This code is clear because the function is short, it abstracts an obvious concept (the creation of the first line), and the only parameterization involved maps directly to the problem domain (changing the day).

The second sub-problem is to create the list of gifts for a given day. In this case we can leverage the inherent recursion in the poem's structure to organize the code in a function that creates a list of gifts by adding the last gift to a smaller list of gifts:

```java
static String[] GIFTS = { "a partridge in a pear tree",
                          "two turtle doves", ... };

static String allGifts(int day) {
  if( day == 0 ) {
    return "and " + GIFTS[0];
  }
  else {
    return GIFTS[day] + "\n" + allGifts(day-1);
  }
}
```

The allGifts function provides a classic implementation of a recursive algorithm. In this case, the code's structure is explicit because it trivially realizes a foundational strategy in computing.

At this point the only thing left it to put the poem together by assembling the twelve verses. Here the only small issue is that in the first verse, we do not add the conjunction *and* in front of *a partridge*. No matter how small a program, it can be difficult to completely avoid annoying corner cases.

```java
static String poem() {
  String poem = firstLine(0) + GIFTS[0] + "\n\n";
  for( int day = 1; day < 12; day++ ) {
    poem += firstLine(day) + allGifts(day) + "\n\n";
  }
  return poem;
}
```

At a glance, we see the overall structure of the code: a special case for the first verse, then an iteration through the remaining eleven verses, where each verse is created by concatenating the output of two functions: one to create the first line, and the other to create the list of gifts.

1.1 Defining Software Design

Software design is a mysterious activity. For many software development projects, if you ask for "the design" for the software system, you may get a blank look. The "design" is not necessarily something you can retrieve and look at. Similarly, very few people walk around with the title of "software designer". In that sense, designing software is not like designing furniture or clothing.

There are many definitions of software design, each with a different focus. The word *design* is also both a verb and a noun, which adds to the ambiguity because it can thus refer to both a process (*to design*) and the outcome of this process (*a design*). My working definition of software design (the process) is *the construction of abstractions of data and computation and the organization of these abstractions into a working software application*. At first this may sound overly restrictive, but when we consider everything that the term *abstraction* can mean (variables, classes, objects, etc.), we see that we are afforded quite a bit of flexibility for interpreting what software design means.

In practice, the design process is essentially one of decision making. *Should we use a list or a stack? What services should this interface offer? Where should this error be handled?* Considering design as decision making leads to the concept of a *design space*. A design space can be imagined as an n-dimensional geometric space where each dimension corresponds to a design quality attribute. Typical design quality attributes for software include understandability, reusability, and ease of implementation. Within such a design space, each specific design decision (or coherent set of decisions) corresponds to a coordinate in the space that represents the consequence of the decision. Figure 1.3 illustrates the idea with two dimensions. In practice, any design decision is likely to be good in some dimension, but less good in other dimensions, something we call a *design trade-off*.

Two sub-spaces of the design space that are useful to consider are the space of *possible solutions*, and the space of *acceptable solutions*. We can observe that the theoretically optimal solution, which best satisfies all dimensions at the same time, is unlikely to be possible. Design is a decision process for which there is rarely a single "right answer", only solutions that are better or worse in some dimensions (including some solutions that are pretty bad in most dimensions).

The concept of a design space may make it look like selecting a design decision is a systematic, almost mathematical process. This is not the case. Where the analogy breaks down is that a geometric space is completely defined, whereas the reality of software design is rife with uncertainty. First, not all possible decisions are known and, in complex situations, there may be an infinity of them. Second, estimating to what extent a design decision fulfills a given quality attribute (e.g., understandability) is a very approximate process. Consequently, there is no standard formula for arriving at a point in the design space. In most realistic software development contexts, it will not be the case that to design and implement a software requirement, we can follow a pre-determined set of steps. Software design is a highly *heuristic* process: it consists of iterative problem-solving guided by experience, general principles, and design techniques. In fact, the heuristic nature of the software design process is what makes it an exciting creative activity.

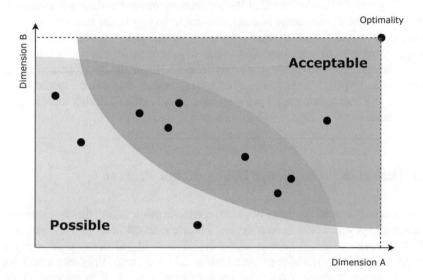

Fig. 1.3 A hypothetical design space

The quality attributes that constitute the dimensions of the design space also correspond to the general goals of design. One of the most important goals for software design is to reduce the complexity of software, which means making it easier to understand. Cleanly-designed code that is easy to understand is less error-prone and also easier to modify. Messy code obscures the important decisions of its original developers. When developers ignore existing design constraints, they risk modifying code in a way that does not agree with the original structure, and thereby introduce errors and generally degrade the quality of the code. The problem of modifying code in a way that does not respect the original structure has been called *ignorant surgery* (see Further Reading).

In general, the relative importance of design goals depends on the context in which a piece of software is being designed. A *design context* is a specific set of requirements and constraints within a domain in which a design solution must be found and integrated. For example, because of economic or contractual reasons, it may be required to design a particular piece of software to maximize its reusability. Or, if a piece of code is intended to be integrated into safety-critical applications, it may be more important to prioritize robustness (i.e., resilience to errors). In this book, I give a lot of importance to the *understandability* quality attribute. I try to emphasize designs where the code itself reveals the underlying design decisions and the *intent* behind these design decisions. The idea of having design decisions be self-evident in code is a property I call *sustainability*.

If we consider that the design process is a series of decisions-making activities about software abstractions, then it follows that a good definition for *a design* or *the design* is the collection of these decisions. This definition for a design artifact is sufficiently general to avoid dictating the medium in which the design is captured. In formal software development settings, this could be an official standardized design document. In less formal contexts, design decisions could be stored in the code, diagrams, or various documentation pages associated with the project. In the extreme, design decisions could exist only in the head of the developers who made them. Because people tend to forget or misremember, this latter approach is best kept to a minimum. Section 1.3 provides an overview of how design knowledge can be captured.

1.2 Design in the Software Development Process

Design is only one of the many activities that take place during the development of a software system. There is an abundant literature on different process models for software development. A *process model* describes (and sometimes prescribes) how the different steps required to create a system are organized. Different process models offer different ways of doing things for different reasons. In the early days of the software engineering discipline it was believed that a *planning-heavy* process, exemplified by the waterfall software process model, was the desirable way to build high-quality software. However, in the mid-1990s this belief was challenged by a movement towards a more organic approach to software development, also called *agile development*. In practice, ideas about how to best develop software keep evolving, and in the end the important things are to have a development process in the first place, and for that process to be well-adapted to the type of system being developed and the organization that develops it. For example, the process used by an organization to develop a prototype for a video game would probably be different from the process used to develop banking or aeronautical software.

The issue of devising, adapting, or even following a software development process is not the main focus of this book. However, even when beginning to learn about software design, it is useful to have a general idea of software development processes, if only to stay oriented in the wide and buzzword-laden realm of technology.

One concept of the software development process literature that is related to software design is the idea of a software development *practice*. A practice is a well-understood way of doing something to achieve a certain benefit. An example of a practice many programmers are familiar with is *version control* (the use of software tools to keep track of changes to software development artifacts). Another example of software development practice is *pair programming* (writing code as a team of two in front of a single computer). In this book I refer to a number of software development practices that directly support good design, including the use of *coding conventions* (see Appendix B) and *refactoring* (see below).

Another concept of software development processes that is relevant to software design is that of the *iteration*. As discussed in Section 1.1, when searching for a design solution, it is common practice to iterate over various alternatives. However, iterations also take place at a more macroscopic level in software development, in the sense that the design of the system may be periodically extended, reviewed, and/or improved. In some cases, the design can even be improved without any change to the observable behavior of the system. Improving the design of code without changing its functionality is the software development practice known as *refactoring*. There are various reasons why refactoring can become necessary or desirable. One reason is that the original developer did not really get it right, and after working with the code for a while it becomes apparent that a different design would be better. Another reason is that we might want to add modules and features that do not integrate well with the existing design, so we first refactor the design to prepare it so that it better supports the later addition of new code. A third reason is to reduce accumulated design weaknesses. As part of maintaining the code (e.g., to fix bugs), developers occasionally implement quick and dirty solutions that do not align properly with the existing design. This phenomenon is known as accumulating *technical debt*. By not investing the effort necessary to code a clean solution, the team effectively borrows development effort from the future. If allowed to accumulate, too much technical debt can threaten the viability of the project, just like the risk of bankruptcy incurred by excessive borrowing in the financial sense. When technical debt is incurred in a project, refactoring is a way to pay it back, and good software development teams will periodically refactor their code. Thus, software design is in continual evolution.

1.3 Capturing Design Knowledge

A design (or design solution) is a collection of decisions, each of which is the result of a search process through a design space for a particular design problem, or context. This definition naturally leads to the question of what a design decision looks like. Informally, we could say that a design decision is a statement about how to do a particular thing, ideally coupled with the reason for this statement. An example would be: *We will store the appointments in a linked list because we will mostly be performing additions to the list.* For this decision to even exist, it has to be in at least one developer's brain at some point. We thus have a first medium for storing design decisions: a person's brain. For small projects, this could be sufficient. However, given the ephemerality of human memory, it can often be worthwhile to record important design decisions externally. This opens up the question of how to capture design knowledge. This fundamental question has been the subject of debate and academic and industry research for decades. Entire books have been written on the topic. Given that the present book is not one of them, the following is a concise summary of the options for externalizing design knowledge:

- **Source code:** Many design decisions can be captured directly in the source code. The example above, of selecting a linked list as a data structure, would be one case. The advantage of source code is that it is a formal language whose rules are checked by the compiler. Unfortunately, source code is not a good substrate for capturing the *rationale* of design decisions. For this purpose, code comments can be of some assistance.
- **Design documents:** Design decisions can be captured in documents specifically aimed at capturing such design decisions. There exists a wide variety of formats for documents about software, from standardized design documents to blog posts. Design documents may also include diagrams, which are another way to represent design decisions.
- **Email, discussion platforms, and version control systems:** Design information can be captured in email and comments stored in software development tools, such as issue management systems and version control systems.
- **Specialized models:** In certain software development projects, developers use formal models to specify many aspects of the software. These models can then be automatically converted into code in a programming language. Such an approach is called *generative programming* or *model-driven development* (MDD). In model-driven development, the models serve as design documents. As a software construction approach, model-driven design and development is outside the scope of this book.

Because the level of design abstraction covered by this book remains close to the source code, many of the design decisions discussed will be at least partly reflected in the code. Subsequent chapters will also contain many diagrams and accompanying text that document design decisions.

The Unified Modeling Language

There will often be situations where we need to discuss design problems and solutions that are cumbersome, inconvenient, or too complex to describe using either source code or natural language. For this purpose we can use a specialized *modeling language*. This situation is not limited to software. For example, describing instrumental music in plain language is near-impossible: instead, we use musical notation.

Historically, many different modeling languages and notations have been developed for representing, at an abstract level, various aspects of a software system. This disparity was, however, an obstacle to adoption because of the overhead involved in interpreting models expressed in an unfamiliar notation. Thankfully, in the mid-1990s the main software modeling notations were merged into a single one, the Unified Modeling Language (UML), which was subsequently adopted as a standard by the International Organization for Standardization (ISO).

The UML is a modeling language organized in terms of different types of diagrams intended to illustrate different aspects of software. Examples of design information than can be neatly captured in the UML include relationships between classes (e.g., A inherits from B), changes in the state of an object (e.g., the list object goes from *Empty* to *Non-Empty* when the first element is added), and sequences of calls dispatched on objects (e.g., a.m1() results in a call to b.m2()).

Not all development teams use the UML. However, those who do use it in different ways for different reasons. For example, UML can be used to produce formal design documentation in waterfall-type development processes. Others use the UML to describe enough of the software to be able to automatically generate the code from the models, following the idea of generative programming. In this book, I use the UML simply for *sketching* design ideas. The diagrams included in this book are not expected to be automatically transformable into code. I also use the smallest subset of the modeling language necessary, and introduce the notation progressively.

An important thing to remember about UML diagrams is that they are *models*. This means that they are not intended to capture every single detail of a solution. Ideally, a UML diagram will focus on illustrating a *single main idea* and only include the relevant information. In UML diagramming it is a common practice to leave out the parts of a system and details that are not directly relevant to the point being illustrated.

1.4 Sharing Design Know-How

Capturing knowledge about the design of a particular system is one thing, but how do we capture general know-how about the design process? Software design is influenced by the skills and experience of the designer, and this type of heuristic knowledge is not easy to synthesize and package for dissemination. In earlier days, organized approaches to disseminate design know-how centered around comprehensive *design methods*, which prescribed a sequence of steps and the use of specialized charts and other instruments. Such approaches peaked in the 1980s, and were replaced with adaptations suited to object-oriented programming, a paradigm that was then quickly gaining adoption. Comprehensive object-oriented design methods themselves peaked in the mid-1990s. At that time, it was being observed that some elements of design solutions tended to recur between many object-oriented applications.

Design Patterns

The idea of reusing elements of object-oriented design was captured in the concept of a *design pattern* in the book *Design Patterns: Elements of Reusable Object-Oriented Software* [6]. This book, often referred to as the *Gang of Four* book from the author list, is one of the most influential software design books in existence. Following the concept of an architectural pattern originally proposed by an architect named Christopher Alexander, the book describes 23 patterns for addressing common software design problems. Since then, countless other patterns have been

documented. The idea to capture abstract design solutions that address specific problems was a breakthrough for software engineering, because it provided a practical
way to convey design know-how and experience without the requirement to adopt
a comprehensive design method. To this day, design patterns and close variants of
the concept have been a dominant way to capture design know-how. There currently
exist countless design catalogs for different programming languages, in the form of
books and websites.

According to the Gang of Four, a pattern has four essential elements:

> The *pattern name* is a handle we can use to describe a design problem, its solutions, and
> consequences in a word or two. Naming a pattern immediately increases our design vocab-
> ulary. It lets us design at a higher level of abstraction. Having a vocabulary for patterns lets
> us talk about them with our colleagues, in our documentation, and to ourselves...
>   The *problem* describes when to apply the pattern. It explains the problem and its con-
> text...
>   The *solution* describes the elements that make up the design, their relationships, respon-
> sibilities, and collaborations. The solution doesn't describe a particular concrete design or
> implementation, because a pattern is like a template...
>   The *consequences* are the results and trade-offs of applying the pattern... [6]

In this book, I present a subset of the original patterns by integrating them in the
flow of the material when they become relevant. I do not reproduce the structured
description that can be found in other pattern catalogs. I instead use a lightweight
description for a pattern that focuses on the link between the problem and solution,
and I include a discussion of important design decisions related to the pattern. I also
prefer to refer to the problem as the *context* for applying a pattern, because design
problems can sometimes be difficult to isolate. Finally, I will sometimes express
the solution embodied by a pattern as a UML diagram that captures the name of
the *abstract elements* of the pattern. Because these elements are abstract, I prefer
to refer to them as a *solution template* rather than a solution. A typical task when
attempting to apply a design pattern in a context is to map the abstract elements of
the solution template to concrete design elements in the code. In the text, the name
of design patterns are set in SMALL CAPS FONT. This is to indicate that a term refers to
a well-defined design concept, as opposed to a general use of the term. For example,
one design pattern is called the *Strategy* pattern. Instead of continuously referring
to it as the *Strategy design pattern*, I will refer to it as the STRATEGY, which will
distinguish it from the concept of a *strategy* as a general problem-solving approach.

Because solution templates for design patterns can be looked up in any number
of resources, the most important skill to develop with respect to design patterns is
to know where to apply them. For this reason, my coverage of design patterns emphasizes the rationale for using a pattern and a discussion of its strengths and weaknesses in different contexts, and de-emphasizes the focus on solution templates. One
potential pitfall when first learning about design patterns is to get over-enthusiastic
and try to apply them everywhere. Like all other elements of design solutions, a particular instance of a design pattern will occupy a specific point in the design space,
with attendant benefits and drawbacks. If I can make one generalization about the
use of design patterns, it is that employing one tends to make an overall design
more flexible. Sometimes, this flexibility is exactly what we need. At other times, it

is overkill and leads to unnecessary structures and clutter in the code. In other words, using a particular design pattern in a particular way in a given context is a design decision which, like most other design decisions, should be critically assessed.

Design Antipatterns

An interesting take on the idea of a design pattern is that of a design *antipattern*. Just as it can be observed that some design solution elements recur between applications, it is also the case that recognizable flaws can be abstracted from many similar cases and catalogued. This influential idea took hold around the turn of the millennium in a popular book on refactoring, which documents 22 antipatterns as motivation to refactor the corresponding code [5]. Typical antipatterns include problems such as DUPLICATED CODE†, LONG METHOD†, and others that will be covered in this book. For reasons similar to design patterns, antipatterns are set in SMALL CAPS†, but are followed by a dagger symbol to distinguish them from actual patterns. Design antipatterns are also known as *code smells*, or *bad smells* (in code), to convey the idea of a symptom that something is not quite right.

Insights

This chapter introduced software design and placed it in the general context of software development projects.

- The verb *to design* refers to the process we follow when we design software, and the noun *a design* refers to the outcome of this process;
- The process of software design is the construction of abstractions of data and computation and the organization of these abstractions into a working software application;
- There is rarely a single right answer to a design problem, only solutions that are better or worse in some dimensions;
- A design artifact is an external representation of one or more design decisions;
- Design is only one of many activities that take place during the development of a software system. Software development follows a process that can vary from organization to organization, and vary from planning-heavy to agile. Development processes typically involve iterations;
- A software development practice is a well-understood way of doing something to achieve a certain benefit. Examples include version control, coding conventions, and refactoring;
- Design knowledge can be captured in source code, code comments, specialized documents, discussion forums, and models;
- The Unified Modeling Language, or UML, is a modeling language organized in terms of different types of diagrams. Using UML can be an effective way to illustrate different aspects of software without getting caught up in details;

- A design pattern captures an abstract design solution that is applicable in a common design context. The description of a design pattern includes a name, a description of the design problem or context it addresses, a solution template, and a discussion of the consequences of applying the pattern;
- A design antipattern is an abstract description of a common design flaw.

Further Reading

The paper *Software Aging* by David L. Parnas [12] introduces the term *ignorant surgery* and provides a compelling motivation for the benefits of maintaining good design in software. Parnas is one of the early contributors to the software engineering discipline. Chapter 1 of the book *Clean Code: A Handbook of Agile Software Craftmanship* by Robert C. Martin [7] discusses the various ills of bad or "messy" code. My short paper titled *Sustainable Software Design* discusses in more detail what it means for design decisions to be self-evident [14].

Chapter 1 of the book *UML Distilled, 3rd Edition* by Martin Fowler [5] provides a more comprehensive introduction to the UML. Fowler distinguishes between three modes for using the UML: as sketches for design, as a blueprint for creating an application, and as source code that can be executed. Sketching is the mode employed in this book.

The original book on design patterns is *Design Patterns: Elements of Reusable Object-Oriented Software* by Erich Gamma, Richard Helm, Ralph Johnson, and John Vlissides [6]. This book is often referred to as the *Gang of Four* book. Because it predates the UML, the notation it uses for capturing software designs may feel a bit foreign. Nevertheless, it is a timeless reference work.

The book *Refactoring: Improving the Design of Existing Code*, also by Martin Fowler [3] is the main reference on the practice of refactoring. It introduces the idea of design antipatterns (which are called *code smells* in the book). Robert C. Martin also includes a list of bad smells in Chapter 17 of *Clean Code*, cited above.

Chapter 2
Encapsulation

Concepts and Principles: Abstraction, assertion, class, design by contract, encapsulation, immutability, information hiding, input validation, interface, object diagram, scope.
Patterns and Antipatterns: INAPPROPRIATE INTIMACY†, PRIMITIVE OBSESSION†.

An essential technique in software design is to decompose a system into distinct, manageable abstractions. However, there is little value in decomposing a piece of software into several parts if each part depends on all the other parts in a tangled mess of interactions. For a decomposition to be useful, the resulting abstractions have to be well isolated from each other. For good design, an idea that should be inseparable from that of software abstraction is *encapsulation*.

Design Context

We start our exploration of software design by considering how to effectively represent a deck of playing cards in code. This representation would be necessary for most computer card games, for example the Solitaire game used as a sample application. In the common card deck used as a running example, there are 52 distinct cards and any given card can be completely defined by its *suit* (Hearts ♡, Spades ♠, Diamonds ◇, Clubs ♣) and its *rank* (Ace, 2, 3, ..., 10, Jack, Queen, King). A software structure to represent a deck of cards should therefore be able to represent any sequence of any number of distinct cards between 0 and 52. The two main operations required of a deck of cards is to *shuffle* it and to *draw* cards from it. Shuffling randomly reorders the cards in the deck. In the domain of card games, *drawing* a card means to remove a card from the deck (typically from the top). This opera-

© Springer Nature Switzerland AG 2022
M. P. Robillard, *Introduction to Software Design with Java*,
https://doi.org/10.1007/978-3-030-97899-0_2

tion is not to be confused with the action of depicting the card on a user interface component.

2.1 Encapsulation and Information Hiding

The idea of *encapsulation* is to enclose something as if it were in a capsule. For example, we can think of a nut, which is encapsulated in its shell. The shell, or capsule, serves as protection. In software design we encapsulate both data and computation to limit the number of contact points between different parts of the code. Encapsulation has several benefits: it makes it easier to understand a piece of code in isolation, it makes the use of the isolated part by the rest of the code less error-prone, and it makes it easier to change one part of the code without breaking anything. In software design, the equivalent of a shell is the general concept of an *interface*.

Encapsulation is related to the principle of *information hiding*, which has been around since the early 1970s. Following the principle of information hiding, encapsulated structures should only reveal the minimum amount of information that is necessary to use them, and hide the rest. A typical example of information hiding is an implementation of a stack abstract data type (ADT) whose interface only provides `push` and `pop` operations. This minimal interface allows *client code* to make use of the stack structure, but decisions on how to store elements in the stack remain hidden from the code that uses the stack. I use the term *client code* to refer to any code that refers to a code element that is not part of the definition of this element. The term *code* in *client code* is especially important, because here *client* does not refer to a customer or user of a software project. Which part of the code qualifies as *client code* will depend on the situation at hand. In many cases, the details of the client code will not really matter in the discussion of the design ideas I present.

Although encapsulation and information hiding are very general principles for software design, there exist specific techniques that we can use to help ensure our code respects these principles. The rest of this chapter presents some of these techniques.

2.2 Encoding Abstractions as Types

As our first design task, we define the abstractions that are necessary to represent a deck of cards. An *abstraction* is a conceptual building block for a software system. Examples of common abstractions in computing include data structures (for example, stack, list) and operations (sorting, iterating). However, abstractions can also refer to ideas in the problem domain, such as *playing card*. With the term *defining an abstraction*, I mean deciding what the abstraction represents, and what it will look like in terms of source code. In the case of a deck of cards, the first part of the process is straightforward, because the concepts we need to represent in code (a playing card, a deck of cards) are well-defined in the real world. This will not always be the case.

Essentially, a deck of cards is an ordered collection of playing cards. We could use any standard data structure to represent this collection (an array, a list, etc.). However, what would such a collection hold? What is a card? In the code, we can represent a playing card in many different ways. For example, we could use an integer between 0 and 51 where the value represents a certain card according to a convention. For example, Clubs could have numbers 0–12 in increasing rank, Hearts 13–25, etc.:

```
int card = 13;        // 13 = The Ace of Hearts
int suit = card / 13  // 1 = Hearts
int rank = card % 13; // 0 = Ace
```

This approach would also require us to have similar conventions to represent suits and ranks, as illustrated on the second and third lines.[1] To avoid having to continually divide and multiply numbers that represent cards to switch between suits, we could also represent a card as a pair of values, the first one encoding the suit, and the second one encoding the rank (or vice-versa):

```
int[] card = {1,0}; // The Ace of Hearts
```

While we are at it, we could even decide to represent a card using a combination of six Boolean values. Although extremely inconvenient, this design decision is technically possible to implement: it is an example of a decision that is possible, but not acceptable (see Section 1.1). As it turns out, all three options above have major drawbacks.

First, *the representation of a card does not map to the corresponding domain concept*. To facilitate code understanding and help avoid programming errors, the representation of values should ideally be tied to the concept they represent. For example, the general type int maps to the concept of an integer (a type of number), not that of a playing card. We could define a variable of type int intended to store a playing card, and unwittingly put a value that represents a different entity in it (e.g., the number of cards in the deck). This will not be noticed as an error by the compiler, yet it is likely to lead to intense confusion when executing the code.

Second, *the representation of a card is coupled to its implementation*. If our design decision is that cards should be represented as integers, any location in the code that must store a value that represents a card will refer to an integer. Changing this encoding to something else (for example, the two-element array discussed above) will require discovering and changing every single location where an int variable is used to store a card, and all the code that works with cards as integers.

Third, *it is easy to corrupt a variable that stores a value that represents a card*. In Java a variable of type int can take 2^{32} distinct values. To represent a playing card we only need a tiny subset of these (52 values). Consequently, the overwhelming majority of values we can store in an int variable ($2^{32} - 52$) intended to represent a playing card does not represent any valid information. This opens the door to errors.

---

[1] The modulo operator (%) returns the remainder of the integer division.

The problem would have been even worse had we decided to use a two-element array of type int, which supports $2^{64} + 1$ values.[2]

We can do better. It is generally a bad idea to try to shoehorn domain concepts into basic general types like int, String, and so on. Ideally, these types should only be used to hold values that are proper values of the type. For instance, the int type should only be used to hold actual integers (and perhaps very similar concepts, such as currency). Similarly, Strings should be used only to hold sequences of characters meant to represent text or text-like information, as opposed to being some encoding of some other concept (e.g., "AceOfClubs"). The tendency to use primitive types to represent other abstractions is a common problem in software design that has been captured by the antipattern PRIMITIVE OBSESSION†.

To apply the principle of information hiding, we instead organize our code to *hide* the decision of how exactly we represent a card. We hide this decision behind an interface specifically tied with the concept of a card. In programming languages with a strong support for types, such as Java, this is typically accomplished through the use of types. In our case, to properly represent a card in code, we define our own type Card as a Java class:

```
class Card {}
```

As we will see below, the use of a specific type to represent a card will allow us to hide the decision of how we represent a card internally. However, although we now have a class Card, we still need to decide how to represent a card within the class. All options are back on the table. We could do simply:

```
class Card {
  int aCard; // 0-51 encodes the card
}
```

This class defines a single instance variable aCard of type int. The name of the instance variable includes the prefix a as part of a coding convention detailed in Appendix B. Client code can refer to this variable through *dereference* (see Section A.2), for example:[3]

```
Card card = new Card();
card.aCard = 28;
```

Although using a class somewhat links the value a bit better to the domain concept of a card, the other problems are still present. First, it is still possible to corrupt the representation of a card. Second, the decision to represent this value as an int is not exactly hidden, given that client code would be accessing the variable directly through a dereference of the instance variable. Let us then tackle the issue of representing the card internally. The next section handles the issue of hiding this decision.

---

[2] The additional value comes from the fact that array-typed variables can also be null.

[3] Technically, this code only compiles if placed in a method declared in a class that is in the same package as class Card. This detail is not important here. Section 2.3 explains where class members can be accessed in the code.

Two key observations can help us arrive at a better way to encode a card. First, the value of a playing card is completely and exactly defined in terms of two sub-concepts: its suit (e.g., Clubs) and its rank (e.g., Ace). So, we can take the process of decomposition one step further, and define abstractions for ranks and suits. Following the same logic as above, primitive values are not a good match for encoding these abstractions, so we prefer to use a dedicated type. However, here the second important observation comes into play: the rank of a playing card can only be one of 13 distinct values, which are known in advance and can be enumerated. In the case of suits, the number of values is even smaller (four). The best tool at our disposal to encode such abstractions is the *enumerated type*:

```
enum Suit {
   CLUBS, DIAMONDS, SPADES, HEARTS
}
```

In Java, enumerated types are a special kind of class declaration. The identifiers listed in the declaration of the enumerated type are globally available constants (see Section A.3 in the appendix). These constants store a reference to an object of the class that corresponds to the enumerated value. For example,

```
Suit suit1 = Suit.CLUBS;
Suit suit2 = Suit.CLUBS;
boolean same = suit1 == suit2; // same == true
```

Enumerated types are a perfect fit in our situation. They meet all our design requirements, because variables of type Suit and Rank are directly tied to their corresponding concept of rank and suit, and variables of these types can only take values that are meaningful for the type.[4] Enumerated types are a simple yet effective feature for creating or implementing robust designs. They help avoid PRIMITIVE OBSESSION† and generally make the code clearer and less error-prone.

The code below completes our definition of class Card as a combination of a rank and a suit value. It assumes that each enumerated type is defined in its own file.

```
enum Suit {
   CLUBS, DIAMONDS, SPADES, HEARTS
}

enum Rank {
   ACE, TWO, ..., QUEEN, KING
}

class Card {
   Suit aSuit;
   Rank aRank;
}
```

Now that we have a reasonable type to represent a playing card in the code, we return to the issue of representing a deck of cards, and follow the same line of thinking. Because a deck is just a collection of cards, we could represent a deck of cards as a List of Cards:

---

[4] With the unfortunate exception of null. See Section 4.5.

```
List<Card> deck = new ArrayList<>();
```

However, the disadvantages of this approach are the same as the disadvantages of representing a playing card as an `int` value:

- A list of cards is not strongly tied to the concept of a deck. It could represent any list of cards, e.g., the cards in one of the piles created while playing Solitaire, the cards discarded as part of the game, etc.
- Using a list of cards ties the representation of a deck in the program with its implementation. If we decide later to replace the list by, say, an array, we would have to change all the corresponding source code locations.[5]
- The structure can easily be corrupted: a simple deck of cards can hold a maximum of 52 cards, without duplicates. A list allows one to put any number of cards in the structure, including duplicates.

A better way to approach the representation of a deck of cards in our code is to also define a proper type for it:

```
class Deck {
  List<Card> aCards = new ArrayList<>();
}
```

Although it may seem redundant to define a new class to hold just one instance of an `ArrayList`, this decision helps avoid many of the problems discussed above. The new type `Deck` specializes the list and ties it directly to its corresponding domain concept. It also becomes possible to hide the decision of how the cards are stored. The remainder of this chapter presents the details of how to achieve this hiding in practice.

Code Exploration: JetUML · Dimension

Avoiding PRIMITIVE OBSESSION† *with a small abstraction.*

This boxed paragraph, called a Code Exploration, is the first discussion of design decisions based on the code of the sample applications. The left part of the title is the name of the sample application, and the right part is the name of the class discussed. See Appendix C for instructions on how to access the relevant code easily.

At first glance, class `Dimension` looks exceedingly simple: a pair of integer values, one to represent a width, one to represent a height. Why bother, since these values can be accessed individually (using methods `width()` and `height()`)? Would it not be simpler to just use pairs of integers? Is this not excessive effort to avoid a case of PRIMITIVE OBSESSION†? The answers to these questions are not to be found in the definition of the class itself, but rather by looking at all the places in the code where `Dimension` is used. The rationale

---

[5] Disturbingly, replacing the list by a `Stack` on the right-hand side of the assignment in the listing would actually work because in Java `Stack` is a subtype of `List`. In Chapter 7, I explain why this is disturbing.

for encoding the concept of a *dimension* explicitly is threefold: to be able to return both related values as one object, to avoid the possibility of invalid dimensions (e.g., with negative values), and to prevent errors caused by flipping the width and the height. Of course, these have to be provided in the right order in a constructor call, but once a `Dimension` object is created, the risk of flipping the two values is eliminated.

Code Exploration: Solitaire · Card

A complete version of the `Card` class.

This chapter has used the creation of a deck of cards as a running example, so it is worth pointing out class `Card` in the Solitaire project. Some of the code in the class implements more advanced features that I will return to in Chapter 4, including the static members and the private constructor. Ignoring these, however, the basic structure of the class is identical to the one discussed in this section: two fields of enumerated types to represent the card's rank and suit, respectively, as well as two accessor methods to obtain these values from a `Card` object.

2.3 Scopes and Accessibility

Encoding abstractions as types is only the first step in the process of encapsulation. Once we have types we feel are good abstractions for our design, we need to ensure that these types are effective in hiding information from client code. At this point we have determined that four types are necessary to represent a deck of cards in code: `Deck`, `Card`, `Rank`, and `Suit`. Each of these types defines a set of possible values and a set of operations on these values. We now turn to the problem of specifying the values these types can take and the operations on these types so as to achieve good encapsulation of both the values and computation.

In Java and most other object-oriented languages, an *object* is a mechanism to group variables together and access their values through the process of dereferencing (see Section A.2 in the appendix). Without encapsulation, any variable that forms part of an object can be accessed indiscriminately. For example, given the following code:

```
class Deck {
  public List<Card> aCards = new ArrayList<>();
}

class Card {
  public Rank aRank = null;
  public Suit aSuit = null;
}
```

we could use our objects as follows:[6]

```
Deck deck = new Deck();
deck.aCards.add(new Card());
deck.aCards.add(new Card());
deck.aCards.get(1).aRank = deck.aCards.get(0).aRank;
System.out.println(deck.aCards.get(0).aSuit.toString());
```

Because of the complete lack of encapsulation, we can make unprincipled use of the internal implementation of our types. Without major effort, this kind of code almost invariably leads to bugs, simply because the number of ways to misuse the structures greatly exceeds the number of ways to use them properly. For example, although it may not be immediately apparent, the code above, when executed, raises a `NullPointerException`. With good encapsulation, it should be near-impossible to misuse one of our types.

The idea of encapsulation is to hide the internal implementation of an abstraction behind an interface that tightly controls how an abstraction can be used. Designing good abstractions and good interfaces for these abstractions are tandem tasks that underlie most of software design. Designing good interfaces can be tricky and requires a combination of different mechanisms and techniques. We start with one of the simplest, *access modifiers*. Access modifiers are Java keywords that control what parts of the code can *access* certain program elements (e.g., classes, fields, methods). The idea of restricting access to fields is very similar to that of visibility and *scope* for local variables. In most programming languages, a *scope* is a lexical region that acts as a sort of boundary for variables. In Java, scopes are defined using curly braces. The following code fragment:

```
public static void main(String[] args) {
  { int a = 0; }
  { int b = a; }
}
```

has a compilation error because in the second assignment, the reference to a cannot be resolved because, according to Java scoping rules, it is not visible in the second scope. In this tiny example, the scoping restriction may look like a limitation. However, it is actually a powerful feature. To understand what happens in the second statement, we only need to track down references to variables that are in scope (as opposed to every code location). We can do the same with classes.

---

[6] This code is not defined in any method because its exact location does not matter. For example, the code could be placed in a `main` method.

In Java, it is possible to control the visibility of classes and class members (and in particular fields) through the use of access modifiers. In this chapter, I only focus on the distinction between the `public` and `private` access modifiers.[7] Members marked `public` are visible anywhere in the code. In the example above, because the field `aCards` of class `Deck` is `public`, the variable `aCards` of any object of type `Deck` is visible from any code that has a reference to the object. In contrast, members marked `private` are only visible within the scope of the class, namely, between the left curly brace that begins the declaration of the class body and the last right curly brace of the class declaration.

A general principle for achieving good encapsulation is to use the narrowest possible scope for class members. Thus, instance variables should almost always be `private`. Also, `public` methods should reveal as little as possible about implementation decisions meant to be encapsulated. A revised design for class `Card` that respects this guideline is as follows:

```java
public class Card {

  private Rank aRank;
  private Suit aSuit;

  public Card(Rank pRank, Suit pSuit) {
    aRank = pRank;
    aSuit = pSuit;
  }

  public Rank getRank() {
    return aRank;
  }

  public Suit getSuit() {
    return aSuit;
  }
}
```

This class properly encapsulates the representation of a playing card because client code cannot interact in any way with the internal representation of a card. In fact, with this design it is possible to change the representation of the card to use a single field of type `int`, or an enumerated type (say, `PlayingCard`), without requiring *any* change to the client code.

As a mechanism for software design, access modifiers serve a dual purpose. First, they express the *intent* of the developer about where certain structures are meant to be used. Second, they support the automatic enforcement of the stated intent through compilation. In an ideal design, the intent of the developer should be clear, or at least not egregiously ambiguous. Access modifiers also help provide us with our first working definition of an type's interface in Java. In general, an interface to a class consists of the methods of that class that are accessible to another class. For

---

[7] The other two are `protected` and *default* (absence of a modifier). Members with default visibility are accessible by code in classes declared in the same package. The `protected` modifier is discussed in Chapter 7.

now, we will keep things simple and consider that the interface to a class is the set of its public methods. This is only a starting point, and we will be refining this definition of interface as we go along, and in particular in Section 3.1. For now, what is important is that the public methods of a type (a class) represent what client code can do with objects of the type, and the design of all other (non-public) fields and methods remains hidden from that client.

2.4 Object Diagrams

An object diagram is a type of UML diagram (see Section 1.3) that represents objects and how they refer to each other. Whenever a `new` statement is executed, an object of a class is created and a reference to this object is returned and can be passed around. It can often be useful to visually represent the resulting graph of objects and their inter-dependent references, especially when groups of objects are structured or organized in sophisticated ways, or when relations between objects are especially important.

I introduce a slight enhancement to official UML object diagrams, so as to provide a representation of an object's fields and values that resembles the kind of data-structure diagrams often used in introductory computer science classes. In an object diagram, a rectangle represents an object, with its name and type indicated as `name:type`. Both name and type information are optional, but in general it is useful to have at least one of the two. In UML diagrams in general, the name of objects (as opposed to classes) are underlined. Objects can contain *fields*, which are just like fields in a Java program. Fields can contain a value of a primitive type or a value of a reference type (see Section A.1 in the Appendix). When the value is a reference type, it is represented as a directed arrow to the object being referenced. Let us consider the diagram of Figure 2.1:

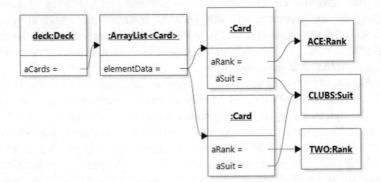

Fig. 2.1 Object diagram showing a detailed model of the object graph for a deck of cards

This diagram models an instance of the `Deck` class named `deck`. It would have been fine to omit this name and simply indicate `:Deck` in the rectangle, as in the case of `ArrayList<Card>`, which is anonymous. This `deck` has a field `aCards` whose current value is a reference to an `ArrayList<Card>` object. The `ArrayList<Card>` object's `elementData` field references two `Card` instances. Here, because `ArrayList` is a library type, it is necessary to have knowledge of the source code of the library to accurately model objects of this class. However, for a design sketch, using the actual name is not critical. To model internal properties of library types without looking up all their implementation details, it is often sufficient simply to make up evocative names. For example, the diagram would be just as informative if the field had been named `data` or `elements`.

Through modeling, we can skip over some details. In reality, in an instance of `ArrayList` the `elementData` field refers to an array of `Object`-typed cells that contain the actual data. This information is not useful here, and we link directly to the contained data. It is also worth noting how the list refers to two cards, and not three or four or 52. Another important point about object diagrams is that they represent a *snapshot* in the execution of a program. Here it was at the point where the list had two cards. For the purpose of communicating design information, including only two cards is sufficient to illustrate that a deck is a list of cards, so it would not be worth it to depict a snapshot of the program when the deck contains more cards. The two `Card` instances, however, are modeled in full detail. The values of enumerated types are distinguished by name, as they should be, and the enumerated value `Suit.CLUBS` is *shared* between two cards. I will cover reference sharing in more detail in Chapter 4.

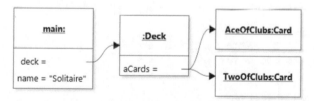

Fig. 2.2 Object diagram showing a simplified model of the object graph for a deck of cards

The second example diagram (Figure 2.2) illustrates some of the additional modeling simplifications we can do, when appropriate. First, I added an untyped object named `main`. This "object" is actually a trick for representing a method body. Object diagrams do not have an explicit notation to represent code statements that form the body of a method declaration. However, this can be achieved through untyped objects by observing that, from the point of view of the diagram, an object and a method body are simply collections of variables (instance variables in the first case, local variables in the second). A second difference is that the `Deck` object is now anonymous, and the name `deck` is used to represent the *variable* in which a reference to an object (any object) is stored, as opposed to a specific object. Third, the `main` method contains a `name` variable that stores a string. In Java, strings are technically instances of the reference type String. To be strictly accurate, we should represent a string value as a reference to an instance of class String that has a reference to an array of char values, each with one letter. That level of detail would be both superfluous and annoying, so we just show the string literal. A fourth important difference is that the ArrayList has been abstracted away. In this diagram, we see that a deck somehow keeps track of a number of cards, but how these are stored internally is not represented. The cards could be in an array, a list, whatever. Although in some cases (such as in the next section) the details may be important, it is often the case that details of internal data structures are superfluous. Finally, the value of the Card instances are represented artificially by using an evocative name for the objects, instead of modeling the field values. This does not mean that these Card instances do not have the aRank and aSuit fields, it just means this detail has been elided from the diagram.

2.5 Escaping References

The use of the visibility restrictions for fields using the private keyword provides a basic level of encapsulation, but it by no means ensures an iron-clad protection of internal structures. We explore this problem by returning to the issue of storing an aggregation of Card objects within an instance of a Deck object. Let us assume we decided to implement a Deck as a list of cards using Java's ArrayList type.[8]

```
public class Deck {

    private List<Card> aCards = new ArrayList<>();

    public Deck() {
      /* Add all 52 cards to the deck */
      /* Shuffle the cards */
    }

    public Card draw() {
      return aCards.remove(0);
    }
}
```

So far, the only way to use an instance of Deck from code outside the class is to *draw* a card from the deck: there are no other members (methods or fields) that could be referenced outside the class. The class is thus very well encapsulated, but also very limited it the services it can offer. Let us assume the client code needs to inspect the content of the deck. We could simply add a *getter* method to the class:

---

[8] It may appear that Stack could be a better choice, but I prefer to avoid this type because its implementation is victim of a design flaw discussed in Chapter 7.

```
public class Deck {

  private List<Card> aCards = new ArrayList<>();

  public List<Card> getCards() {
    return aCards;
  }
}
```

Unfortunately, this solution solves the problem of providing access to the content of the deck at a great cost: it allows a reference to the private internal list of cards to *escape* the scope of the class, thus granting access to internal elements of the class from outside the class. For example:

```
Deck deck = new Deck();
List<Card> cards = deck.getCards();
cards.add(new Card(Rank.ACE, Suit.HEARTS));
```

Here, the reference to the list of cards held within an instance of `Deck` *escaped* into the scope of the client code, which can then use it to mess things up, for example by adding an additional Ace of Hearts.

Clearly, declaring fields private is insufficient to ensure good encapsulation. If a class is well encapsulated, it should not be possible to change the data stored by an object without going through one of its methods. In turn, to achieve this encapsulation quality, it is also necessary to prevent references to internal structures to escape the scope of the class. There are three main ways in which a reference to a private structure can escape the scope of its class: returning a reference to an internal object, storing an external reference internally, or leaking references through shared structures.[9]

Returning a reference to an internal object

This problem is demonstrated above through the use of the getter method. It is not a good idea to automatically supply getters and setters for each field because, as in this case, it may result in a degradation of encapsulation. Figure 2.3 shows the effect of this escape.

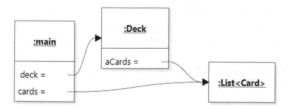

Fig. 2.3 Effect of leaking references outside the class scope

---

[9] A fourth, more indirect, way is to use metaprogramming. See Section 5.4.

Although an object is a collection of variables, in the context of design, these variables correspond to an abstraction. Having a class that is mostly accessed through getters and setters points to a design weakness, because the abstraction the object represents is not effective. This problem is also known as the INAPPROPRIATE INTIMACY† antipattern, because its symptom is that classes "spend too much time delving in each others' private parts" [3]. To the extent possible, objects should interact with each other using methods that involve abstractions above individual instance variables. In the case of the `Deck` class, this means prohibiting access to the internal list of cards, which constitutes a "private part".

Storing an external reference internally

The problem with returning a reference to an internal object is that this reference becomes shared by the client code. A similar problem is to introduce this sharing by using a reference to an external object to initialize the internal state of another object. For example, if we have a setter method for the content of the deck:

```
public class Deck {

  private List<Card> aCards = new ArrayList<>();

  public void setCards(List<Card> pCards) {
    aCards = pCards;
  }
}
```

the reference will already be *escaped* as soon as it is assigned to the field:

```
List<Card> cards = new ArrayList<>();
Deck deck = new Deck();
deck.setCards(cards);
cards.add(new Card(Rank.ACE, Suit.HEARTS));
```

Here, we can corrupt the state of the deck from the scope of the client code, for example by adding an Ace of Hearts. From an object graph perspective, the outcome of this code is similar to the one caused by leaking a reference through a getter method, as illustrated in Figure 2.3.

A similar version of this problem is to set the content of the deck from a constructor, as opposed to a setter method:

```
public class Deck {
  private List<Card> aCards = new ArrayList<>();

  public Deck(List<Card> pCards) {
    aCards = pCards;
  }
}
```

Although the leak uses a different type of programming language element (constructor vs. setter method), the result is identical.

Leaking references through shared structures

The issue of escaping references is complex because references can escape through
any number of shared structures, which may not always be obvious. Although a bit
contrived, the following example shows how this could come about:

```java
public class Deck {
  private List<Card> aCards = new ArrayList<>();

  public void collect(List<List<Card>> pAllCards) {
    pAllCards.add(aCards);
  }
}
```

with the corresponding client code:

```java
List<List<Card>> allCards = new ArrayList<>();
Deck deck = new Deck();
deck.collect(allCards);
List<Card> cards = allCards.get(0);
cards.add(new Card(Rank.ACE, Suit.HEARTS));
```

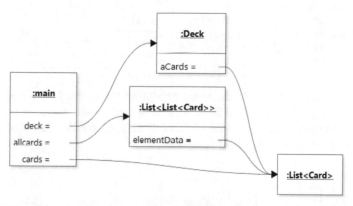

Fig. 2.4 Effect of leaking references through a shared structure

Figure 2.4 illustrates the result. Unfortunately, automatically detecting escaping
references is a difficult program analysis problem, and there currently does not exist
any production tool that can accomplish it for Java. Preventing the escape of references from the class scope is currently a manual process that relies on rigourous
programming and code inspection practices. Section 2.7 introduces techniques for
exposing some carefully selected information encapsulated by an object, without
leaking references to internal structures.

2.6 Immutability

One of the major design insights of this chapter is that to ensure good encapsulation, it should not be possible to modify the internal state of an object without going through its methods. Section 2.5 discussed the issue of escaping references, and how they threaten encapsulation. There is, however, one situation where leaking a reference to an internal object is harmless: when the object is immutable (i.e., impossible to change). Let us consider the following code:

```
class Person {
  private String aName;

  public Person(String pName) {
    aName = pName;
  }

  public String getName() {
    return aName;
  }
}

public class Client {
  public static void main(String[] args) {
    Person person = new Person("Anonymous");
    String name = person.getName();
  }
}
```

The implementation of class `Person` clearly violates the advice given in Section 2.5 (of not returning references held in private fields), given that `Person.getName()` returns a reference to the value of an instance variable. We can also represent this situation with an object diagram (Figure 2.5):

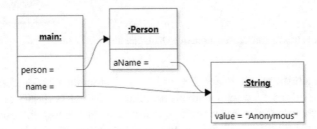

Fig. 2.5 Illustration of a shared reference to a `String` instance

However, a crucial notice in the reference documentation of the `String` library type changes things considerably:

> Strings are constant; their values cannot be changed after they are created. [...] Because String objects are immutable they can be shared.

Because it is not possible to change the data encapsulated by a `String` instance after its creation, sharing a reference to a `String` that forms the internal data encapsulated by an other object is harmless, as it will not be possible to change the object using the reference. This applies to any immutable object.

Objects are *immutable* if their class provides no way to change the internal state of the object after initialization. By extension, I call a class that yields immutable objects an *immutable class*.[10] Unfortunately, in Java and most other programming languages, there is no mechanism to guarantee that a class yields immutable objects. For the designer of a class, the only way to ensure immutability is to carefully design the class to prevent any modification (e.g., by providing no setter methods, leaking no reference, etc.). When relying on library classes (such as `String`), unless we are willing to personally inspect the source code of the class, we have to trust the documentation. Generally speaking, immutable objects have many advantages. In the context of this chapter, the immediate benefit is to support sharing information encapsulated in an object without breaking encapsulation. Chapter 4 provides additional insights that can help with the design of immutable classes. For now, it is sufficient to say that immutability is a desirable design property in many cases.

Let us conclude this brief introduction to immutability by defining class `Card` to be immutable. First, we rely on our two enumerated types `Rank` and `Suit` which we assume to be immutable.[11] With the following declaration, class `Card` will be immutable:

```
public class Card {
  private Rank aRank;
  private Suit aSuit;

  public Card(Rank pRank, Suit pSuit) {
    aRank = pRank;
    aSuit = pSuit;
  }

  public Rank getRank() {
    return aRank;
  }

  public Suit getSuit() {
    return aSuit;
  }
}
```

In this definition of the class, the only way to set the values of the two instance variables is through the constructor call which, by definition, is only executed once for each object. The fields are private, so they cannot be accessed from outside the

---

[10] This is a slight abuse of language because, technically speaking, it makes no sense for a class to be immutable. However, *immutable class* is a more convenient term than *class that yields immutable objects*.

[11] Simple enumerated types, which only enumerate values, are immutable. Although it is technically possible to define enumerated types that are *not* immutable, this is not a good idea. See Chapter 4.

class. There are only two methods. Although they are public, neither changes (or *mutates*) the state of the object. Finally, although the methods return a reference to the content of a field, the type of these fields is immutable, so it will not be possible to change the state of the referenced objects in any case. The class is thus immutable.[12]

Code Exploration: JetUML · Rectangle

Creating objects derived from immutable objects.

In addition to numerous query methods (e.g., `getX()`, `getHeight()`, `getCenter()`), the interface of this class also includes methods that create *new* `Rectangle` instances as derivatives of the implicit parameter. For instance, `translated(int, int)` returns a new instance of `Rectangle` that is a translated version of the implicit parameter. Note the subtle difference in naming: the method is called `translated` instead of `translate`, because `translate` would imply the translation of the implicit parameter. This approach is necessary because, being immutable, it is not possible to directly translate the implicit parameter. The pattern of "modifying" an immutable object by returning a modified version of the (unmodified) implicit parameter is common. The library class `String` provides many examples, such as `substring(int)`, which returns a new `String` instance that is a substring of the object on which the method is called. One will note that the declaration of the class is prefixed with the mention `@Immutable`. This part of the source code is an *annotation*. Annotations are described in detail in Section 5.4. For now however, it is important to know that this code element does not *make* the class immutable: it simply serves as a structured piece of documentation.

2.7 Exposing Internal Data

In many cases the objects of the classes we define will need to expose part of the information they encapsulate to other objects. How can we do this without breaking encapsulation? As often in software design, there are different options, each with its strengths and weaknesses. For sake of discussion, let us consider that we want to design our `Deck` class so that it is possible to find out what cards are in a deck.

```
public class Deck {
  private List<Card> aCards = new ArrayList<>();
}
```

---

[12] To make the immutability of the class even more explicit, the keyword `final` could be placed in front of the `class` keyword, as well as before the type of both fields. The use of `final` instance variables is introduced in Chapter 4, and the use of `final` classes is introduced in Chapter 7.

As discussed above, adding a getter method that simply returns aCards is out of the question, as this allows code outside the class Deck to modify the internal representation of a Deck instance.

Extended interface

One solution is to extend the interface of the class to include access methods that only return references to immutable objects. In our case, we could accomplish this goal by adding two methods to the Deck class:

```
public int size() {
  return aCards.size();
}

public Card getCard(int pIndex) {
  return aCards.get(pIndex);
}
```

If class Card is immutable, this solution fulfills its mandate. However, it is somewhat inelegant if client code typically needs to access all the cards in the deck. In such a situation, the code would become cluttered with calls to size() and for loops going over all indexes. Code might also need to be written to check that the argument to getCard is not out of bounds, and so on.

Returning Copies

Another option, which mimics returning a reference to the field aCards without breaking encapsulation, is to return a *copy* of the list stored in aCards. Thus, we could add a new method:

```
public List<Card> getCards() {
  return new ArrayList<>(aCards);
}
```

This code relies on the behavior of the constructor ArrayList(Collection), which creates a new ArrayList and initializes this list with all the elements in the collection, in the same order. Thus, a client would receive a reference to a different list of cards, with the same cards, as illustrated in Figure 2.6.

Assuming Card is immutable, we have a valid solution to expose the content of a Deck to clients. Figure 2.6 shows the result of executing:

```
public static void main(String[] pArgs) {
  List<Card> cards = deck.getCards();
}
```

We see that it is not possible to change the internal state of Deck from a reference to its cards. There are other strategies for returning a copy of a data structure or a wrapper for it. Ultimately, the details of the implementation do not matter as much as

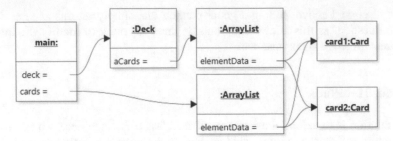

Fig. 2.6 Reference to a copy of a list of cards

the central idea, which is to return a different object that has all the same information as the internal structure we wish to keep encapsulated.

Although it looks like a simple idea, copying objects is actually a tricky topic, because it requires deciding how deep to copy the object graph. So far, we assumed that Card objects were immutable, so it was sufficient to perform a shallow copy. A shallow copy of a list is a copy of the list with shared references to the elements in the original list (that is, the elements are not copied). But what if Card instances were mutable? In this case the above solution would not offer good encapsulation, because it would become possible to change the state of a deck without going through its interface, for example:

```
public static void main(String[] pArgs) {
  Deck deck = new Deck();
  deck.getCards().get(0).setSuit(Suit.HEARTS);
}
```

With mutable Card instances, to implement the copying solution correctly, we need to go one step further and copy all cards when we copy the list of cards encapsulated within a Deck instance. In turn, this introduces a new requirement, namely, to find a clean way to copy card objects.

A common technique for copying objects is to use a *copy constructor*. The idea is to design a constructor that takes as argument an object of the same class, and (usually) to copy matching field values:

```
public Card(Card pCard) {
  aRank = pCard.aRank;
  aSuit = pCard.aSuit;
}
```

In fact, the code above, where we use new ArrayList<>(aCards), is an example of a copy constructor for ArrayList. To perform a deep(er) copy of our list of cards now becomes slightly more involved:

```
public List<Card> getCards() {
  ArrayList<Card> result = new ArrayList<>();
  for( Card card : aCards ) {
    result.add(new Card(card));
  }
  return result;
}
```

However, this extended solution ensures that encapsulation would be preserved even with mutable `Card` objects. Java provides other mechanisms that support copying objects, including its *cloning* mechanism (see Section 6.6), metaprogramming (see Section 5.4) and its *serialization* mechanism (not covered in the book).

Other Strategies

Copying objects is only one of many strategies for exposing information internal to an object while maintaining encapsulation. The Java class library provides another option through the use of *unmodifiable view collections*. An unmodifiable view is an unmodifiable wrapper for an underlying collection of objects. For example, the library method `Collection.unmodifiableList(List)` returns an unmodifiable wrapper around a list. As an alternative to copying a list, we could do:

```
public List<Card> getCards() {
  return Collections.unmodifiableList(aCards);
}
```

Other strategies will be covered later in the book. These include iterators (see Section 3.5) and streams (see Section 9.6).

Code Exploration: JetUML · Diagram

Using unmodifiable collections in practice.

A `Diagram` object holds a collection of root nodes and a collection of edges. Client code can access these collections through the methods `rootNodes()` and `edges()`. These two methods return the corresponding collection wrapped in an unmodifiable view using the library method `Collections.unmodifiableList`.

2.8 Input Validation

One of the benefits of encapsulation is to make it difficult or impossible for client code to corrupt the value of a variable. Following the principles and guidelines presented in this chapter helps us achieve this goal. Let us consider the following implementation of class `Card`.

```
public class Card {
  private Rank aRank;
  private Suit aSuit;

  public Card(Rank pRank, Suit pSuit) {
    aRank = pRank;
    aSuit = pSuit;
  }

  public Rank getRank() {
    return aRank;
  }

  public Suit getSuit() {
    return aSuit;
  }
}
```

The encapsulation provided by this class is very good, but there remains a crack in the shell it provides: it is possible to create a new card with a null reference:

```
Card card = new Card(null, Suit.CLUBS);
```

For most use cases where a representation of a playing card is required, this would be incorrect. At least, I am not aware of any card game that involves a "null of Clubs". We thus corrupted the variable. Section 4.5 provides an extended discussion of the issue of null references, but for now we focus on the general problem of avoiding the creation of an invalid instance of class Card. For this purpose, one strategy is to modify the code that provides our functionality of interest so that it checks that the input is valid, and reports an error otherwise. In Java we typically use exception handling for this purpose (see Section A.8 in the appendix):

```
/**
 * ...
 * @throws IllegalArgumentException if pRank or pSuit is null
 */
public Card(Rank pRank, Suit pSuit) {
  if( pRank == null || pSuit == null) {
    throw new IllegalArgumentException();
  }
  aRank = pRank;
  aSuit = pSuit;
}
```

With this code, any attempt to create a Card instance with a null reference for either of the two fields will result in an exception being thrown. When an exception is thrown, the constructor does not complete normally and no new object is created. For this reason, it is now impossible to create an invalid Card object as a result of calling the class's constructor.

An important consequence of this input validation is that now the null check becomes an integral part of the implementation of the constructor. Like any other kind of functionality, users of the code should be aware of how a method or constructor behaves in response to its input. For this reason, it is necessary to document this behavior carefully. In the example above, the information about the exception being raised is provided using Javadoc's @throws tag.

It is important to remember that, in object-oriented programming, the object that is the target of a method call is also an input to the method. As such, this input may need to be validated as well. Let us consider a slightly more complete version of the Deck class where we have added an implementation of a draw() method, along with a method to check whether the deck is empty:

```java
public class Deck {
  private List<Card> aCards = new ArrayList<>();

  public boolean isEmpty() {
    return aCards.isEmpty();
  }

  public Card draw() {
    return aCards.remove(aCards.size() - 1);
  }
}
```

Calling method draw() on an instance of Deck that contains no card will result in an exception being thrown by method remove, which will propagate out of method draw(), causing it to terminate abnormally. This situation, however, is very different from the case above. In our Card constructor, we *explicitly* designed our code to detect a null reference being passed as argument, and to throw an exception in response. The code comment reflects this design decision In the case of draw(), the exception is raised because we misuse a library method in our implementation by passing *it* an invalid input. The resulting exception is IndexOutOfBoundsException. One sloppy way to deal with the situation would be to simply document the exception as follows:

```java
/**
 * ...
 * @throws IndexOutOfBoundsException if isEmpty()
 */
public Card draw() {
  return aCards.remove(aCards.size()  1);
}
```

This approach, however, has two major drawbacks: it abuses the exception handling mechanism, and it violates the principle of information hiding. A good design principle for exception handling is that exceptions should only be used for unpredictable situations. In the case of method remove, this means passing it an unknown value, which turns out to be out of bounds for the underlying list. However, this is not our situation, because we can always determine with complete certainty whether aCards.size()-1 will be valid (by calling isEmpty()). As for information hiding, the reason why propagating IndexOutOfBoundsException violates the principle is that the fact that cards in the deck are stored in an indexed sequence is no longer a secret. Although the implications are not dramatic, the encapsulation of class Deck can be improved by avoiding this information leak. A solution that avoids both problems is thus to implement an explicit check, similarly to how we have done with the `Card` constructor. In this case, because the illegal argument is the implicit argument (the object that is the target of the call), it is clearer to use `IllegalStateException`. Chapter 4 discusses the concept of object state in more detail.

```
/**
 *  ...
 * @throws IllegalStateException if the deck is empty
 */
public Card draw() {
  if( isEmpty() ) {
    throw new IllegalStateException();
  }
  return aCards.remove(aCards.size() - 1);
}
```

Input validation is one option for ensuring that we only construct valid objects and use them in valid ways. As usual, this design decision has both benefits and drawbacks. The main benefit, as we have seen, is that the class is very robust: client code can no longer corrupt the internal values in an object. The consequence, however, is that we have shifted the responsibility of the client code from *input valida-tion* to *error handling*. Presumably, if the client code is written so that it is possible to raise an exception, it should also catch this exception:

```
try {
  card = deck.draw();
} catch( IllegalStateException exception ) {
  // Recover
}
```

Another important consequence of input validation is that now we have additional input validation code to test, document, and maintain within our classes. In some cases, this extra burden may not be justified. For example, if we only create new cards in one location in the code, where it is clear that no null values are used, then the error-handling machinery for protecting against the possibility of null inputs would be excessive. In the next section, I describe a systematic way to think about input validity.

Code Exploration: JetUML · Version

Input validation when it is really needed.

Class `Version` represents a specific JetUML release number, for example, `2.1`. The method `parse(String)` of this class shows a good example of a case where input validation is typically necessary. Because the input value is read from a file, we do not know what to expect. For example, a buggy program may have written the file with an invalid version number. The implementation of `parse` thus ensures that the input is valid, and throws an `IllegalArgumentException` if it is not the case, this time supplying an error message to the constructor of the exception.

2.9 Design by Contract

In the previous section, I pointed out the need for input validation to ensure that client code does not misuse an object. However, input validation may not be necessary if the client code is written in a way that precludes erroneous values. For example, the following code creates all the cards in the Clubs suit:[13]

```
List<Card> clubs = new ArrayList<>();
for( Rank rank : Rank.values() ) {
  clubs.add( new Card(rank, Suit.CLUBS));
}
```

With code like this, no null reference can ever be provided as argument to the Card constructor, and we could consider omitting input validation. Unfortunately, the fact that the responsibility for ensuring that valid values are used in a program can rest either on the implementation of a class or on its client code creates a major source of ambiguity. Let us again consider the interface of the Card constructor:

```
public Card(Rank pRank, Suit pSuit)
```

Without additional information, the following interpretations are possible about the behavior of this constructor:

- It validates the input and throws an exception if it is null, but this fact is not documented;
- It validates the input, but does something else if it is null (for example, use a default value);
- It does *not* validate the input, expects the client code to *only* pass valid values, and breaks in some undefined way if it receives invalid arguments;
- It does *not* validate the input, and client code can create cards with null values as long as it does not use a card for which either the rank or suit is null.

Ambiguity of this nature can very easily destroy the quality of a design, render code incomprehensible, and upset developers using it. Observing that the problem comes from the ambiguity about what is or should be a legal value for the arguments of the Card constructor, one natural solution is to define method and constructor signatures so that the ambiguity is minimized or eliminated.

The idea of *design by contract* is to follow a principled approach to the specification of interfaces. Although, in practice, method signatures already specify much of what is needed in an interface, they also leave room for ambiguity, as was shown by the example above. Diligent programmers can help eliminate ambiguities by stating the precise range of allowed values in a method's documentation. This is certainly better than nothing. However, design by contract goes further and provides a formal framework for reasoning about complete interface information. There is a lot to say about design by contract, so to keep things tractable I only provide an overview of a simplified version of the approach.

---

[13] Method values() is a static method available for all enumerated types. It returns an array that contains all the enumerated values for the type in declaration order.

The main idea of design by contract is for method signatures (and related documentation) to provide a sort of contract between the client (the caller method) and the server (the method being called). This contract takes the form of a set of *preconditions* and a set of *postconditions*. A precondition is a predicate that must be true when a method starts executing. The predicate typically involves the value of the method's arguments, including the state of the target object upon which the method is called. Similarly, postconditions are predicates that must be true when the execution of the method is completed.[14] Given preconditions and postconditions, the contract is basically that the method can only be expected to conform to the postconditions if the caller conforms to the preconditions. If a client calls a method without respecting the preconditions, the behavior of the method is undefined. In practice, design by contract is a great way to force us to think about all possible ways to use a method.

In the sample applications (see Appendix C) I follow a lightweight version of design by contract where preconditions are specified using Java statements in the comments using the Javadoc @pre tag and postconditions are specified using the tag @post.

```
/**
 * @pre pRank != null && pSuit != null
 */
public Card(Rank pRank, Suit pSuit) {
    // ...
}
```

It is possible to make pre- and postconditions (and any other predicates) *checkable* in Java using the assert statement:

```
public Card(Rank pRank, Suit pSuit) {
    assert pRank != null && pSuit != null;
    aRank = pRank; aSuit = pSuit;
}
```

The assert statement evaluates its predicate expression and raises an Assertion-Error if the result is false.[15]

Correctly implemented, design by contract helps prevent the tedious idiom of *defensive programming* where corner cases (such as null references) are checked for everywhere in the code. Additionally, the technique supports clear *blame assignment* while debugging: If a precondition check fails, the client (caller method) is to blame. If a postcondition check fails, the actual method being called is to blame. More generally, assert statements are a simple yet powerful tool to increase code quality and they can be used anywhere, not just for pre- and postconditions. Whenever an assertion check fails, we know exactly where the problem is, and we can thus save on debugging time.

---

[14] The complete approach also involves the concept of *invariants*. In theory, invariants are predicates that are expected to remain true at all times. In the practice of design by contract, it is sufficient for invariants to be true at method entry and exit points.

[15] Assertion checking is disabled by default in Java, so to use this properly it is necessary to add -ea (enable assertions) as a VM parameter when running Java.

A final note about design by contract is that the addition of preconditions to a method's interface actually relieves us of the requirement to handle the condition. Hence, the code below is not properly designed because it *both* states that null references are not a valid input *and* handles them in a consistent way (by raising an exception). If a method checks for a certain type of input (like null references) and produces a well-defined behavior as the result, then this is part of the method's interface specification. When designing method interfaces, it is important to decide whether the method will be in charge of rejecting illegal values, or whether these will simply be specified as invalid. These are two different design choices. In the same vein, it must be emphasized that the `assert` statement is not a compact way to implement input validation. `AssertionError`s are not meant to represent the presence of invalid values in a running program. Rather, they point to a design or implementation flaw in the code.

```
/**
 * @pre pRank != null && pSuit != null
 */
public Card(Rank pRank, Suit pSuit) {
  if( pRank == null || pSuit == null ) {
    throw new IllegalArgumentException();
  }
  // ...
}
```

Code Exploration: JetUML · Rectangle

Design by contract in practice.

The methods of class `Rectangle` provide examples of different types of preconditions. To call the constructor, the arguments must not be less than zero. The methods that take a reference type as argument (for example, `contains(Point)` and `contains(Rectangle)`) require that this argument be non-null. Other design decisions were possible. For example, it would have been possible to accept `null` as an argument to `contains`, and return false when this argument is provided. A downside of this alternative is that is makes the interface ambiguous: if `false` is returned, is it because the point was not contained in the rectangle, or because the point was not actually a point, but `null`? Section 4.5 provides additional reasons why null values are best avoided.

Code Exploration: Solitaire · Deck

Preconditions on the state of the target object.

The interface to method `draw` illustrates how preconditions can be a function of the state of the object. The interface of class `Deck` requires that the deck not be empty before `draw` is called. Here, this precondition can be expressed in terms of another method, `isEmpty()` (by negating the return value).

Insights

This chapter focused on how to follow the principles of encapsulation and information hiding when defining classes.

- Use classes to define how domain concepts are represented in code, as opposed to encoding instances of these concepts as values of primitive types (an antipattern called PRIMITIVE OBSESSION†);
- Use enumerated types to represent a value in a collection of a small number of elements that can be enumerated;
- Hide the internal implementation of an abstraction behind an interface that tightly controls how an abstraction can be used. Declare fields of a class `private`, unless you have a strong reason not to. Similarly, declare any method `private` if it should not be explicitly part of the type's interface;
- Ensure that the design of your classes prevents any code from modifying the data stored in an object of the class without using a method of the class. In particular, be careful to avoid leaking references to private fields of the class that refer to mutable objects;
- To provide information about the internal data in an object without violating encapsulation, strategies include extending the interface of the class, returning copies of internal objects, or using unmodifiable views;
- Object diagrams can help explain or clarify the structure of complex object graphs, or how references are shared;
- Make classes immutable if possible. In Java, it is only possible to ensure that a class is immutable through careful design and inspection;
- Input validation can be used to ensure that the objects of a class are created and used properly. However, this extra code comes at a cost as it needs to be documented, tested, and maintained.
- Use design by contract to avoid ambiguity in method signatures, and thereby help prevent the possibility that client code will misuse an instance of a class.

Further Reading

Chapter 6 of the book *Software Architecture: A Comprehensive Framework and Guide for Practitioners* by Vogel et al. [17] provides a well-organized overview of the different principles of software design, and how they are related. For a more historical perspective, the seminal paper on the principle of information hiding is Parnas's 1972 *On the Criteria to be Used in Decomposing Systems into Modules* [11]. The article contrasts two designs for a text-processing system, and argues for the superiority of the design that realizes information hiding over a sequential processing decomposition.

The section titled *Enum Types* in the Java Tutorial [10] provides additional insights on how enumerated types work. In Item 50 of the book *Effective Java* [1], Bloch discusses the creation of defensive copies of internal object encapsulated by a class .

The article *Applying Design by Contract*, by its inventor Bertrand Meyer, provides an accessible overview of the technique [8].

Chapter 3
Types and Interfaces

Concepts and Principles: Class diagram, coupling, extensibility, function objects, interface, Interface Segregation Principle, interface type, iterator, polymorphism, reusability, separation of concerns, specification, subtyping;
Patterns and Antipatterns: ITERATOR, STRATEGY, SWITCH STATEMENT†.

In the previous chapter we saw how to define well-encapsulated classes, but conveniently left out the question of how objects of these classes would interact. We now start addressing this question. Interactions between objects are mediated through interfaces. The term *interface* is overloaded in programming: it can have different meanings depending on the context.

Design Context

The examples in this chapter concern the design of a class library to allow client code to instantiate and use a deck and other collections of card objects to support the development of card games.

3.1 Decoupling Behavior from Implementation

An *interface* to a class consists of the methods of that class that are accessible (or visible) to another class. What methods are accessible depends on programming language rules that take into account access modifiers and scopes (see Section 2.3). For now, we define the interface to a class as the set of its public methods (I will extend this definition in Chapter 7). Let us consider the following code:

© Springer Nature Switzerland AG 2022
M. P. Robillard, *Introduction to Software Design with Java*,
https://doi.org/10.1007/978-3-030-97899-0_3

```
public class Client {
  private Deck aDeck = new Deck();
}

public class Deck {
  public void shuffle() { ...  }
  public Card draw() { ... }
  public boolean isEmpty() { ... }
}
```

The interface of class Deck consists of three methods. The code in other classes can interact with objects of class Deck by calling these and only these methods. Here we would say that the interface of class Deck is fused, or *coupled*, with the class definition. In other words, the interface of class Deck is just a consequence of how we defined class Deck: there is no way to get the three services that correspond to the three methods of the class, without interacting with an instance of class Deck. In our example, to shuffle the deck, client code will need to invoke method shuffle() of a field or local variable of type Deck: there is no other option.

There can be, however, situations in which we may want to *decouple* the interface of a class from its implementation. These are situations in which we want to design the system so that one part of the code can depend on the availability of a service, without being tied to the exact details of how this service is implemented. Given that we are designing a library that can be used to build different card games, we note that many card games require the user to draw cards, but not necessarily from a standard deck of 52 cards. For example, some games might require drawing cards from an aggregation of multiple decks of cards, from a set of cards of only one suit, from ordered sequences of cards, etc. Let us consider the following code that draws cards from a deck up to a required number.

```
public static List<Card> drawCards(Deck pDeck, int pNumber) {
  List<Card> result = new ArrayList<>();

  for( int i = 0; i < pNumber && !pDeck.isEmpty(); i++ ) {
    result.add(pDeck.draw());
  }

  return result;
}
```

This method can only be used with sequences of cards that are an instance of class Deck. This is a pity, because exactly the same code could be useful for any object that has the two required methods draw() and isEmpty(). Here it would be useful to specify an abstraction of an interface without tying it to a specific class. This is where Java *interface types* come in. In Java, interface types provide a *specification* of the methods that it should be possible to invoke on an object. With interface types, we can define an abstraction CardSource as any object that supports a draw() method and an isEmpty() method:

```
public interface CardSource {
  /**
   * Returns a card from the source.
   *
   * @return The next available card.
   * @pre !isEmpty()
   */
  Card draw();

  /**
   * @return True if there is no card in the source.
   */
  boolean isEmpty();
}
```

This interface declaration[1] lists two methods, and includes comments that specify the behavior of each method. The specification of `draw()` includes the precondition that the method can only be invoked if `isEmpty()` is false. This precondition is provided to support the use of design by contract (see Section 2.9), and takes into account the existing state of the object. Because interface method declarations are a specification and not an implementation, details of what the method is expected to perform are very important. With a method implementation, it could always be possible to inspect the code (if we have access to it) and infer the specification. This is not an ideal situation, but it is better than nothing. With interface methods, though, reverse-engineering what the method does is not possible. In Java terminology, methods that do not have an implementation are called *abstract methods*.[2] To tie a class with an interface, we use the `implements` keyword.

```
public class Deck implements CardSource {
  ...
}
```

The `implements` keyword has two related effects:

- It provides a formal guarantee that instances of the class type will have concrete implementations for all the methods in the interface type. This guarantee is enforced by the compiler.
- It creates a subtype relationship between the implementing class and the interface type: here we can now say that a `Deck` is a type of `CardSource`.

The subtype relation between a concrete class and an interface is what enables the use of *polymorphism*. In plain language, polymorphism is the ability to have different shapes. Here, `CardSource` is an abstraction that can present itself in different

---

[1] There is an important distinction between the general concept of an *interface*, and the specific `interface` construct in Java. When the difference is clear from the context, I simply use the term *interface*. When necessary, I use the expression *interface type* to refer to the Java construct.

[2] Prior to Java 8, all interface methods were automatically abstract. With Java 8, this is no longer true, because interfaces can include default and static methods, which have an implementation. Nevertheless, it remains a good practice to thoroughly document the expected behavior of interface methods.

concrete shapes. Each concrete shape corresponds to a different implementation of the `CardSource` interface.

For polymorphism to be useful, it is important to remember that according to the rules of the Java type system, it is possible to assign a value to a variable if the value is of the same type or a *subtype* of the type of the variable. Because the interface implementation relation defines a subtype relation, references to objects of concrete classes declared to implement an interface can be assigned to variables declared to be of the interface type. For example, because class `Deck` declares to implement interface `CardSource`, we can assign a reference to an object of class `Deck` to a variable of type `CardSource`, as such:

```
CardSource source = new Deck();
```

Taking this idea further, this means we can make our implementation of the `draw-Cards` method much more *reusable*:

```
public static List<Card> drawCards(CardSource pSource, int pNum){
  List<Card> result = new ArrayList<>();
  for( int i = 0; i < pNum && !pSource.isEmpty(); i++ ) {
    result.add(pSource.draw());
  }
  return result;
}
```

The method is now applicable to objects of any class that implements the `Card-Source` interface.

Another illustration of the use of polymorphism is the use of concrete vs. abstract types in the Java Collections Framework.

```
List<String> list = new ArrayList<>();
```

`List` is an interface that specifies the usual services (add, remove, etc.), and `ArrayList` is an implementation of this service that uses an array. But we can replace `ArrayList` with `LinkedList` and the code will still compile. Even though the details of the list implementation differ between `ArrayList` and `LinkedList`, they both provide exactly the methods required by the `List` interface, so it is permissible to swap them. Polymorphism provides two useful benefits in software design:

- *Loose coupling*, because the code using a set of methods is not tied to a specific implementation of these methods.
- *Extensibility*, because we can easily add new implementations of an interface (new "shapes" in the polymorphic relation).

3.2 Specifying Behavior with Interface Types

Typical design questions related to interfaces include: *do I need a separate interface?* and *what should this interface specify?* There are no general answers to such questions, because in each case the task is to determine if interfaces can help us solve a design problem or realize a particular feature. One good illustration of both the purpose and usefulness of interfaces in Java is the Comparable interface.

One obvious task to be implemented in the Deck class is to shuffle a deck of cards. This can be realized trivially with the help of a library method.

```
public class Deck {
  private List<Card> aCards = new ArrayList<>();

  public void shuffle() {
    Collections.shuffle(aCards);
  }
}
```

As its name implies, the library method shuffle randomly reorders the objects in the argument collection. This is an example of code reuse because it is possible to reuse the library method to reorder any kind of collection. Here reuse is easy because to shuffle a collection, we do not need to know anything about the items being shuffled.

But what if we want to reuse code to *sort* the cards in the deck? Sorting, like many classic computing problems, is supported by many existing quality implementations. In most software development situations, it would not be acceptable to hand-craft one's own sorting algorithm. The Java Collections class conveniently supplies us with a number of sorting functions. However, if we opportunistically try the following without further consideration:

```
List<Card> cards = ...;
Collections.sort(cards);
```

we are rewarded with a possibly cryptic compilation error.[3] This should not be surprising, though, because how exactly is a library method supposed to know how we want to sort our cards? Not only is it impossible for the designers of library methods to anticipate all the user-defined types that can be invented, but even for a given type like Card, different orderings are possible (e.g., by rank, then suit, or vice-versa).

The Comparable<T> interface helps solve this problem by defining a piece of behavior related specifically to the comparison of objects, in the form of a single compareTo(T) abstract method. The specification for this method is that it should return 0 if the implicit argument is equal to the explicit argument, a negative integer if it should come before, and a positive integer if it should come after. Given the existence of this interface, the internal implementation of Collections.sort can now rely on it to compare the objects it should sort. Conceptually, the internal code of the sort implementation looks a bit like this:

```
if( object1.compareTo(object2) > 0 ) ...
```

So, from the point of view of the implementation of sort, it really does not matter what the object is, as long as it is *comparable* with another object. This is a great example of how interfaces and polymorphism support loose coupling: the code of

---

[3] *The method sort(List<T>) in the type Collections is not applicable for the arguments (List<Card>).* Results can vary on different compilers.

`sort` depends on the minimum possible piece of functionality required from its argument objects. This is a good general insight on how to define interface types. Ideally, they should capture the smallest cohesive slice of behavior that is expected to be used by client code. For this reason, many interface types in Java are named with an adjective that ends in *-able*, a suffix that means *fit to be*.... Besides `Comparable`, examples include `Iterable`, `Serializable` and `Cloneable`.

To make it possible for us to sort a list of cards, we therefore have to provide this *comparable* behavior and declare it with the `implements` keyword:

```
public class Card implements Comparable<Card> {
  public int compareTo(Card pCard) {
    return aRank.ordinal() - pCard.aRank.ordinal();
  }
}
```

This minimal implementation sorts cards by ascending rank, but leaves the order of suits undefined, which leads to unpredictability. A more useful implementation of the `Comparable` interface would provide a well-defined total ordering.

Because Java interfaces are types, the type-checking mechanism that is part of the compilation process makes it possible to detect that a `List<Card>` object cannot be passed to `Collections.sort` unless the `Card` class declares to implement the `Comparable<Card>` interface. How this happens is outside the scope of this book because it requires a good understanding of the typing rules for Java generic types (see Section A.6 in the appendix).

Many other library types that have a so-called *natural* ordering implement the `Comparable` interface. This includes `String` (with lexicographic order) but also many other pervasive types. In particular, Java enumerated types implement `Comparable` by comparing instances of an enumerated type according to their ordinal value. With this knowledge in hand, we observe that our implementation of `Card.compareTo`, above, actually re-implements reusable behavior provided by the enumerated types. We thus have an opportunity to simplify our code:

```
public class Card implements Comparable<Card> {
  public int compareTo(Card pCard) {
    return aRank.compareTo(pCard.aRank);
  }
}
```

Using small interfaces encourages the respect of a software design principle called *separation of concerns*. The idea of separation of concerns is that one abstraction should map to a single *concern* (or area of interest) for developers. In designs that do a poor job at separation of concerns, we find concerns to be *tangled* within an abstraction (a method for example), and/or *scattered* across multiple different abstractions. Here the use of the `Comparable` interface is a good example of effective separation of concerns: the code to compare cards is entirely contained within a clearly defined and identified abstraction (the `compareTo` method), which does only one thing.

3.3 Class Diagrams

Designs where the important concerns revolve around the definition of types and relations between types can become overwhelming to describe in code, and are more easily captured through a diagram. Class diagrams represent a *static*, or *compile-time*, view of a software system. They are useful to represent how types are defined and related, but are a poor vehicle for capturing any kind of *run-time* property of the code. Class diagrams are the type of UML diagrams that are the closest to the code. However, it is important to remember that the point of UML diagrams is not to be an exact translation of the code. As models, they are useful to capture the essence of one or more design decisions without having to include all the details.

Class diagram have an extensive associated notation. In a class diagram, there is typically more going on than, say, in an object diagram. I only use a subset of the notation in this book. The Further Reading section includes references for UML class diagrams. Figure 3.1 shows the main concepts used in this book. In the figure, all quotes are taken from *The Unified Modeling Language Reference Manual, 2nd edition* [15]. The interpretation of the concepts of aggregation, association, and dependency will become clearer as we progress through the chapters. For now, it is sufficient to know that these concepts represent that two classes are somehow related. The concept of navigability, represented with an arrow head, models how code supports going from objects of one type to objects of another type. Navigability can be unidirectional (as shown), bidirectional, or unspecified.

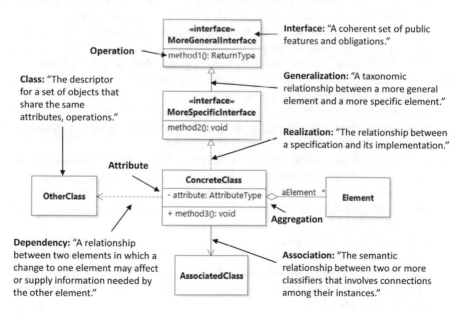

Fig. 3.1 Selected notation for class diagrams

Figure 3.2 shows an example of a class diagram that models some of the key relations between the design elements for a card game that we have seen so far. We can observe the following:

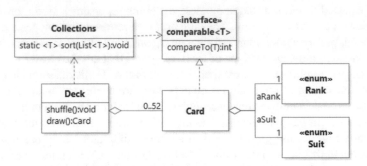

Fig. 3.2 Sample class diagram showing key decisions in the design of a Deck class

- The box that represents class Card *does not have attributes* for aRank and Suit because these are represented as aggregations to Rank and Suit enumerated types, respectively. It is a modeling error to have *both* an attribute *and* an aggregation to represent a given field.
- The methods of class Card are not represented. Because they are just the constructor and accessors, I judged this to not be very insightful information. It would not be wrong to include them, but it would clutter the diagram.
- In the UML, there is no good way to indicate that a class *does not have* a certain member (field or method). To convey the information that Card does *not* have setters for the two fields, it would be necessary to include this using a note.
- Representing generic types is a bit problematic, because in some cases it makes more sense to represent the type parameter (Comparable<T>) and in some other cases it makes more sense to represent the type instance (Comparable<Card>). In this diagram I went with the type parameter because I wanted to show how Collections depends on Comparable in general.
- All UML tools have some sort of limitations one needs to get around. For simplicity, JetUML (see Appendix C) does not have different font decorations (such as underlines) to distinguish between static and non-static members. To indicate that a method is static in JetUML, we can prefix the members's name with the keyword static.
- The model includes cardinalities to indicate, for example, that a deck instance will aggregate between zero and 52 instances of Card. Typical values for an association's cardinality include a specific number (for example, 1), the wildcard ∗ (which means zero or more), and ranges such as M..N (which means between M and N, inclusively).

3.4 Function Objects

In practice, an interface type often defines only a subset of the operations of the classes that implement it. This scenario is exemplified by `Comparable`: the complete implementation of `Card` comprises methods, such as `getSuit()` and `getRank()`, that add to the slice of behavior required by the `Comparable` interface. There are other situations, however, where it is convenient to define classes that specialize in implementing *only* the behavior required by a small interface with only one method.

Let us continue with the problem of comparing cards. Implementing the `Compara-ble` interface allows instances of `Card` to compare themselves with other instances of `Card` using one strategy, for example, by comparing the card's rank, and using suits to break ties. What if we are designing a game where we need to sort cards according to different strategies, and occasionally switch between them? One could tweak the code of `compareTo`, for instance by relying on a global variable that stores the required strategy and switching the comparison strategy based on this flag. However, harebrained schemes of this nature have many drawbacks. In our case, using such a flag variable would degrade the separation of concerns between representing a card and knowledge of how the card should be sorted, and generally make the code harder to understand.

In fact, the use of this kind of switching is considered a design antipattern called SWITCH STATEMENT†.[4] A more promising solution is to move the comparison code to a separate object. This solution is supported by the `Comparator<T>` interface. The abstract method in this interface is `compare` (as opposed to `compareTo`).[5]

```
int compare(T pObject1, T pObject2)
```

As for `Comparable`, `Comparator` is a generic type, so in the above declaration, `T` refers to a type parameter that must be instantiated (with type `Card` for example). Besides the slight name difference, the most notable difference is that the method takes two arguments instead of one. Indeed, its specification is very similar to that of `compareTo`, except that instead of comparing the implicit parameter (the `this` object) with an explicit parameter, it compares two explicit parameters with each other. Not surprisingly, library methods were also designed to work with this interface. For example: `Collections.sort`:

```
Collections.sort(List<T> list, Comparator<? super T> c)
```

This method can sort a list of objects that do not necessarily implement the `Comparable` interface, by taking as argument an object guaranteed to be able to compare two instances of the items in the list. One can now define a *rank first* comparator:

---

[4] There is evidence of the antipattern whether or not an actual `switch` statement is used, because the latter can be trivially emulated through `if-else` statements.

[5] As of Java 8, this interface provides an intimidating list of methods. These are not important here. In Chapter 9 I revisit this interface to explain how we can leverage some of the additional methods.

```
public class RankFirstComparator implements Comparator<Card> {
  public int compare(Card pCard1, Card pCard2) {
    /* Comparison code */
  }
}
```

and another *suit first* comparator:

```
public class SuitFirstComparator implements Comparator<Card> {
  public int compare(Card pCard1, Card pCard2) {
    /* Comparison code */
  }
}
```

and sort[6] with the desired comparator:

```
Collections.sort(aCards, new RankFirstComparator());
```

In this scenario, an instance of Comparator is simply an object that provides the implementation for a single method. Such objects are referred to as *function objects*. Their interface typically maps one-to-one to that of an interface type.

The use of comparators (and similar function objects) introduces many interesting design questions and trade-offs. First, if comparator classes are defined as standalone top-level Java classes, the code of their compare method will not have access to the private members of the objects they compare. In some cases the information available from getter methods is sufficient to implement the comparison, but in other cases implementing the compare method will require access to private members.

In such cases, one option to give comparator classes access to private members of the classes they compare is to declare the comparator classes as *nested classes* (see Section 4.10) of the class that defines the objects being compared:

```
public class Card {
  static class CompareBySuitFirst implements Comparator<Card> {
    public int compare(Card pCard1, Card pCard2) {
      /* Comparison code */
    }
  }
}
```

To client code, the impact of this change in design is minimal: the only difference is the additional qualification of the name of the comparator class:

```
Collections.sort(aCards, new Card.CompareBySuitFirst());
```

Another option is to define comparator classes as *anonymous classes*. In cases where the comparator is only referred to once, this makes a lot of sense:

---

[6] As of Java 8, method sort is also available on the Collection (no 's') interface. However, to preserve the symmetry with the use of the Comparable<T> interface, I retain this version.

```
public class Deck {
  public void sort() {
    Collections.sort(aCards, new Comparator<Card>() {
      public int compare(Card pCard1, Card pCard2) {
        /* Comparison code */
      }
    });
  }
}
```

A third option is to use *lambda expressions*. Lambda expressions are a form of anonymous functions. These and related mechanisms form the topic of Chapter 9. However, since it is possible to implement a very close equivalent to the code above using lambda expressions, I provide it here. The basic idea is based on the observation that to supply a comparator, not only do we not need to name a class because it is only an implementation of the Comparator interface, we also do not need to name the method, because it is only an implementation of compare. How this code actually works is explained in Chapter 9.

```
public class Deck {
  public void sort() {
    Collections.sort(aCards, (card1, card2) ->
      card1.getRank().compareTo(card2.getRank()));
  }
}
```

In the two examples above, we have brought back the problem of encapsulation, because the code in the anonymous class that implements the comparison is defined outside of the Card class. We can solve this with the help of a static *factory method*. The term *factory method* refers to methods whose primary role is to create and return an object.

```
public class Card {
  public static Comparator<Card> createByRankComparator() {
    return new Comparator<Card>() {
      public int compare(Card pCard1, Card pCard2) {
        /* Comparison code */
      }
    };
  }
}
```

A final question is whether a comparator should store data. For example, instead of having different comparators for sorting cards by rank and suit, we could define a UniversalComparator that has a field of an enumerated type that stores the desired type of comparison. Although this solution is workable, it can lead to code that is harder to understand, for reasons explained in Section 3.7 and further discussed in Chapter 4.

3.5 Iterators

A common requirement when designing a data structure is to gain access to a collection of encapsulated objects without violating the principle of information hiding. For example, if we are designing a type of represent a deck of cards, we may need to give client code access to the cards in the deck. This problem was originally introduced in Section 2.7, where the solution proposed was to return copies of the internal data. For example, to return a copy of the list of cards encapsulated within a `Deck` instance. One issue with this solution is that it can subtly leak information about the way a structure is stored internally (or at least, give the impression that it leaks this information). For example, if we choose to return a deck's cards as a `List`:

```
public List<Card> getCards() { ... }
```

code using the `Deck` may start relying on the operations defined on a list, or make the assumption that cards are internally stored in a list within a `Deck`. To achieve an even higher level of information hiding, it would be better to allow client code access to the internal objects of another object, without exposing anything about the internal structure of the encapsulating object. This design feature is supported by the concept of an *iterator*. The concept of an iterator is very general, and iterators are employed in many programming languages.

In Java, iterators are easy to use, but understanding how they work requires being aware of a careful coordination between at least three types of objects. Iterators also provide an example of the use of interfaces types and polymorphism.

To support iteration we must first have a specification of what it means to iterate. As usual, this specification is captured in an interface: in this case the `Iterator` interface. This interface defines two abstract methods: `hasNext()` and `next()`. So, according to the rules of subtyping, once a piece of code gains access to a reference to an object of any subtype of `Iterator`, the client code can iterate over it, independently of what the actual class of the object is. To enable iteration over the cards of a `Deck`, let us simply redefine the `getCards` method to return an iterator instead of a list:

```
public Iterator<Card> getCards() { ... }
```

This way, to print all the cards in a deck, we can do:

```
Iterator<Card> iterator = deck.getCards();
while( iterator.hasNext() ) {
  System.out.println(iterator.next());
}
```

Although this design achieves our decoupling goal, we can generalize it to great effect. A first important insight is that in most software systems there will be different types of objects that it would be useful to iterate over. Lists are an obvious example. In our case we also have a `Deck`. The issue with the iterator system as we have it now, though, is that different classes define a different way to obtain an iterator. For class `List`, it is through the method `iterator()`. For our `Deck` class, it is through method `getCards()`. Although the behavior in both cases is identical (return an iterator), the *name* of the service is different. We can solve this issue with another interface. The `Iterable<T>` interface specifies the smallest slice of behavior necessary to make it possible to iterate over an object. To be able to polymorphically iterate over an object, the only thing we need from this object is that it supplies an iterator. So the only abstract method of the `Iterable` interface is `Iterator<T> iterator()`.

We can make our `Deck` class iterable by implementing the `Iterable<Card>` interface and renaming the `getCards()` method to `iterator()`:

```
public class Deck implements Iterable<Card> {
  public Iterator<Card> iterator() {
    ...
  }
}
```

This way, an instance of `Deck` can be supplied anywhere an `Iterable` interface type is expected. Figure 3.3 shows the main elements of the iterator design so far.

Fig. 3.3 Class diagram for the design of an iterator

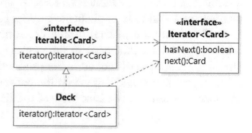

One of the main ways to use `Iterable` objects in Java is in an *enhanced for loop*, also know as a *foreach* loop:

```
List<String> list = ...;

for( String string : list ) {
  System.out.println(string);
}
```

The above code is just syntactic sugar for:

```
List<String> list = ...;

for(Iterator<String> iter = list.iterator(); iter.hasNext(); ) {
  String string = iter.next();
  System.out.println(string);
}
```

To iterate over a deck, we can now do:

```
for( Card card : deck ) {
  System.out.println(card);
}
```

The way the enhanced `for` loop works is that, under the covers, it expects the rightmost part of the loop head to be an instance of a class that is a subtype of `Iterable` (or an array type, which is a special case).

The final issue to solve to complete our iterator-based design for `Deck` is to find a way to return an instance of `Iterator` when the `iterator()` method is called. Although it would be possible to hand-craft our own user-defined class that implements the `Iterator<Card>` interface, we can observe that the `List` contained within a `Deck` is also `Iterable`, and the `Iterator` it returns does everything that we want.

```
public class Deck implements Iterable<Card> {
  private List<Card> aCards;

  public Iterator<Card> iterator() {
    return aCards.iterator();
  }
}
```

Strictly speaking, this idiom can violate the encapsulation of class `Deck` because interface `Iterator<T>` includes a method `remove()` that can be optionally implemented (and which is implemented by `ArrayList`). Consistent with the book's goal of focusing on general design concerns with minimum coverage of the libraries, I overlook this case. In the context of the book, it can be assumed that `Iterator#remove()` is not used. For production code, how to best avoid the encapsulation problem would depend on the context. One option is to return the iterator obtained from an unmodifiable view of the list with a call such as:

```
return Collections.unmodifiableList(aCards).iterator().
```

Representing the implementation of the `Iterator` interface in the UML is not obvious given our reliance on an instance of an unknown concrete type. Although we know that the type returned by `List.iterator()` is some subtype of the `Iterator` interface, we do not know the name of the class that ultimately implements this interface. In fact, this may be an anonymous class, in which case, by definition, there is no name. So the fact to reckon with at this point is that we do not know the type. However, we cannot really write *Unknown* in a class in a class diagram, because this would indicate that the name of the class is known, and it is *"Unknown"*, which is very confusing. For now, I will assume that the type is anonymous and indicate this fact with the UML *stereotype* (`<<anonymous>>`), leaving the name blank. In the UML, a stereotype is a variation on an element type, with the name of the variation placed in angle brackets.

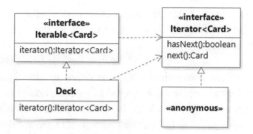

Fig. 3.4 Class diagram of the complete iterator design

3.6 The ITERATOR Design Pattern

The previous section introduced the use of iterators as a way to provide access to
a collection of objects encapsulated within another object without violating the information hiding properties of this object. This solution is a common design pattern
called, not surprisingly, the ITERATOR. The *context* for ITERATOR is to

> Provide a way to access the elements of an aggregate object sequentially without exposing
> its underlying representation. [6]

The *solution template* for ITERATOR can be best captured by the class diagram in
Figure 3.5, which is simply an abstraction of the solution presented in Figure 3.4.

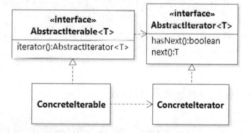

Fig. 3.5 Class diagram of the solution template for ITERATOR

An important difference to notice between the solution template in Figure 3.5
and its concrete realization in Figure 3.4 is that the solution template does not refer to the Java library interfaces `Iterable` and `Iterator`. Although they can be
supported by libraries, design patterns are abstract solution elements that can be realized in code independently of specific library implementations. For this reason,
the solution template simply indicates that to apply the ITERATOR pattern in practice,
one needs a type to fulfill the *roles* of `AbstractIterable` and `AbstractIterator`,
and similarly with their concrete implementation. This being said, in Java there are
very few variants of ITERATOR. Because only subtypes of `Iterable` can be used in
the enhanced `for` loop, there is a strong incentive to actually use `Iterable` as the

AbstractIterable, which forces the use of Iterator as the ConcreteIterator. The remainder of the mapping is almost automatic, as the ConcreteIterable is whatever one wants to iterate over.

How to create the ConcreteIterator is one design decision that yields more possibilities, but the most convenient option is often to simply return the iterator supplied by the data structure (e.g., ArrayList.iterator()), possibly wrapped in an immutable view (see Section 3.5). In some cases, it might be necessary to combine elements from various collections and iterate over them, or iterate in an order different from that of the collection holding the elements to iterate over. In such cases, the simplest option is often to create a new collection with the desired elements in the right order, and to return that collection's iterator.

Code Exploration: Solitaire · CardStack

A basic application of the ITERATOR *pattern.*

Class CardStack illustrates the simplest possible application of the ITERATOR in Java. The class represents a stack of cards, which I made it possible to iterate over from bottom to top. As expected, the class implements interface Iterable<Card> and declares a method iterator(). Because, by project-wide convention, iterators are not used to remove cards from the underlying collection, I chose to return the iterator of the underlying collection as the return value of CardStack#iterator(). In the class, an Iterable<Card> is also used to define the type of the argument to one of the constructor: CardStack(Iterable<Card>). This decision maximises the flexibility of the constructor, by allowing it to take as input any type of object that can be iterated over for Card objects.

3.7 The STRATEGY Design Pattern

One of the major benefits of interfaces and polymorphism is to promote flexible designs. One example of a flexible design enabled by interfaces is the use of a Comparator instance by the Collections.sort(...) method, as introduced in Section 3.4. The use of function objects such as comparators to customize the behavior of another part of the code (e.g., the sorting behavior) is recognized as one application of a more general idea called the STRATEGY design pattern. The *context* for STRATEGY is to:

> Define a family of algorithms, encapsulate each one, and make them interchangeable. Strategy lets the algorithms vary independently from clients that use it. [6]

This is a very general definition, especially given that there is no agreed-upon definition for what a *family of algorithms* is. Fortunately, the *solution template* for STRATEGY provides a clarification for object-oriented code: algorithms in the same family implement the same interface.

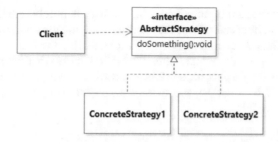

Fig. 3.6 Solution template for STRATEGY

The STRATEGY looks exceedingly simple. In fact in many cases it can be indistinguishable from a basic use of polymorphism. I find it useful to think of a part of the design as an application of STRATEGY when that part of the design is focused on allowing the switch between algorithms. One example, illustrated in Figure 3.7, is the use of different card comparators for a deck of cards. Another example is the implementation of different automatic playing strategies, as will be further discussed in the Code Exploration section below.

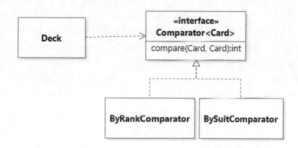

Fig. 3.7 Sample instantiation of a STRATEGY

Although nominally simple, in practice applying a STRATEGY requires thinking about many design questions:

- Does the `AbstractStrategy` need one or multiple methods to define the algorithm? Typically the answer is one, but in some cases it may be necessary to have more methods.
- Should the strategy method return anything or have a side-effect on the argument?
- Does a strategy need to store data?
- What should be the type of the return value and/or method parameters, as applicable? Ideally we want to choose these types to minimize coupling between a strategy and its clients.

Figure 3.7 shows an example instantiation of STRATEGY for the context of comparing cards. Here the design of the `AbstractStrategy` is already decided because we are reusing the `Comparator` interface. This strategy is purely functional as it does not have any side-effect and returns the result of applying the comparison algorithm. At this point it should become clearer that implementing the `Comparator` interface as a `UniversalComparator` that holds a value to decide what kind of comparison to do, does not really respect the spirit of the STRATEGY because the actual strategy would be selected by changing the state of an object, as opposed to changing the concrete strategy object.

Code Exploration: Solitaire · PlayingStrategy

Applying the STRATEGY *to implement game-playing strategies.*

In Solitaire, the package `ai` provides an elaborate example of the STRATEGY pattern. Interface `PlayingStrategy` defines a method `computeNextMove` that is called by a `GameModel` instance when the player uses the *auto-play* feature. With the auto-play feature, the software makes a decision of how to play the next move in the game, as opposed to waiting for the user to play a move. Any class that implements `PlayingStrategy` can provide a decision-making behavior for making a move. The package contains two examples of strategies. The `NullPlayingStrategy` never does anything, and always returns a so-called *null move*. The purpose of this code is explained in Section 4.5. The `GreedyPlayingStrategy` selects the move with the most immediate impact on the game. To implement a different strategy, for example one that uses probabilities in the decision-making process, a developer creates a new class that implements `PlayingStrategy` and assign an instance of this class in the initialization of field `GameModel.aPlayingStrategy`.

3.8 Dependency Injection

So far in this chapter we have seen how to use interface types so that classes that use a service can be decoupled from the actual implementation of the service. Continuing with our example of the comparator, let us say we are designing a version of our `Deck` of cards that can be sorted in various ways. Applying the STRATEGY pattern described in the previous section, our code should look like this:

```
public class Deck {
   private List<Card> aCards = new ArrayList<>();
   private Comparator<Card> aComparator = /* initialize */;

   public void sort() {
     Collections.sort(aCards, aComparator);
   }
}
```

In the code above, various options are possible for initializing the comparator (that is, the concrete strategy). One option is to call the constructor of the desired comparator when initializing the field:

```
private Comparator<Card> aComparator = new ByRankComparator();
```

There are two issues with this approach. First, it does not allow the client code to easily switch the comparison strategy. To switch the comparison strategy, it would be necessary to modify the source code of the Deck class and recompile it. Second, this design introduces a *dependency* between the Deck class and a specific comparator implementation. Figure 3.8 illustrates the problem.

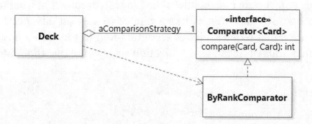

Fig. 3.8 Introducing a dependency between a client class and an implementation class

One variant of this solution could be to use an anonymous class in the definition of the comparator:

```
private Comparator<Card> aComparator = new Comparator<Card>() {
  public int compare(Card pCard1, Card pCard2) {
    return pCard1.getRank().compareTo(pCard2.getRank());
  }
};
```

However, this solution exhibits the same problem as the previous one: it does not allow us to switch the comparison algorithm easily, and the Deck class is still coupled to a specific implementation of the comparison. The only difference is that now this implementation is anonymous.

A solution to both the lack of flexibility of the Deck class and its tight coupling with the comparison strategy is to decouple the creation of the dependency (here, the implementation of the comparator) from the creation of the client of the dependency (here, the Deck class). Instead, we pass in, or *inject*, the dependency into the client class.

```
public class Deck {
  private Comparator<Card> aComparator;

  public Deck(Comparator<Card> pComparator) {
    aComparator = pComparator;
    shuffle();
  }
}
```

This technique is called *dependency injection*. In this way, class `Deck` only has a dependency to the interface type `Comparator<Card>`, and remains decoupled from any specific implementation. The trade-off is that client code of the `Deck` class must now inject this dependency when creating a `Deck`:

```
Deck deck = new Deck(new ByRankComparator());
```

As is the case for design patterns, dependency injection is a general idea and there are many different ways to apply it in practice. For example, one could design various factory methods to instantiate dependency objects, or inject a dependency using an anonymous class, etc. It is also possible to inject the dependency via a setter method instead of the constructor. This alternative, however, is often inferior because it creates object state management challenges, discussed in Chapter 4. Finally, there are also libraries and frameworks available to support advanced dependency injection scenarios that require a lot of configuration. In this book, however, I stick to simple applications of dependency injection such as the one illustrated above.

Code Exploration: Solitaire · GameModel

Injecting a concrete strategy into another object.

The concrete `PlayingStrategy` described in the previous Code Exploration is injected into the `GameModel` via its constructor. The application is assembled in method `start()` of class `Solitaire`. In this method, we see the creation of the concrete strategy and its injection into the `GameModel`:

```
GameModel model = new GameModel(new GreedyPlayingStrategy());
```

3.9 The Interface Segregation Principle

Throughout this chapter we saw the various benefits of defining specialized interfaces that specify a small and coherent slice of behavior that clients depend on. This way, client code is not coupled with the details of an implementation, and only depends on the methods it actually requires. For example, code that processes cards can only depend on a `CardSource` interface with two methods, and can therefore be reusable with any class that can provide these methods. Similarly, the `Collections#sort(...)` method works because it can rely on just the fact that the items in the collection are `Comparable`. This idea is actually an instance of a general design principle called the *Interface Segregation Principle (ISP)*. Simply put, the ISP states that *client code should not be forced to depend on interfaces it does not need*.

The idea of the ISP is easier to explain by presenting a situation where the principle is *not* respected. We can consider again the code in Section 3.1 where `drawCards` takes a `Deck` as argument:

```
public static List<Card> drawCards(Deck pDeck, int pNumber) {
  List<Card> result = new ArrayList<>();

  for( int i = 0; i < pNumber && !pDeck.isEmpty(); i++ ) {
    result.add(pDeck.draw());
  }
  return result;
}
```

In Section 3.1 I argued that this was a suboptimal design because it tied an interface with its implementation. Well, let us say we split the two by declaring an IDeck interface:

```
public interface IDeck {
  void shuffle();
  Card draw();
  boolean isEmpty();
}

public class Deck implements IDeck...
```

which we rely on in drawCards:

```
public static List<Card> drawCards(IDeck pDeck, int pNumber)
```

This effectively decouples interface from implementation, and supports the use of drawCards with non-Deck sources. However, this design also forces drawCards to statically depend on a method it does not need, namely, shuffle. What if we might want to draw cards from a source that cannot be shuffled? For this reason, the CardSource solution initially presented in Section 3.1 did respect the ISP, and only included methods draw and isEmpty in interface CardSource.

To push on this idea of ISP a bit, let us assume that there might be places in the code that only shuffle an object. To support this slice of behavior, we would define an interface Shufflable with a single method shuffle(). Figure 3.9 shows a maximally flexible separation of concerns for class Deck, with three different interfaces that capture three cohesive slices of behavior that are supported by class Deck, and three client code locations (represented by Client1-3) interested in different combinations of these services.

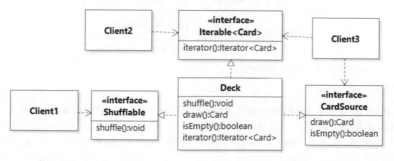

Fig. 3.9 Interface segregation in practice

This design has loose coupling, which is great. However, this loose coupling has one major disadvantage for cases where a client might be interested in more than one slice of behavior. This situation is represented in Figure 3.9 by `Client3`, which needs to both iterate over an `Iterable<Card>` *and* draw some cards from the source. How can we express this combination, since in Java it is only possible to specify a single type for a variable? For example, if we pass an instance of `CardSource` to a method of interest and wish to iterate over the cards, we have to venture into inelegance:

```
public void displayCards(CardSource pSource) {
  if( !pSource.isEmpty() ) {
    pSource.draw();
    for( Card card : (Iterable<Card>) pSource) {
      ...
    }
  }
}
```

In fact this is not only inelegant, but also unsafe, because it could be possible to provide an argument to `displayCards` that is *not* a subtype of `Iterable`. A better solution to this issue is offered directly by the type system, in the form of subtyping. In Java, interfaces can be declared to extend each other, with the semantics that if A extends B, types that implement A must provide implementations for all the methods declared in B as well, transitively. By extending interfaces, we can more easily support combinations of services while respecting the ISP. In our scenario, if it is observed that a lot of the code that uses `CardSource` also uses `Iterable<Card>`, *but not the other way around*, then we can declare `CardSource` to be a subtype of `Iterable<Card>`, as illustrated in Figure 3.10.

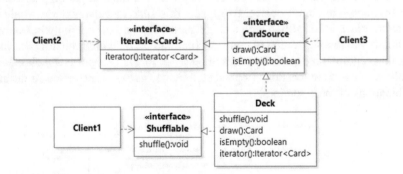

Fig. 3.10 Example of interface extension

In principle, the same reasoning could apply in the reverse situation: if we notice that most code that uses `Iterable<Card>` also uses `CardSource` *but not the other way around*, it would make sense to declare `Iterable<Card>` to extend `CardSource`. In practice, however, this is not possible because `Iterable<T>` is a library type, which it is not possible to modify. For this reason, there are also large amounts of code that depend on it without depending on `CardSource`, rendering the situation a mere theoretical possibility. Finally, software designs can be hard to get right immediately. It may be the case that two segregated interfaces end up always being used together in the client code. In such a situation, it is possible that application of the ISP went too far, and it might be worth considering fusing two interfaces back into one, by collecting all method declarations into a single interface.

Code Exploration: Solitaire · GameModel

Using the Interface Segregation Principle when applying the STRATEGY.

In Solitaire, the STRATEGY is used via interface `PlayingStrategy`, which defines a method `computeNextMove`. To decide how to make a move, a strategy object needs some information about the game. This information is provided as a parameter to the strategy method. All the information about an on-going game is stored in an instance of `GameModel`. This is a large class which declares both accessor methods and methods that can change the state of the game. Hence, by passing an instance of `GameModel` to a strategy object, the code of the strategy object would be able to modify the state of the game. This is excessive coupling, because in the design the playing strategies are only supposed to compute a move, not actually do the move. To make this constraint clearer, I used the Interface Segregation Principle as follows. Class `GameModel` implements an interface `GameModelView` that declares *only* the methods of `GameModel` that provide information about the game without changing anything. The effect of this decision is to have a type that *narrows* the interface of `GameModel` to only include query methods. I then declared the type of the parameter of `computeMove` to be `GameModelView`. This way, although it is still actually an instance of `GameModel` that is provided to strategy objects, the limited interface makes it clear that the code of strategy objects is only meant to query the state of the game, not change it.

Code Exploration: JetUML · DiagramElement

Organizing interfaces into a hierarchy to serve different usage contexts.

A diagram in JetUML contains different diagram elements that are either nodes or edges. I used interface types `Node` and `Edge` to specify the expected behavior of these elements. However, certain parts of the code, like the `Clipboard` class, need to deal with diagram elements in general, independently of whether they are nodes or edges. To accommodate this flexibility, I defined an additional interface, `DiagramElement`, which is extended by both `Node` and `Edge`. The behavior for general elements, nodes specifically, and edges specifically, is thus segregated into different interface types. This allows the various client code locations to work with the most appropriate abstraction for the diagram element objects they needs to handle.

Insights

This chapter focused on how to use interfaces and polymorphism to achieve extensibility and reuse.

- Use interface types to decouple a specification from its implementation if you plan to have different implementations of that specification as part of your design;
- Define interface types so that each type groups a cohesive set of methods that are likely to be used together;
- Organize interface types as subtypes of each other to create flexible groupings of behavior;
- Use library interface types, such as `Comparable`, to implement commonly expected behavior;
- Use class diagrams to explore or capture important design decisions that have to do with how classes relate to each other;
- Consider function objects as a potential way to implement a small piece of required functionality, such as a comparison algorithm. Function objects can often be specified as instances of anonymous classes, or as lambda expressions;
- Use iterators to expose a collection of objects encapsulated within another without violating the encapsulation and information hiding properties of this object. This idea is known as the ITERATOR design pattern;
- Consider using the STRATEGY pattern if part of your design requires supporting an interchangeable family of algorithms;
- Use dependency injection to decouple a client class that uses some abstractions from the creation of these abstractions;
- Make sure that your code does not depend on interfaces it does not need: break up large interface types into smaller ones if you find that many methods of a type are not used in certain code locations.

Further Reading

The definitions for the notation of the class diagram shown in Figure 3.1 are adapted from *The Unified Modeling Language Reference Manual* [15], which is one of the most comprehensive resources available on UML. Chapter 3 of *UML Distilled* [5] provides a more concise overview of the notation and semantics for this type of diagram. The Gang of Four book [6] has the original, detailed treatment of the ITERATOR and STRATEGY patterns.

Chapter 4
Object State

One of the most difficult things to reason about when looking at a program is state changes. Which operations can have a side-effect? On which path can data flow? What impacts what? This chapter clarifies what object state is and how we can manage to keep control over its state in a principled way.

Design Context

In this chapter, I continue the discussion of how to design abstractions to effectively represent a deck of cards in code (see the Design Context section of Chapter 3 for details).

4.1 The Static and Dynamic Perspectives of a Software System

There are different ways we can look at a software system. One way is in terms of the software elements declared in the source code and the relations between them. For example, a Deck class declares a field aCards that is a list of Card instances. This is a *static* (or compile-time) perspective of the system. The static perspective is best represented by the source code or a class diagram. A different, but complementary, way to look at a system, is in terms of objects in a running software system. For

© Springer Nature Switzerland AG 2022
M. P. Robillard, *Introduction to Software Design with Java*,
https://doi.org/10.1007/978-3-030-97899-0_4

example, at one point a `Deck` instance contains three cards, then one card is drawn, which leads to the instance of `Deck` containing two cards, etc. This is the *dynamic* (or *run-time*) perspective on the software. The dynamic perspective corresponds to the set of all values and references held by the variables in a program at different points in time. It is what we see in a debugger while stepping through the execution of the code. The dynamic perspective cannot easily be represented by any one diagram. Instead, we rely on object diagrams, state diagrams (introduced in this chapter), and sequence diagrams (introduced in Chapter 6). The static and dynamic perspectives are complementary in software design. Sometimes it is best to think of a problem and solution in static terms, sometimes in dynamic terms, and sometimes we really need both. This duality between the static and dynamic perspectives on a software system is akin to the wave-particle duality for representing the phenomenon of light in physics:

> It seems as though we must use sometimes the one theory and sometimes the other, while at times we may use either. [...] We have two contradictory pictures of reality; separately neither of them fully explains the phenomena of light, but together they do.
> —Albert Einstein and Leopold Infeld, *The Evolution of Physics*

To paraphrase for software design: It seems as though we must use sometimes the one perspective and sometimes the other, while at times we may use either. We have two *complementary* pictures of a software system; separately neither of them fully explains the phenomena of software, but together they do. This chapter focuses on understanding important *dynamic* properties of software.

4.2 Defining Object State

An important concept when thinking of a design in terms of run-time objects is that of *object state*. Informally, the state of an object refers to the particular pieces of information the object represents at a given moment. It is generally useful to distinguish between *concrete state* and *abstract state*. The concrete state of an object is the collection of values stored in the object's fields. For example, we can consider a `Player` object which, for now, only holds a score for the player in a scored game of Solitaire:

```
public class Player {
    private int aScore = 0;
}
```

The cardinality of the set of possible concrete states for `Player` is 2^{32}, or about 4 billion states.[1] We usually refer to the set of possible states for a variable or object as its *state space*. As soon as objects have fields of reference types, the cardinality (or size) of the state space explodes dramatically. For example, the state space of a `Deck` instance includes all possible permutations of any number of cards in the

---

[1] In Java a variable of type `int` is allocated 32 bits of storage.

deck, a number in the range of 2.2×10^{68}. This is an enormous number.[2] With class `Player`, adding an `aName` field of type `String` blows up the size of the state space to something that is only limited by the computing environment. For this reason, when designing software, it is more practical to think in terms of abstract states.

In principle, an abstract state is an arbitrarily-defined subset of the concrete state space. For example, considering the simple version of `Player` without the `aName` field, *Even Score* could be an abstract state for a `Player` instance that groups the roughly 2^{31} states that represent a score that is an even number. Likewise, for an instance of the `Deck` class, the abstract state *Three Kings* could represent any possible configuration of the deck where exactly three cards of rank `Rank.KING` are present. These two examples illustrate the fact that because abstract states are *arbitrary* partitions of the state space, they can really be defined as anything, no matter how whimsical. It should however be evident that neither of these two example abstract states would be particularly useful to design a realistic software system. In practice, the software design task of state space partitioning is to define abstract states that correspond to characteristics that will help construct a clean solution. A more useful abstract state for `Player` would be *Non-zero Score*, and one for `Deck` would be *Empty* (no cards in the deck), which in the latter case happens to correspond to a single concrete state. When the distinction is necessary, I use the term *meaningful* abstract state to indicate abstract states that capture states that impact how an object would be used. For example, the abstract state *Empty* is meaningful because it is not possible to draw a card from an empty deck. In contrast, the abstract state *Three Kings* is not meaningful because, at least in a game of Solitaire, whether a deck contains three kings or not has no impact on the game play and is not related to any design or implementation decision. Unless otherwise noted, future references to the term *abstract state* assume that we are talking about meaningful abstract states.

A special case when thinking about object state is that some objects do not store any values. For example, function objects (see Section 3.4), often do not have any fields besides constants. In this case, we talk about *stateless* objects. When the contrast is important, we can refer to objects that have state as *stateful* objects. Another property of objects that is related to their state is mutability (see Section 2.6). This chapter is concerned with objects that are both mutable and stateful. In the case of immutable objects, the boundary between statefulness and statelessness becomes blurry, because in practice they only have a single state.

---

[2] Computed as $\sum_{k=0}^{52} \frac{52!}{(52-k)!}$.

4.3 State Diagrams

UML *state diagrams*[3] are useful to represent how objects can, during their lifetime, transition from one abstract state to another as a reaction to external events
(typically, method calls). They represent a *dynamic* view of a software system. The
annotated diagram in Figure 4.1 shows all the state diagram notation used in the
book.

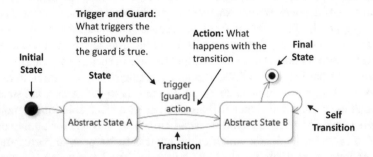

Fig. 4.1 Selected notation for state diagrams

The example in Figure 4.2 illustrates both the notation and purpose of UML state
diagrams. It models some of the important abstract states of an instance of a class
Deck that represents a deck of 52 playing cards. Even this simple diagram captures
key information about the design of the Deck class.

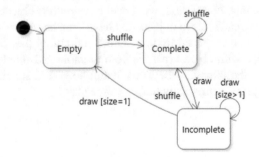

Fig. 4.2 State diagram for an instance of Deck

The abstract state *Empty* is annotated as the *initial state*, which allows us to infer
that the constructor returns a reference to a new Deck object with no cards in it.

---

[3] The official name of the diagram is *UML state machine diagram*. In this book I use the simpler
form *state diagram*.

In state diagrams, *absence of a transition* usually means that the absent transition is not possible (i.e., invalid) for that state. Here we can see that we cannot draw cards from an empty deck. The transitions are annotated with names that correspond to methods of the class Deck. The only legal transition out of the *Empty* state is shuffle which brings the object in the *Complete* state. From this it can easily be inferred that *Complete* is a shorthand for *Complete and shuffled* (in this particular design).

The shuffle transition out of the *Complete* state illustrates the idea of *self transitions*, namely, events that do not result in a change of abstract state. The only legal transition out of the *Complete* state is draw, which inevitably brings the deck object to an *Incomplete* state.

It is also possible to attach to a transition an *action* that describes what happens as the result of the transition. The action that corresponds to the draw event is *remove card from the deck*. The action information is optional and here I chose to leave it out of the diagram because it seemed redundant with the name of the event (considering that *to draw* is a synonym of *to remove* in the context of card games).

The two transitions out of the *Incomplete* state illustrate the importance of *guards*, because here without the concept of a guard we would not be able to model the distinction between a draw event that leads to the *Empty* state, and a draw event that keeps the object in the *Incomplete* state. The language I use for modeling guards does not follow a formal specification, but I nevertheless like to specify guards using pseudo-code that is very close to what could be reasonably tested on an instance of the object. Here the guard would assume the presence of a size() method in the Deck class.

Finally, this diagram does not include any *final state*. The final state model element is used to specify if an object *must* be in a certain state at the end of its lifetime. In Java, this means when all references to the object are eliminated, and the object becomes available for garbage collection. In many designs, objects can end their life (stop being used) in any state. In this latter case, the final state model element does not apply.

An important benefit of state diagrams is that they allow us to self-evaluate the impact of design decisions on the complexity of the abstract state space that must be considered when working with an object. Here the state space is very simple (three states) because of the decision to bundle the deck initialization code together with the shuffling code. Separating this behavior into distinct initialize and shuffle events, or including a sort event, leads to a much more complicated abstract state space for the object (see Figure 4.3 for an example).

Another important benefit of state diagrams is that they support systematically exploring the abstract behavior of an object of a given class. When modeling the state of an object, a good practice is to visit each state and consider each possible type of transition. This simple procedure is an excellent way to avoid overlooking certain paths through the code (e.g., shuffling an incomplete deck).

When getting started with modeling object states with state diagrams, one common tendency is to use the state diagram notation to model a type of data flow information, where states represent processing, and arrows represent the flow of data

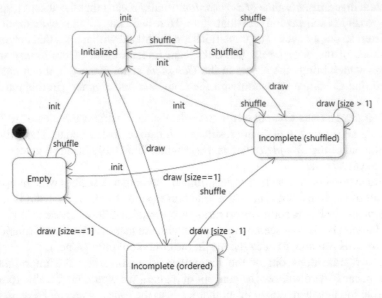

Fig. 4.3 State diagram for an instance of `Deck` where initialization and shuffling are separate operations

between processing stages. This is an incorrect use of the notation.[4] A good tip for avoiding this pitfall is to think about the names of the states. If the names assigned to states include verbs or generally feel like they are describing actions (for example, *draw card*), it is probably a sign that the diagram does not represent a good model of the state space.

Finally, it is worth noting that the concept of state diagram is very similar to that of *deterministic finite automata (DFA)*. This is not a coincidence, as both notations are intended to model some sort of stateful phenomenon. However, the purpose of each notation is different. DFAs are strict theoretical representations meant to fully and precisely describe computation models, whereas state diagrams involve communicating more abstract ideas about software to support software development activities such as software design, testing, and documentation. State diagrams can omit certain elements, but DFAs cannot.

---

[4] For which a better match is an activity diagram, which is, however, not covered in this book.

4.4 Designing Object Life Cycles

As the result of method calls, a stateful and mutable object will transition between different abstract states. The state diagram model of an object can also be referred to as its *life cycle*, because it describes the "life" of an object, from its initialization to its abandonment and eventual destruction by the garbage collector. The idea of a life cycle is similar to that of humans, which are created (somehow), then go through various stages of life (childhood, adolescence, etc.). However, in contrast to humans and most types of biological organisms, where stages of life occur once in a given sequence, the life cycle of objects depends on their design, and can get very complex. Object life cycles can include actual cycles, different paths through the abstract state space, and dead ends. As the complexity of the class grows (in terms of number of abstract states), the life cycle of instances of the class can become impossible to understand, even with the help of state diagrams. The contrast between Figure 4.2 and Figure 4.3 shows how an object life cycle can gain in complexity, even as a consequence of a seemingly small design change.

Objects with a complex life cycle are difficult to use, difficult to test (see Chapter 5), and their design and implementation is error-prone. A good design principle to avoid objects with complex life cycles is thus to *minimize the state space of objects* to what is absolutely necessary for the object to conduct its business. In practice, this means designing the class so that it is both impossible to put the object in an invalid or useless state, and that there is no unnecessary state information.

Invalid and Useless States

Some states in the state space might simply be a consequence of how an object is designed or implemented, without there being any use for an object in that state in a given software system. For example, in a game of Solitaire, there is no use for an unshuffled deck of cards. A design where a fresh instance of `Deck` must be first initialized, then shuffled, introduces two abstract states, and all the consequent complexity visible in Figure 4.3, without any benefit. In some cases, eliminating some states from the life cycle of an object may seem like reducing the versatility of a class (*what if we need this one day?*). This is an argument that can be made in some situations. However, it is always important to consider the cost (in terms of software developer time spent understanding code, writing tests, and fixing bugs). Often, this kind of SPECULATIVE GENERALITY† is not worth the cost.

Unnecessary Stateful Information

Another common bad practice when designing objects is to *cache* stateful information in instance variables, typically for convenience, presumed performance efficiency, or both. This point is best illustrated with an example. Because this example is so simple, the argumentation may seem ridiculous. However, I have seen the problem it represents countless times in code.

The implementation of the `Deck` class we have been discussing so far stores cards in a list and provides a method `size()` to allow client code to determine the number of cards in a deck.

```java
public class Deck {
  private List<Card> aCards = new ArrayList<>();

  public int size() {
    return aCards.size();
  }
}
```

A developer with a keen eye for efficiency might observe that in a typical execution of the Solitaire application, method `size()` is called numerous times on an instance of `Deck` of the same size. For example, it may be possible to call `deck.size()` ten times and receive the same value, before `deck.draw()` is called (which changes the size of the deck). Every time, a call to `deck.size()` results in a "useless" call to `aCards.size()`! Instead, would it not be more efficient to store the size directly in the deck, and return it?

```java
public class Deck {
  private List<Card> aCards = new ArrayList<>();
  private int aSize = 0;

  public int size() {
    return aSize;
  }

  public Card draw() {
    aSize--;
    return aCards.remove(aCards.size());
  }
}
```

This design decision is an example of the classic computing trade-off between space and time: save a bit of time at the cost of a bit of extra memory. However, except in the case of genuine long-running operations (such as device input/output), the savings in terms of execution time and the cost in terms of memory tend to be insignificant, whereas the significant losers are the simplicity, elegance, and understandability of the code.

Similarly to a misplaced concern about performance, another common reason for storing redundant information in fields is convenience (e.g., when a value is difficult to obtain through other fields of an object). This case is more difficult to illustrate with simple code examples. The general principle, however, applies widely: to the extent possible, information should not be stored in an object unless it uniquely contributes to the intrinsic value represented by the object. A violation of this principle often constitutes an instance of the TEMPORARY FIELD† antipattern.

4.5 Nullability

One aspect of most programming languages that gets in the way of designing clean state spaces and life cycles for objects is the possibility to assign the value `null` to a variable of a reference type. In Java (and many similar languages, such as C++), `null` is a special value that indicates, in a troublesome way, *the absence of value*. For example, if we assign `null` to a variable:

```
Card card = null;
```

we are in effect stating that the variable `card` is of a reference type `Card`, but that it refers to... nothing! This is a big problem because variables of reference types are intended to be dereferenced:

```
System.out.println(card.getRank());
```

Unfortunately, because, with a reference to nothing, there is nothing to dereference, the result is the dreaded `NullPointerException`, the obvious symptom of innumerable bugs in Java software. Generally speaking, relying on the null reference can cause a lot of harm. In fact, the inventor of the null reference, Tony Hoare, is reported to have stated his regret at implementing this feature (see Further Reading). In terms of low-level design, null references are a problem because of how difficult it is to think about all possible program paths that may lead to a null dereference. More generally, however, null references are a liability for software design because of their inherent ambiguity. Depending on the situation, a null reference in the state of an object could be interpreted to mean:

1. That a variable is temporarily un-initialized, but is expected to become initialized in a different abstract state for the object. For example, in class `Deck`, we could assign to the field `aCards` the value `null` until the deck is shuffled;
2. That a variable is incorrectly initialized because the programmer overlooked a path through the code where the variable had to be initialized;
3. That the value is a flag that purposefully represents the absence of a useful value in the normal life cycle of an object;
4. That the value is some sort of other flag that must be interpreted in a special way.

To avoid unnecessarily enlarging and complicating the state space of an object with dangerous null references, a recommended best practice is to design classes so that null references are simply not used. How to realize this goal in practice depends on whether there is a need to model the absence of a value for a variable or not. The Solitaire application is an example of code base that does not use the null reference anywhere.

No Need to Model Absent Values

If it is possible to design a class to avoid any abstract state where a certain variable does not have a value, it is greatly desirable to design the class to forbid this eventuality. For example, normal playing cards *must* have a rank and a suit, so there is really no reason to allow null references for either instance variable.

```
public class Card {
  private Rank aRank; // Should not be null
  private Suit aSuit; // Should not be null

  public Card(Rank pRank, Suit pSuit) {
    aRank = pRank;
    aSuit = pSuit;
  }
}
```

We can ensure that variables are not assigned a null reference by using either one of two approaches: *input validation* (Section 2.8), or design by contract (Section 2.9). With input validation, everywhere a variable can be assigned, we check whether the input value is a null reference and throw an exception if that is the case:

```
public Card(Rank pRank, Suit pSuit) {
  if( pRank == null || pSuit == null) {
    throw new IllegalArgumentException();
  }

  aRank = pRank;
  aSuit = pSuit;
}
```

With design by contract, we stipulate, using a precondition, that `null` is not a valid value for a variable and, optionally, check that the precondition is respected with an `assert` statement:

```
/**
 * @pre pRank != null && pSuit != null;
 */
public Card(Rank pRank, Suit pSuit) {
  assert pRank != null && pSuit != null;
  aRank = pRank;
  aSuit = pSuit;
}
```

In either case, if the `Card` constructor is the only place where `aRank` and `aSuit` can be assigned, we have effectively ensured that the value stored in either variable will not be a null reference.

Modeling Absent Values

In many situations, the domain concept we are trying to model will require that we make a provision for the fact that there may not be a value. As an example, let us consider a variant of class `Card` where an instance can also represent a *joker*. In many card games, a joker is a special card that has no rank and no suit. To flag a card as a joker, a simple approach is to add a `aIsJoker` field to its declaration:

```
public class Card {
  private Rank aRank;
  private Suit aSuit;
  private boolean aIsJoker;

  public boolean isJoker() { return aIsJoker; }
  public Rank getRank() { return aRank; }
  public Suit getSuit() { return aSuit; }
}
```

Here the logic to determine whether a card represents a joker is simple enough, but what should we do with its rank and suit? As usual, many options are possible. We can review three:

- *Null references:* We could just ignore the advice offered in this section and assign null to aRank and aSuit. This means it would be possible to call (for example) card.getRank().ordinal() on a joker, and get a NullPointerException.
- *Bogus values:* We could assign an arbitrary, meaningless value for the rank and suit of a joker (e.g., Ace of Clubs). However, this is both confusing and dangerous. A part of the code could erroneously request the rank of a joker, and receive the value Rank.ACE, which makes no sense. It is easy to imagine how tracking down this bug could be lengthy and annoying.
- *Special values of an enumerated type:* We could add an INAPPLICABLE enumerated value to both Rank and Suit, and assign these values to the corresponding fields for instances of Card that represent jokers. In my opinion, this solution is slightly better than the two above, but it still has some clear weaknesses. First, it is a conceptual abuse of the idea of enumerated types, where each value is enumerated. Although technically that is what it is, conceptually INAPPLICABLE is not a valid value in the enumeration, but rather a flag that indicates that we do not have a value. Second, although we have four ranks and 13 suits, this solution will yield five and 14 enumerated values for each type, respectively. This discrepancy will muck up any code that relies on the ordinal values of these types (such as the initialization of a deck of cards), and introduce opportunities for off-by-one errors.

Fortunately, there are better solutions for avoiding the use of null references to represent absent values.

Optional Types

One solution is to use an *optional type*. In Java, optional types are supported by the Optional<T> library class. The Optional class is a generic type that acts as a wrapper for an instance of type T, and which can be empty. To make a value of type T optional for a variable, we declare this variable to be of type Optional<T>. In our case:

```
public class Card {
  private Optional<Rank> aRank;
  private Optional<Suit> aSuit;
}
```

To represent the absence of a value of the variable, we use the value returned by `Optional.empty()`. So, to create a constructor that instantiates a `Card` that represents a joker, we could have:

```
public class Card {
  private Optional<Rank> aRank;
  private Optional<Suit> aSuit;

  public Card() {
    aRank = Optional.empty();
    aSuit = Optional.empty();
  }

  public boolean isJoker() { return !aRank.isPresent(); }
}
```

To create an instance of `Optional` that represents an actual value, we do `Optional.of(value)` if `value` is not (ever) expected to be null, and `Optional.ofNullable(value)` if `value` can be null (in which case `Optional.empty()` will be stored instead). To get the value wrapped by an instance of `Optional`, we call `get()`.

Using `Optional` in this way, we can both shed the dangerous use of null references and cleanly represent the absence of a value. The one main consequence, however, is that the two fields no longer have the types likely to be desired by the client code. While the client will probably be interested in working with values of type `Rank` and `Suit`, the fields of the class now store values of type `Optional<Rank>` and `Optional<Suit>`. To get around this issue, two main alternative are possible:

- *Change the interface of class `Card`* so that `getRank()` and `getSuit()` return `Optional<Rank>` and `Optional<Suit>`, respectively. This requires client code to call `get()` everywhere the actual instance is needed, which can be cumbersome.
- *Unwrap the optional within `getRank()` and `getSuit()`*, which preserves the interface but requires clients to ensure that they do not call the methods on a card that represents a joker (something that could be specified using design by contract, for example). This last solution is starting to look a lot like the use of null references, but it is technically safer, because calling `get()` on an empty instance of `Optional` will raise an exception immediately when the value is misused, as opposed to potentially propagating a null reference through the execution of the code.

Code Exploration: JetUML · TypeNode

Using optional types.

Class `TypeNode` illustrates a classic scenario for using optional types. In Jet-UML, type nodes represent class and interface diagram elements in a class diagram. They can optionally be located in a package node. Correspondingly, the class declares a field `aContainer` to store a reference to the package node that contains the object. In this case, using an optional type as the type of the container makes perfect sense, because it supports a feature that is actually optional. If the type node is not contained in any node, `!aContainer.isPresent()`. In this case, I implemented the access to the optional value using design by contract, by specifying that the getter method `getParent()` can only be called if the node has a parent (that is, a container).

The NULL OBJECT Design Pattern

There exists a second solution for avoiding the use of null references to represent absent values, which avoids the issue of unpacking wrapper objects. This solution uses a special object to represent the null value. For this reason, this idea is called the NULL OBJECT design pattern. Using a NULL OBJECT to represent a null value relies on polymorphism, so it is only applicable to situations where a type hierarchy is available. Because `Card` objects are not a subtype of any other user-defined type, we cannot use it to model a joker. To explore the NULL OBJECT pattern, let us consider a different scenario, where a `CardSource` in client code could be unavailable. `CardSource` is an interface that defines methods `draw()` and `isEmpty()` and that it is implemented by the `Deck` class (see Section 3.1).

The main idea of NULL OBJECT is to create one special object to represent the absent value, and to test for absence using a polymorphic method call. Figure 4.4 captures the solution template as applied to the problem of handling potentially absent card sources.

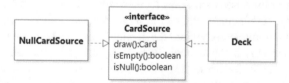

Fig. 4.4 Class diagram showing the `CardSource` interface with support for the NULL OBJECT pattern

In this design, one method was added to the original `CardSource` interface to determine if we are dealing with the null object, and one class was added to represent the null object. As expected, `isNull()` returns `false` for objects of any concrete type except `NullCardSource`, and `true` for the instance of `NullCardSource`. Client code can then use this idiom to handle absent card sources:

```
CardSource source = new NullCardSource();
...
CardSource source = getSource();
if( source.isNull() ) {...}
```

With the features of Java 8, a NULL OBJECT solution can be implemented efficiently by only modifying the interface at the root of the type hierarchy. First, we use a *default* method to avoid having to change all card source classes to implement `isNull` simply to return `true`. In Java, default methods are methods that have an implementation in the interface which is applicable to instances of all implementing types. To have a minimal impact on the rest of the code, we can also implement the NULL OBJECT as a constant in the interface by using an anonymous class.[5]

```
public interface CardSource {

  CardSource NULL = new CardSource() {
    public boolean isEmpty() {
      return true;
    }
    public Card draw() {
      assert !isEmpty();
      return null;
    }
    public boolean isNull() {
      return true;
    }
  };

  Card draw();
  boolean isEmpty();
  default boolean isNull() { return false; }
}
```

With this solution, there is no longer a need for a separate `NullCardSource` class. Client code that must indicate an absent card source can simply use the reference available through `CardSource.NULL` instead. Because a NULL `CardSource` behaves just like any other card source, many special cases can be avoided. It is worth noting how this includes the call to `draw`: because calling `draw` on the NULL card source will automatically violate the precondition; the fact that we return a null reference afterwards is inconsequent. In fact, in an ideal application of the NULL OBJECT, a check method such as `isNull()` should not even be necessary. In our case, for example, because all client code that works with a card source must check for emptiness first, obtaining a NULL card source is indistinguishable from obtaining an empty one. For this reason, in practice we could dispense with the `isNull()` method altogether, and leverage polymorphism to its fullest to yield a clean design without corner cases.

---

[5] Fields declared in interfaces are implicitly public and static.

Code Exploration: Solitaire · NullPlayingStrategy

Applying the NULL OBJECT *pattern.*

Class `NullPlayingStrategy` demonstrates two related applications of the NULL OBJECT pattern. First, the class itself is a null object value that represents the absence of a playing strategy. Injecting the `GameModel` class with this type of strategy is a clean way to disable the auto-play feature without flags or corner cases. Second, the class realizes the pattern by overriding method `getLegalMove` to return a null object for the `Move` class hierarchy. The null `Move` is declared in the initialization of `GameModel.NULL_MOVE`. Predictably, a null move represents the absence of an action in the game.

4.6 Final Fields and Variables

In Section 4.4, I argued that one useful principle to follow when designing a class is to keep the abstract state space for objects of the class to the minimum necessary for the objects of the class to provide the services expected of them. For example, a well-designed `Deck` class has three meaningful abstract states, not ten. Because object state is just an abstraction of the combination of values taken by the fields of an object, the way to realize the principle in practice is to limit the number of ways in which the field values can be updated. We already saw, in the previous section, how avoiding null references whenever possible can help us reach this goal. An even stricter constraint for keeping the abstract state space of objects nice and small, is to prevent changing the value of a field after initialization, so that the value of the field remains constant.

This constraint can be made explicit through the use of the `final` keyword placed in front of a variable declaration (which includes the declaration of instance variables). If we declare the fields `aRank` and `aSuit` to be `final` in class `Card`:

```
public class Card {
  private final Rank aRank;
  private final Suit aSuit;

  public Card( Rank pRank, Suit pSuit) {
    aRank = pRank;
    aSuit = pSuit;
  }
}
```

then the fields can be assigned a value *only once*, either in the initializer part of their declaration, or directly in the constructor (as in the example).[6] Attempting to

---

[6] In practice, field initialization code (the right-hand side of the equal sign in a field declaration) gets executed as part of constructor call anyways.

reassign the value of the field anywhere else in the code leads to a compilation error. The `final` keyword thus goes a long way in limiting the state space of an object, because any field marked as `final` can only take a single value. In the case of class `Card`, making both `aRank` and `aSuit final` effectively renders objects of the class immutable, because there are no other fields.

An important thing to keep in mind with the use of the `final` keyword, however, is that for reference types, the value stored in a variable is a *reference* to an object. So, although it is not possible to reassign a `final` field, it is certainly possible to change the state of the object referenced (if the object is mutable). Let us illustrate this point by making field `aCards` of class `Deck final`:

```
public class Deck {
  private final List<Card> aCards = new ArrayList<>();
}
```

A fresh instance of class `Deck` is shown in Figure 4.5.

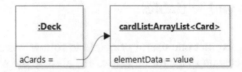

Fig. 4.5 Instance of class `Deck`

Because field `aCards` is `final` (something not visible on the diagram), we can be sure that the reference held in the field will *always* refer to the one `ArrayList` named `cardList` on the diagram. In other words, it will not be possible for this arrow to point anywhere else. However, we can (and need to) change the state of `cardList`, for example to initialize it with all the cards. Thus, although final fields can be very helpful in restricting the state space of an object to make it easier to understand the behavior of the object at run time, they do *not* make the referenced objects immutable.

The discussion above was concerned mainly with *instance* variables. However, local variables (including method parameters) can also be declared to be `final`. As opposed to fields, however, the case for making local variables final is much less clear because they are not long-lived.[7] There is one fairly technical special case where local variables must not be reassigned (see Section 4.10), but even then the variable does not need to be explicitly marked with the `final` keyword.[8] I occasionally declare a variable `final` to make my intent clear that the variable is not and should not be reassigned. This is only really useful for long and/or complex methods that may be a bit difficult to understand. Ideally, this should be a rare scenario, because well-designed methods are short and simple (and an overly LONG METHOD† is a recognized antipattern).

---

[7] Local variables only exist for the duration of the execution of code in their scope.

[8] Since Java 8, local variables that are not reassigned are considered *effectively final* by the compiler.

4.7 Object Identity, Equality, and Uniqueness

Three important concepts to keep in mind when designing object life cycles are those of *identity*, *equality*, and *uniqueness*.

Identity refers to the fact that we are referring to a particular object, even if this object is not in a variable. In terms of programming environments, the identity of an object usually refers to its "memory location", or "reference/pointer to". However, in modern programming systems the memory management of objects is heavily abstracted, and for this reason it is best to think in terms of object identity. Most integrated development environments supply a convenient handle to represent an object's identity. For example, in the Eclipse debugger this is represented by the object id.

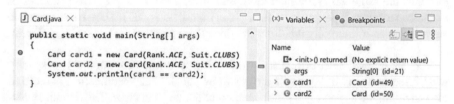

Fig. 4.6 Representation of object identity in the Eclipse debugger

In the small example of Figure 4.6 two `Card` objects are created, and consequently result in two distinct objects with two distinct identities, represented with internal object identifiers 49 and 50 (on the right, in the *Value* column). In the object diagram of Figure 4.7, the `main` method is represented as an object with two fields in place of local variables. The diagram shows how object identity corresponds to both object model elements and the references to these objects. If, for instance, a reference to the `Card` object with id 49 is added to a list, there will be two locations that refer to a single shared identity.

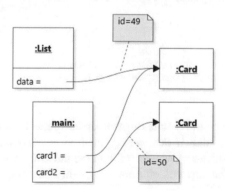

Fig. 4.7 Object identity example

The last statement in the `main` method in Figure 4.6, is a reminder that in Java, the `==` operator returns `true` if the two operands evaluate to the same value. In the case of values of reference types, *the same value* means referring to the same object (identity). So here the statement returns `false` because, although both cards represent an Ace of Clubs, they are references to different objects.

The situation above, where two different `Card` objects represent the Ace of Clubs, illustrates the concept of *object equality*. In the general case, *equality* between two objects must be programmer-defined because the meaning of equality cannot always be inferred from the design of the object's class. In very simple cases (like objects of class `Card`), one could say that two objects are equal if all their fields have the same value. However, for many objects of more complex classes, this would be too strict. For example, if some objects cache values or have non-deterministic or unspecified internal representations, they could be "equal" in the practical sense, without having *precisely* the same value for each field, transitively. For example, two instances of a set abstract data type (such as Java's `Set`) must be equal if they have the same elements, even if internally the order in which these elements are stored is different.

For this reason, Java provides a mechanism to allow programmers to specify what it means for two objects of a class to be equal. This specification is realized by *overriding* the `equals(Object)` method of the `Object` class. The default implementation of the `equals` method defines *equality* as *identity*. In other words, if the `equals` method is not redefined for a class, `a.equals(b)` is practically the same as `a == b`.[9] In many situations, like our example of playing cards, this is not what we need, and we must supply our own implementation of the `equals` method. Implementations of `equals` can usually follow this example as a template:

```
public boolean equals(Object pObject) {
  if( pObject == null ) {
    return false; // As required by the specification
  }
  else if( pObject == this ) {
    return true; // Standard optimization
  }
  else if( pObject.getClass() != getClass()) {
    return false;
  }
  else {
    // Actual comparison code
    return aRank == ((Card)pObject).aRank &&
      ((Card)pObject).aSuit == aSuit;
  }
}
```

I will revisit some of the details of the overriding mechanism in Chapter 7. For now, it suffices to say that if the `equals` method is *redefined* in a class, calling `equals` on an object of this class will result in the redefined version being executed, and thus implement the custom definition of equality. In our case,

---

[9] Except in the case where `a == null`. The `==` operator will correctly compare null values, but if a is null, `a.equals(b)` will raise a `NullPointerException`.

```
card1.equals(card2)
```

will return `true`.

A crucial constraint when overriding `equals` is that any class that overrides `equals` must also override `hashCode` so that the following requirement is respected:

> If two objects are equal according to the `equals(Object)` method, then calling the `hashCode` method on each of the two objects must produce the same integer result.
> —Reference documentation for `Object#equals`

This constraint is necessary because, among other things, many classes of the Collections framework rely interchangeably on equality testing and on an object's hash code for indexing objects in internal data structures.

A final consideration related to identity and equality is the concept of *uniqueness*. In our example code, we could rightfully wonder what is the point of tolerating duplicate objects that represent exactly the same card (e.g., Ace of Clubs). A sometimes useful property for the objects of a class is *uniqueness*. Objects of a class are unique if it is not possible for two distinct objects to be equal. If the objects of a class can be guaranteed to be unique, then we no longer need to define equality, because in this specific case, equality become equivalent to identity and we can compare objects using the `==` operator. Strict guarantees of uniqueness are almost impossible to achieve in Java due to mechanisms such as metaprogramming (see Section 5.4) and *serialization*.[10] However, in practice, the use of two design patterns, presented below, and the conscious avoidance of metaprogramming and serialization, provide a good enough guarantee of uniqueness that can help simplify some designs.

Code Exploration: JetUML · Dimension

Implementing `equals` *and* `hashCode`.

Class `Dimension` provides an example of a class that yields objects that are not unique, given that it is possible to create two distinct objects that represent exactly the same dimension (width and height). The class thus provides a fairly typical implementation of the `equals` and `hashCode` methods, which allows client code and library classes to take into account that dimension objects can be equal.

4.8 The FLYWEIGHT Design Pattern

The FLYWEIGHT pattern provides a way to cleanly manage collections of low-level immutable objects. Although sometimes used to address performance concerns, FLYWEIGHT is also valuable to ensure the uniqueness of objects of a class.

---

[10] *Serialization* involves converting an object into a data structure that can be stored outside a running program, and then reconstructed later. The reconstruction of a serialized object almost invariably leads to a copy of the serialized object being created.

The *context* for using FLYWEIGHT is when instances of a class are heavily shared in a software system. For example, Card objects in the Solitaire application are referenced in many different classes.

The idea that underlies the pattern's solution template is to manage the creation of objects of a certain class, called the *flyweight* class. Instances of the flyweight class are called flyweight objects. The crucial aspect of the FLYWEIGHT is to control the creation of flyweight objects through an *access method* that ensures that no duplicate objects (distinct but equal) ever exist. The three main components necessary to realize this constraint are:

1. A *private constructor* for the flyweight class, so clients cannot control the creation of objects of the class;
2. A static *flyweight store* that keeps a collection of flyweight objects;
3. A static *access method* that returns the unique flyweight object that corresponds to some identification key. The access method typically checks whether the requested flyweight object already exists in the store, creates it if it does not already exist, and returns the unique object.

For example, we could decide to make the Card class a flyweight. Let us first consider the non-flyweight version:

```
public class Card {
    private final Rank aRank;
    private final Suit aSuit;

    public Card(Rank pRank, Suit pSuit ) {
        aRank = pRank;
        aSuit = pSuit; }

    /* Includes equals and hashCode implementations */
}
```

Instances of this class are clearly not flyweights, given that it is possible to use the constructor to create two instances that are distinct but equal:

```
Card card1 = new Card(Rank.ACE, Suit.CLUBS);
Card card2 = new Card(Rank.ACE, Suit.CLUBS);
System.out.println(String.format("Same?: %b; Equal?: %b",
    card1 == card2, card1.equals(card2)));
```

To implement Step 1 of the solution template, we simply change public for private in front of the constructor. This prevents client code from creating new Card instances arbitrarily. Now we need to figure out a way for code outside of class Card to get instances of the class. Before tackling this question (Step 3 in the solution template), let us create a store for flyweight Card instances (Step 2 in the solution template). The two main decisions to make to realize this step are choosing a data structure to hold the instances, and deciding where to locate this structure in the code.

It is important to note that with design patterns, each application of the pattern can involve different implementation details. A solution template is just that: an overview of the main structures. For the FLYWEIGHT in particular, the implementation of the flyweight store and access method can exhibit much variability, depending on the details of the flyweight class.

In our specific case, because playing cards can be completely indexed in terms of two keys (rank and suit), I will store them in a two-dimensional array. As to where this array should be located, an obvious choice is to hold it as a static field in class Card so that we can make it private and use methods of class Card to access it. The following code shows the definition of the flyweight store and an implementation of its initialization.

```
public class Card {
  private static final Card[][] CARDS =
    new Card[Suit.values().length][Rank.values().length];

  static {
    for( Suit suit : Suit.values() ) {
      for( Rank rank : Rank.values() ) {
        CARDS[suit.ordinal()][rank.ordinal()] =
          new Card(rank, suit);
      }
    }
  }
}
```

Because objects that represent playing cards are relatively small in number (52) and completely known in advance, I also chose to pre-initialize the flyweight store with a static initializer block.[11] This implementation is only one example of a FLYWEIGHT implementation. Even for the same context (playing cards), many other alternatives are possible. For example, it would be possible to store flyweights in lists or hash tables.[12] With the current solution, accessing the collection with a correct index is guaranteed to produce the requested card. For example:

```
CARDS[Suit.CLUBS.ordinal()][Rank.ACE.ordinal()];
```

will return the (assumed unique) instance of Card that represents the Ace of Clubs.

The code above is only correct if it is placed within the scope of class Card, because CARDS is private. To grant access to cards to code outside the class, we need an access method. In our example, the implementation of this method is trivial:

```
public static Card get(Rank pRank, Suit pSuit) {
  assert pRank != null && pSuit != null;
  return CARDS[pSuit.ordinal()][pRank.ordinal()];
}
```

This method is static given that the flyweight store is static. This makes sense, because it would be bizarre to request a card instance through another card instance. The combination of the flyweight store and corresponding access method is sometimes referred to as the *flyweight factory*. In Java, it is common to use static struc-

---

[11] A block of code that executes once, when the class is first loaded in the run-time environment.

[12] The best choice is probably to use the EnumMap library type, but to get the point across with a minimum of explanation, the array-based solution is more accessible.

tures in the flyweight class as the flyweight factory. However, it is not the only option, as we could easily create a separate class to fulfill this role (called, for example,
`CardFactory`).

For flyweight objects that represent playing cards, the use of the pair (rank, suit)
as the identification key is intuitive. In other scenarios, it can be less obvious what
the identification key should be. For example, for an object of type `Person`, the key
could be a name, an identification number, etc. In any case, the identification cannot
be an instance of the flyweight object itself. In our example with cards, such an
approach would look like:

```
Card card = Card.get(someCard); // INVALID
```

This would mean that to obtain a flyweight object of class `Card`, it would be
necessary to already have that object. Because the only way to get a flyweight object
should be through its access method, this scheme leads to an infinite cycle, and is
thus flawed.

An important concern when implementing the FLYWEIGHT pattern is whether to
pre-initialize the flyweight store, or whether to do this lazily, by creating objects as
they are requested through the access method. The answer is context-dependent. In
general, in cases where there exists a small and finite set of flyweights, it may make
sense to pre-initialize them (as in the example). In other cases, additional logic must
be added to the access method to check whether the object exists in the collection
and, if not, create it based on the key. In this latter case, the access method needs
to be able to access all the information it needs to create the flyweight instance that
corresponds to the requested key. The following code shows the FLYWEIGHT-relevant
portion of a version of the `Card` class where instances are lazily created:

```
public class Card {
  private static final Card[][] CARDS =
    new Card[Suit.values().length][Rank.values().length];

  public static Card get(Rank pRank, Suit pSuit) {
    if( CARDS[pSuit.ordinal()][pRank.ordinal()] == null ) {
      CARDS[pSuit.ordinal()][pRank.ordinal()] =
        new Card(pRank, pSuit);
    }
    return CARDS[pSuit.ordinal()][pRank.ordinal()];
  }
}
```

Finally, it is important to note that the FLYWEIGHT pattern is especially convenient
when used to manage *immutable* flyweight objects. Although it is technically feasi-
ble to apply the pattern to manage a collection of mutable objects, this approach can
easily become error-prone. In any case, it is crucial to ensure that the portion of the
flyweight objects' state that defines the objects' identity cannot be mutated.

Code Exploration: JetUML · Direction

Application of FLYWEIGHT *with multiple access methods.*

Class `Direction` represents a certain direction, in degrees, in a geometric plane. By design, degrees are represented as integers, with a maximum precision of one degree. This decision means that there can be at most 360 distinct directions to represent. I used the FLYWEIGHT to prevent a huge proliferation of `Dimension` objects, with numerous duplicates for the common values that represent the cardinal directions (north, south, etc.). One interesting aspect of this application of the pattern is that the flyweight factory provides multiple access methods. For example, `fromAngle` returns a dimension given an input angle, whereas `fromLine` finds the direction using a line in the plane as input, and `mirrored` finds the direction that is opposite to the input direction.

4.9 The SINGLETON Design Pattern

The SINGLETON design pattern provides a way to ensure that there is only one instance of a given class at any point in the execution of the code. The context for this design pattern is the need to manage an instance that holds, in one place, a cohesive amount of information that different parts of the code need. An example of a potential SINGLETON object in a card game would be the instance that represents the aggregated state of the game. This state could include the deck of cards and the various piles of cards in the game in progress. The solution template for SINGLETON involves three elements:

1. A *private constructor* for the singleton class, so clients cannot create multiple objects;
2. A *global variable* for holding a reference to the single instance of the singleton object.
3. An *accessor method*, usually called `instance()`, that returns the singleton instance. The accessor method is optional, because it is also possible to implement the pattern by declaring the global instance to be a public constant.

In a sample card game, a singleton object that encapsulates the aggregated state of the game, of class `GameModel`, could be implemented as follows:

```
public class GameModel {
  private static final GameModel INSTANCE = new GameModel();

  private GameModel() { ... }

  public static GameModel instance() { return INSTANCE; }
}
```

The SINGLETON pattern differs from FLYWEIGHT in that it attempts to guarantee that there is *a single instance of a class*, as opposed to *unique instances of a class*. Singleton objects are typically stateful and mutable, whereas flyweight objects are preferably immutable.

A typical mistake when implementing the SINGLETON pattern is to store a reference to an instance of the class in a static field called INSTANCE or something like it, without taking proper care to prevent client code from independently creating new objects. In this case, use of the *Singleton* name is harmfully misleading, because users of the code may rely on the fact that the class yields a single instance when in fact it does not.

The classic way to prevent instantiation is to make the class constructor private. However, in *Effective Java* [1], Bloch proposes a controversial trick, namely, to use an enumerated type (Item 3: *Enforce the singleton property with a private constructor or an enum type*). For example, to make a GameModel class a singleton, one could do:

```
public enum GameModel {
    INSTANCE;

    public void initializeGame() {}
}
```

This technically works because the compiler will prevent the instantiation of enumerated types. Although this approach is presented as preferred in *Effective Java*, it is not without detractors. To me, this strategy uses a programming mechanism (enumerated types) for an intent other than originally designed and, as such, it can be confusing. Here the type GameModel is not a finite set of values representing different game models, which is what one would initially expect when seeing an enum designation. I thus recommend sticking to a private constructor to ensure the single-instance constraint.

Now that we know about the SINGLETON, I must mention that this pattern is controversial. While all design decisions involve trade-offs (see Section 1.1), in the case of the SINGLETON, the balance can often tip in favor of the disadvantages. First, a singleton is essentially a global instance, accessible from anywhere in the code. It is thus easy to make unprincipled use of this object, leading to numerous dependencies and code that is hard to understand. Second, singleton objects are difficult to test because they control their own life cycle and live for the entire duration of the application. Chapter 5 discusses testing in detail but, for now, it suffices to say that use of the SINGLETON makes a stateful object difficult to replace when necessary. In many cases, a good alternative for accessing a reference to a unique object is to use dependency injection (see Section 3.8). However, dependency injection does not provide a mechanism for preventing the creation of multiple instantiations of a class. This constraint must be respected with the assistance of methodical programming and documentation. What dependency injection helps achieve, however, is to propagate that single instance to the code that requires it.

Generally, what is important is to be able to recognize situations where only one instance of a class must be present in an application, and to be able to evaluate different strategies for creating and managing this unique instance. In cases where dependency injection or another solution is fit for purpose, it may be preferable to employ it instead of using a SINGLETON. In some cases, however, the SINGLETON may turn out to be the preferable solution.

Code Exploration: Solitaire · GameModel

Managing a single instance without the SINGLETON.

In version 1.0 of Solitaire, I had implemented class `GameModel` as a singleton. Similar to the running example in this section, `GameModel` is the class used to create a single object that holds the complete state of the game. As the pattern dictates, the object was available as a global instance to any other part of the code. For this edition of the book, I refactored `GameModel` to remove the part of the pattern that controls the life cycle of the object. The class is still meant to be instantiated only once, but in version 2.0 of Solitaire, the life cycle is handled differently, to illustrate an alternative to SINGLETON. Specifically, `GameModel` is instantiated once when the application starts (in method `Solitaire#start`), and then injected into the objects that need a reference to it.

Code Exploration: JetUML · ApplicationResources

Using the SINGLETON *for pervasive access to a service.*

Class `ApplicationResources` in JetUML provides a way to obtain the various text strings that appear in the application (for example, button and menu labels). Following the practice of string externalization, these strings are not hard-coded, but stored in a separate configuration file. The class provides an example of the SINGLETON, but with a quirk: there is no `instance()` method. Instead the field storing the singleton instance is called `RESOURCES` and is public. In this case, I compromised on the strict implementation of SINGLETON, mostly for cosmetic reasons. The singleton instance is referred to in over 100 locations in the code. Instead of the cumbersome `ApplicationResources.instance()` reference, I relied on Java's static import mechanism to import the name of the instance field. Because it would not be very meaningful to refer to just `INSTANCE`, however, I named the field `RESOURCES`. This way, the singleton instance of class `ApplicationResources` can be referred to anywhere in the code with the name `RESOURCES` (assuming the mention `import static ...ApplicationResources.RESOURCES;` is present). The fact that `ApplicationResources` is required in a very high number of locations is also a factor that justifies using SINGLETON instead of dependency injection.

4.10 Objects of Nested Classes

A particular state management concern is introduced by the use of nested classes in Java. Nested classes can be divided into two broad categories: *static nested classes* and *inner classes*. In turn, there are two categories of inner classes: *anonymous classes* and *local classes*. The distinction between each of these categories of classes is discussed below. Figure 4.8 summarizes the categories and their relations.

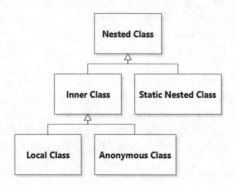

Fig. 4.8 Different categories of Java classes and relations between them. The classifiers in the diagram represent the categories of classes, not source code classes.

Section 3.4 introduced the use of anonymous classes to implement function objects. As it turns out, inner classes can sometimes discretely maintain a reference to other objects. Because this can affect their state space and life cycle in important ways, it is important to know about this feature of the Java language.

Inner Classes

Let us start with inner classes. Inner classes are declared within another class, and used to provide additional behavior that involves an instance of the *enclosing* class, but which for some reason we do not want to integrate into the enclosing class. As an example, let us say we want the option to remember how many times a certain `Deck` instance was shuffled. As usual, there are different ways of doing this. To illustrate how inner classes work, we will define a `Shuffler` class as an inner class of `Deck`:

```
public class Deck {
  public void shuffle() { ... }
  public Shuffler newShuffler() { return new Shuffler(); }

  public class Shuffler {
    private int aNumberOfShuffles = 0;

    private Shuffler() {}

    public void shuffle() {}
      aNumberOfShuffles++;
      Deck.this.shuffle();
    }

    public int getNumberOfShuffles() {
      return aNumberOfShuffles;
    }
  }
}
```

In this example, the first part of the declaration of class Shuffler looks pretty normal: we declare a class Shuffler with a field aNumberOfShuffles and a method shuffle(). However, things get interesting within the code of Shuffler-#shuffle(), where we observe the statement Deck.this.shuffle();. Instances of an inner class automatically get a reference to the corresponding instance of their enclosing class (called the *outer instance*). The outer instance for an inner class is the object that was the implicit parameter of the method where the instance of the inner class was created. This can be confusing at first, so let us run through an execution:

```
Deck deck = new Deck();
Shuffler shuffler = deck.newShuffler();
shuffler.shuffle();
```

The first line creates a new instance of Deck, as usual. The second line calls method newShuffler() on the instance of Deck referred to by variable deck. This method creates a new instance of Shuffler, whose outer instance will be the one referred to by deck. Within an inner class, the outer instance can be accessed through a qualified name that consists of the name of the class of the outer instance, followed by this. So, in our case, Deck.this refers to the outer instance of shuffler. On the third line, it is the method shuffle() of the Shuffler instance that is called, but when this method executes, it then calls the shuffle() method of class Deck on the deck instance using Deck.this. Figure 4.9 illustrates the scenario with an object diagram.

With this design, the deck can be shuffled through the shuffler instance, which will remember how many times the method was invoked. It is also possible to shuffle the deck without going through the shuffler instance, in which case the field aNumberOfShuffles will not be incremented. The important point about this discussion, however, is that the concrete state space of inner classes *adds to* that of the outer instance. Although this can technically lead to increased complexity, it does

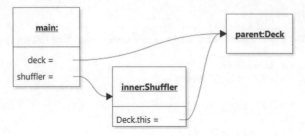

Fig. 4.9 Object graph for an inner class

not have to be so. In good design, the abstract state space of objects of inner classes should abstract the state of the outer instance. This is the case of the Shuffler class, for which the state of the outer instance does not influence how we use the Shuffler instance.

Java also allows the declaration of static nested classes. The main difference between static nested classes and inner classes is that static nested classes are *not* linked to an outer instance. As such, they are mostly used for encapsulation and code organization.

Anonymous Classes

Just like inner classes, local and anonymous classes also have implicit access to additional state information through a reference to their outer instance. Because local classes are rarely used, this section focuses on anonymous classes. However, local classes work in a very similar way. Let us consider the following code for a factory method that creates a Comparator<Deck> instance that compares two decks in terms of the number of cards of a given rank that they have.

```java
public class Deck {
 public static Comparator<Deck> createRankComparator(Rank pRank){
    return new Comparator<Deck>() {
       public int compare(Deck pDeck1, Deck pDeck2) {
          return countCards(pDeck1) - countCards(pDeck2);
       }

       private int countCards(Deck pDeck) {
          /* returns the number of cards in pDeck with pRank */
       }
    };
  }
}
```

For example, in the code below, to see whether deck1 contains more kings than deck2, we could do:

```java
Comparator<Deck> comp = Deck.createRankComparator(Rank.KING);
boolean result = comp.compare(deck1,deck2) < 1;
```

This solution is an example of factory method used to create a function object of type `Comparator`, as explained in Section 3.4. The code is relatively unexciting, except perhaps for one intriguing observation. Upon closer inspection, it appears that the code of method `compare` *declared inside the anonymous class* has access to the parameter `pRank` of `createRankComparator`, which is a *separate method in a separate class*. What could `pRank` possibly refer to when the code is running? Once the `createRankComparator` method returns an object, this object has its own life cycle that is independent from that of the `Deck` object. Yet this is legal, compilable code, that actually works and does what we want.

Because referring to variables in the parent method from an anonymous class is such a useful programming idiom, it is supported by the language. To make this work, when the compiler creates the definition of the anonymous class, it also (invisibly) adds *fields* to the anonymous class, and copies references to each of the local variables referenced in the code of the anonymous class's method into a field. Thus, once an object of the anonymous class is created, the references to the local variables are now stored in fields of the same name in the anonymous class. The object diagram of Figure 4.10 illustrates this idea.

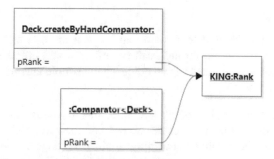

Fig. 4.10 Example of closure modeled by an object diagram

In this diagram the factory method is represented as a separate object with field `pRank` used to represent its parameter. This method returns a completely new object of an anonymous class. So that the `compare` method can still refer to the `pRank` parameter, a field `pRank` is created in the instance of the anonymous comparator, and the value of `pRank` is copied to it. A method definition together with references to its local environment variables is sometimes called a *closure*.[13] As the object diagram shows, it should be clear that closures can lead to shared references between object instances. To prevent unexpected behavior, Java prevents referencing external variables that are reassigned within anonymous classes.[14]

---

[13] In Java, anonymous classes and lambda expressions are not closures in the strict sense because they cannot modify the variables they reference. However, because they are as close as we can get to closures in Java, I employ the term to refer to methods that capture some of the values in non-local variables, as in this case.

[14] Prior to Java 8, local variables referenced within anonymous classes had to be declared `final`. With Java 8 the compiler can infer variables to be *effectively final* without the keyword.

Code Exploration: Solitaire · GameModel

Instances of anonymous classes used as closures.

In class `GameModel`, field `aDiscard` represents a specific type of move in
the game, to discard a card from the deck. How this works with the rest of
the code is the topic of a later chapter. However, the initialization of the field
provides an example of how instances of anonymous classes retain a reference
to their parent class. By instantiating an anonymous subtype of interface `Move`,
the initialization of the field has to provide an implementation for the three
methods of the interface. Part of the explanation is to be found in the code of
method `perform`, which actually performs the discard move. In the code, we
see references to three fields: `aDiscard`, `aDeck`, and `aMoves`. These are *not*
fields of the anonymous class, but fields of its enclosing class, `GameModel`.

Insights

This chapter defined object state, argued that keeping track of all the different abstract states an object can go through can be difficult, and proposed a number of
techniques for designing classes whose objects have simple and well-structured life
cycles.

- For stateful classes, consider using state diagrams to reason systematically about
  the abstract states of the object of the classes and their life cycle;
- Try to minimize the number of meaningful abstract states for objects of a class:
  make sure it is not possible to put the object in invalid or useless states, and
  avoid storing information just for convenience or non-critical performance im-
  provements;
- Avoid using null references to represent legal information in objects and variables; consider using optional types or the NULL OBJECT pattern to represent absent values, if necessary;
- Consider declaring instance variables `final` whenever possible;
- Be explicit about whether objects of a class should be unique or not;
- If objects are not designed to be unique, override the `equals` and `hashCode`
  methods; if objects should be unique, consider using the FLYWEIGHT pattern to
  enforce uniqueness;
- Consider an explicit structure, such as SINGLETON or dependency injection, for
  managing classes that should yield only one instance of a stateful object.
- Remember that additional data can be attached to instances of inner classes, either in the form of a reference to an instance of an outer class, or as copies of
  local variables bundled in a closure.

Further Reading

The Gang of Four book [6] has the original, detailed treatment of the FLYWEIGHT and SINGLETON patterns. Chapter 3 of *Refactoring: Improving the Design of Existing Code* [3] mentions the TEMPORARY FIELD† and LONG METHODS† antipatterns. The entry *Introduce Null Object* in Chapter 8 discusses the idea of NULL OBJECT.

Chapter 10 of *Java 8 in Action* [16] is entitled *Using Optional as a better alternative to null*, and provides more details and examples on the use of the `Optional` type. This is also where I found the anecdote about Tony Hoare. Item 55 in *Effective Java* [1] provides useful insights on when and how to use optional types.

The API documentation for `Object.equals(Object)` and `Object.hashCode()` provide additional information on the meaning of equality in Java. The section on nested classes in the Java Tutorial [10] is a good reference.

Chapter 5
Unit Testing

Concepts and Principles: Annotations, JUnit, metaprogramming, test coverage, test suites, unit testing;

Unit testing is a practice wherein we automatically execute code to check that it does what we think it should. With unit testing, we can build a possibly large collection of tests that can quickly be executed, for instance every time we change the code, to make sure everything that worked still does. Additionally, writing unit tests provides insights into the quality of a design. This chapter introduces mechanisms that facilitate unit testing (metaprogramming and annotations) and presents basic techniques for designing unit tests and evaluating their quality.

Design Context

This chapter discusses the testing of code derived from design elements of the Solitaire sample application. For simplicity, the examples are slightly adapted from the actual project code. The first examples focus on the simple library function `Math.abs(int)`, then a method of the `Suit` enumerated type. Subsequent examples revolve around `FoundationPile`, a class that represents one of the four piles where finished suits are accumulated in the game. The final design problem concerns the partial testing of class `GameModel`, which encapsulates the entire aggregated state of a game of Solitaire in progress.

© Springer Nature Switzerland AG 2022
M. P. Robillard, *Introduction to Software Design with Java*,
https://doi.org/10.1007/978-3-030-97899-0_5

5.1 Introduction to Unit Testing

Software quality problems are often caused by programmers writing code that does not do what they expect, and the programmers remaining ignorant of this mismatch between expectations and reality. As a real example, one bug in JetUML made the directory structure disappear from the file chooser[1] when a user wanted to select the location where to export a file. The offending code statement was in a method in charge of deciding whether to accept a file for display in the file chooser or not:

```
public boolean accept(File pFile) {
  return !pFile.isDirectory() &&
    (pFile.getName().endsWith("." + pFormat.toLowerCase()) ||
     pFile.getName().endsWith("." + pFormat.toUpperCase())));
}
```

At a quick glance, and with insufficient caffeine, this code looks reasonable: *if the file is not a directory and its name ends with a specified extension, in either lower or upper case, accept it.* The idea of the last clause was to avoid exporting images to directories named, for example, `directory.jpg`. Unfortunately, focusing on this unlikely possibility had obscured the more important requirement that we *do* need to show directories in the file chooser. This kind of blind spot is typically how bugs appear. And they really do like to hide in compound conditional statements. Once exposed, the fix was trivial: remove the negation operator and replace the first and operator (`&&`) with an `or` operator (`||`).

One way to detect bugs, and to gain confidence that a part of the code does what we expect, is to *test* it. Testing is a software quality assurance technique that can take many forms. Given that this is an introductory book on software design, I focus on one specific testing approach called *unit testing*. The idea of unit testing is to test a small part of the code in isolation. This way, if a test fails, it is easy to know where to look for problems.

A *unit test* consists of one or more executions of a *unit under test* (UUT) with some input data and the comparison of the result of the execution against some oracle. A UUT is whatever piece of the code we wish to test in isolation. UUTs are often methods, but in some cases they can also be entire classes, initialization statements, or certain paths through the code. The term *oracle* designates the correct or expected result of the execution of a UUT.

For example, the statement: `Math.abs(5) == 5;` technically qualifies as a test. Here the UUT is the library method `Math.abs(int)`,[2] the input data is the integer literal 5, and the oracle is, in this case, also the value 5. The comparison of the result of executing the UUT with the oracle is also called an *assertion*. The name captures the idea that the role of the comparison is to *assert* that the result is what we expect.

When testing instance methods, it is important to remember that the input data includes the *implicit argument* (the instance that receives the method call). As a

---

[1] A graphical user interface component that allows the user to select a file by browsing a view of the file system.

[2] Function to compute the absolute value of an `int` value.

second example that involves an implicit argument, let us consider a version of the
Suit enumerated type that includes an additional method sameColorAs(Suit). In
a standard deck of cards, the Clubs and Spades are *black* suits and the Diamonds
and Hearts are *red* suits.

```java
public enum Suit {
  CLUBS, DIAMONDS, SPADES, HEARTS;

  public boolean sameColorAs(Suit pSuit) {
    assert pSuit != null;
    return (ordinal() - pSuit.ordinal()) % 2 == 0;
  }
}
```

With this design we are not returning the color of a Suit instance, but rather,
whether the suit is of the same color as some other Suit instance. In the case of
a game where the color of a suit does not matter, only whether it is the same color as
some other suit, this design decision makes a lot of sense. Following the principle
of information hiding, we only provide the information that is absolutely needed.
Returning to our example, something to note is that the code was written by a programmer who favors compact code over clarity of intent and robustness. To give
ourselves confidence that this actually works despite the hackery, we can write a
unit test for the method:

```java
public static void main(String[] args) {
  boolean oracle = false;
  System.out.println(oracle == CLUBS.sameColorAs(HEARTS));
}
```

This example makes it clear that although method sameColorAs takes a single *explicit* argument, there are in fact two arguments to the UUT: the explicitly provided
argument (Suit.HEARTS), and the implicit argument: Suit.CLUBS. According to
the definition of a unit test provided above, this main method qualifies as a unit test:
it includes a UUT (Suit#sameColorAs), some input data (CLUBS and HEARTS), an
oracle (false), and an assertion that compares the result with the oracle. Executing
the main method will tell us whether the test passes or not.

    If we wanted to increase the number of inputs we test for sameColorAs, we could
add additional pairs of suits. Because there are only four suits, we could actually test
all possible inputs for sameColorAs with a mere 16 tests. This achievement, called
exhaustive testing, is almost never possible (see Section 5.9). Writing an exhaustive
test for sameColorAs will show that the method works correctly for all possible
inputs. This is fabulous, but only ephemerally so. Source code is not set in stone.
To continue with our scenario, let us say that a different programmer comes along
later and, because of some requirement change, reorders the suits as follows without touching the sameColorAs method (perhaps because its implementation looks
fancy):

CLUBS, SPADES, DIAMONDS, HEARTS;

    In this case, running the test again will immediately reveal a bug introduced by
the fact that sameColorAs relies on an undocumented and unchecked assumption

about the order of enumerated values. This example illustrates the second major benefit of unit tests: in addition to helping detect bugs in new code, they can also check that tested behavior that used to meet some specific expectation still does meet that expectation even after the code changes. Running tests to ensure that what was tested as correct still is (or for detecting new bugs caused by changes) is called *regression testing*.

An important thing to realize about unit testing is what it *cannot* do. Unit testing cannot *verify* code to be correct! When a test passes, it only shows that the one specific execution of the code that is being tested behaves as expected. There are software engineering techniques designed to provide certain guarantees about all possible code executions for a specific code element, but unit testing is not one of them. Section 5.9 provides further justification for why testing is not a verification technique.

5.2 Unit Testing Framework Fundamentals with JUnit

Although it is possible to test a system manually, unit testing is normally done automatically. Because in software development the way to automate anything is to write code to do it, to automate software testing we also write code to test other code. This task is typically supported by a *unit testing framework*.[3] Unit testing frameworks automate a lot of the mundane aspects of unit testing, including collecting tests, running them, and reporting the results. In addition to tools to collect and run tests and display the results, frameworks also include a set of constructs to allow developers to write tests in a structured way and (if they so choose) efficiently. The major constructs supported by testing frameworks are *test cases*, *test suites*, *test fixtures* and *assertions*. The dominant unit testing framework for Java is called *JUnit*. I will introduce the basics of this framework sufficiently to illustrate all of the testing techniques covered in this chapter. However, this chapter is not a tutorial on JUnit, and the Further Reading section provides pointers to additional information and coaching on how to use JUnit.

In JUnit, a unit test maps to a method. The code below illustrates a series of simple unit tests with JUnit.

```
public class AbsTest {
  @Test
  public void testAbs_Positive() {
    assertEquals(5, Math.abs(5));
  }
```

---

[3] The example with the `main` method in the previous section, although it qualifies as automation, was only to illustrate a point, and should not be considered a reasonable way to test production code.

```
@Test
public void testAbs_Negative() {
  assertEquals(5, Math.abs(-5));
}

@Test
public void testAbs_Max() {
  assertEquals(Integer.MAX_VALUE,Math.abs(Integer.MIN_VALUE));
}
}
```

The `@Test` *annotation instance* indicates that the annotated method should be run as a unit test. Section 5.4 explains annotations in more detail. For now, it suffices to say it is a marker we put in the code to mark a method as a unit test. The definition of the `@Test` annotation is defined in the JUnit library.[4] The code example above shows a *test class* (see Section 5.3) that defines three tests, all intended to test the library method `Math.abs(int)`.

To constitute proper tests, test methods should contain at least one execution of a unit under test. The way to automatically verify that the execution of a unit under test has the expected effect is to execute various calls to *assert methods*. Assert methods are different from the `assert` statement in Java. They are declared as static methods of the class `org.junit.jupiter.api.Assertions` and all they do is verify a predicate and, if the predicate is false, report a *test failure*. The JUnit framework includes a graphical user interface component called a *test runner*, which automatically scans some input code, detects all the tests in the input, executes them, and then reports whether the tests passed or failed. Figure 5.1 shows a screenshot of the result of executing all the tests in the test class `TestAbs` (above), using a version of the test runner available through the Eclipse integrated development environment. Two tests passed but one test, `testAbsMax`, failed. Perhaps it seems surprising that the absolute value of `Integer.MIN_VALUE` is not, in fact, `Integer.MAX_VALUE`. This quirk is documented in the Javadoc header for the method:

> Note that if the argument is equal to the value of Integer.MIN_VALUE, the most negative representable int value, the result is that same value, which is negative.

The reason for this design choice is imposed by physical constraints: because one bit of information is used to encode 0, there is no space left available to encode the absolute value of `Integer.MIN_VALUE` in a 32-bit `int` type. In addition to their bug detection potential, unit tests are a great way to surface important but obscure corner cases.

---

[4] The JUnit library must be added to a project's class path before it can be used. This chapter is based on JUnit version 5.

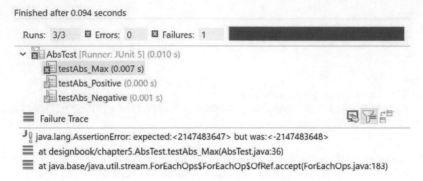

Fig. 5.1 Result of running JUnit using class `AbsTest` in the Eclipse IDE

5.3 Organizing Test Code

A collection of tests for a project is known as a *test suite*. By default, a project's test suite consists of all the unit tests for the production code in the project. However, for various reasons, it may be desirable to run only a subset of different tests at different times (for example, to focus on a specific feature, or save some time). Unit testing frameworks typically provide mechanisms to define arbitrary tests suites or, more generally, to run certain subsets of unit tests. As one example, JUnit provides a `@Suite` construct that allows a developer to list a number of test classes to be executed together. As another example, the JUnit plug-in for the Eclipse IDE allows users to execute the tests for only one package, or even a single test class. Because executing tests is a concern somewhat independent from the issue of designing them, the rest of the chapter focuses on writing the tests themselves.

A common question when building a suite of unit tests is how to organize our tests in a sensible manner. There are different approaches, but in Java a common idiom is to have one test class per project class, where the test class collects all the tests that test methods or other usage scenarios that involve the class. Furthermore, it is common practice to locate all the testing code in a different source folder with a package structure that mirrors the package structure of the production code. The rationale for this organization is that in Java classes with the same package name are in the same *package scope* independently of their location in a file system. This means that classes and methods in the test package can refer to non-public (but non-private) members of classes in the production code, while still being separated from the production code. The figure below illustrates this idea.

Fig. 5.2 Test suite organization for the JetUML sample
application

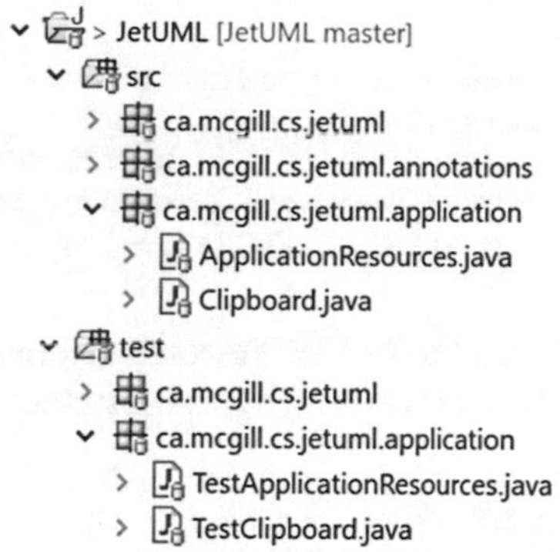

```
∨ 🗁 > JetUML [JetUML master]
   ∨ 📁 src
      > 🎱 ca.mcgill.cs.jetuml
      > 🎱 ca.mcgill.cs.jetuml.annotations
      ∨ 🎱 ca.mcgill.cs.jetuml.application
         > 📄 ApplicationResources.java
         > 📄 Clipboard.java
   ∨ 📁 test
      > 🎱 ca.mcgill.cs.jetuml
      ∨ 🎱 ca.mcgill.cs.jetuml.application
         > 📄 TestApplicationResources.java
         > 📄 TestClipboard.java
```

5.4 Metaprogramming

In the previous section, we saw that to mark a method as a test, we annotate it with
the string `@Test`. The unit testing framework can then rely on this annotation to
detect which methods are tests, and then proceed to execute these methods as part
of the execution of the test runner. This general approach, employed by most unit
testing frameworks, is special in that in requires the code to manipulate other code.
Specifically, the testing framework first scans the code to detect tests, and then executes the code, without having any explicit code for calls to test methods. This strategy is an illustration of a general programming feature called *metaprogramming*.
The idea of metaprogramming is to write code that operates on a representation of
a program's code. Although it may seem confusing at first, metaprogramming is
just a special case of general-purpose programming. When we write code, this code
typically operates on data that represents various things in the world (playing cards,
geometric shapes, bank records, etc.). With metaprogramming, this data happens
to be pieces of software code (classes, methods, fields, etc.). Although metaprogramming is a programming feature, it is instrumental for testing, and can be used
to implement many design ideas. In Java, metaprogramming is called *reflection*,
and library support for metaprogramming features is available through the class
`java.lang.Class` and the package `java.lang.reflect`.

Introspection

The most basic metaprogramming task is to obtain a reference to an object that
represents a piece of code to learn about it, a procedure called *introspection*. In Java,
the class `Class<T>` is the main access point for metaprogramming. For example,
to obtain a reference to an object that represents the `Card` class of the Solitaire
application, we do:

```
try {
  String fullyQualifiedName = "cards.Card";
  Class<Card> cardClass =
    (Class<Card>) Class.forName(fullyQualifiedName);
} catch(ClassNotFoundException e) {
  e.printStackTrace();
}
```

The call to `Class.forName` returns a reference to an instance of class `Class` that represents class `Card`, as illustrated in the object diagram of Figure 5.3.

Fig. 5.3 Instance of class `Class` that represents class `Card`

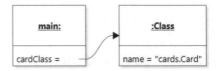

As is evident from the code above, calls to `forName` are brittle: there are many ways in which they can fail. First, we notice that the call is enclosed in a `try-catch` block. Method `forName` declares the checked exception `ClassNotFoundException` and throws it whenever the argument does not correspond to the fully-qualified name of a class on the class path. This may seem easy to prevent in the example above, given the use of a string literal to specify the name of the argument to `forName`. However, any string can be supplied as argument to `Class.forName`, so the requested class name may not even be known at compile time, as in the example below:

```
public static void main(String[] args) {
  try {
    Class<?> theClass = Class.forName(args[0]);
  } catch(ClassNotFoundException e) {
    e.printStackTrace();
  }
}
```

For the same reason, we have to use a *type wildcard* as the instance of the type parameter in the type declaration of the variable that receives the reference supplied by `forName`. In the last example, the variable is declared as `Class<?>`. The exact functioning of the type wildcard is outside the scope of this book, but for now it suffices to say that it acts as a placeholder for any type. In the previous example, because we know exactly which type parameter is appropriate for class `Card`, we can use a downcast instead.

Besides the `forName` library method, Java offers two other ways to obtain a reference to an instance of class `Class` that are less brittle: *class literals*, and through an instance of the class of interest. Both strategies are illustrated in the code below:

```
Class<Card> cardClass1 = Card.class;
Card card = Card.get(Rank.ACE, Suit.CLUBS);
Class<?> cardClass2 = card.getClass();
System.out.println(cardClass1 == cardClass2);
```

The first line shows the use of class literals. In Java, a *class literal* is a literal expression that consists of the name of a class followed by the suffix `.class`, and that refers to a reference to an instance of class `Class` that represents the class named before the suffix. So, `Card.class` refers to the instance of class `Class` that represents class `Card`. Because, in the case of class literals, the argument `T` to the type parameter of `Class<T>` is guaranteed to be known at compile time, we can include it in the variable declaration. Class literals are the least brittle way to obtain a reference to an instance of class `Class`, but they require that we know the exact class to introspect at compile time.

The final way to obtain an instance of class `Class` is through an instance of the class, as illustrated in the second and third lines of the code fragment. As will be explained in detail in Chapter 7, it is possible to call method `getClass()` on any object in a Java program, and the method will return a reference to an instance of class `Class` that represents the run-time type of the object. Because of polymorphism, this type is not known at compile time, so in this case also we have to use the type wildcard in the declaration of the variable.[5] However, because any call to `getClass()` is guaranteed to return a valid reference to an instance of `Class`, the method does not declare to throw an exception.

The last line in the code fragment illustrates a very important property of class `Class`: its instances are unique (see Section 4.7). If executed, the code should always print `true` on the console. Indeed, class `Class` has no accessible constructor, and its instances can be considered to be unique flyweight objects (see Section 4.8).

With metaprogramming, we can introspect any class, including class `Class`. This may at first seem contrived, but it is actually not a special case: class `Class` is just another class. The following code:

```
Class<Class> classClass = Class.class;
```

will produce the object graph illustrated in the diagram in Figure 5.4.

Fig. 5.4 Object graph for an instance of `Class.class`

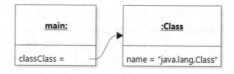

Obtaining an instance of class `Class` is only the first step for introspection. The interface to class `Class` provides numerous methods that can be called to obtain objects that represent the members of the class, its superclass, etc. As one example of endless possibilities, the following code fragment prints the name of all the methods declared in class `String`. This example makes use of class `Method`, a library class intended to represent methods in Java code. Similar classes exist to represent constructors (`Constructor`) and fields (`Field`).

---

[5] In this case it is possible to use a type bound, e.g., `Class<? extends Card>`.

```
for( Method method : String.class.getDeclaredMethods() ) {
  System.out.println(method.getName());
}
```

Program Manipulation

Obtaining information about a code base, or code introspection, only constitutes the most basic form of metaprogramming. However, in many cases we also want to actually manipulate the code of a program. Unlike more dynamic languages, Java does not allow adding or removing members from classes (and objects, by extension). However, in Java it is possible to use metaprogramming features to change the accessibility of class members, set field values, create new instances of objects, and invoke methods. I only provide a small overview of the features most relevant to software testing and design in general. The API documentation of the relevant library classes will provide the catalog of possibilities.

Assuming that our implementation of class Card is a realization of the FLYWEIGHT design pattern and has a private constructor, we will use metaprogramming to get around the pattern and create a duplicate Ace of Clubs.

```
try {
  Card card1 = Card.get(Rank.ACE, Suit.CLUBS);
  Constructor<Card> cardConstructor =
    Card.class.getDeclaredConstructor(Rank.class, Suit.class);
  cardConstructor.setAccessible(true);
  Card card2 = cardConstructor.newInstance(Rank.ACE, Suit.CLUBS);
  System.out.println(card1 == card2);
} catch( ReflectiveOperationException e ) {
  e.printStackTrace();
}
```

In this example, the second statement obtains a reference to an instance of class Constructor that represents the (private) constructor of class Card. To make calls to this constructor *accessible* in a scope outside its class, the third statement changes the accessibility of the constructor, effectively bypassing the private keyword in the code. The fourth statement calls newInstance on the Constructor object. This call makes a new instance of the declaring class of the constructor *represented* by the Constructor instance, as opposed to a new instance of class Constructor. As this is class Card, and the constructor of this class requires two arguments of type Rank and Suit, we pass values of these types to the newInstance call. Because a lot of things can go wrong with a reflective constructor invocation, most of the methods in this example declare to throw checked exceptions of various types, the supertype of which is ReflectiveOperationException.

As a second example of metaprogramming that involves program manipulation, we use metaprogramming to turn a Two of Clubs into an Ace of Clubs. Although this just looks like a neat way to cheat at cards, it is also a technique that can be used to facilitate writing tests (see Section 5.7).

```
try {
  Card card = Card.get(Rank.TWO, Suit.CLUBS);
  Field rankField = Card.class.getDeclaredField("aRank");
  rankField.setAccessible(true);
  rankField.set(card, Rank.ACE);
  System.out.println(card);
} catch( ReflectiveOperationException e ) {
  e.printStackTrace();
}
```

This code works similarly to the previous example, but with one notable difference. Because `rankField` represents a *field* of class `Card`, as opposed to an *instance* of the class, the call to `set` needs to know on *which instance* the field should be assigned a value. Thus, the first argument to `set` is the instance of `Card` on which we want to assign a new value to the field `aRank`, and the second argument is the actual value we want to assign.

Program Metadata

With metaprogramming, it is possible for code to operate not only on data that consists of code elements (e.g., classes, methods, fields), but also on metadata *about* these code elements. In Java and similar languages, it is possible to attach additional information (i.e., meta-information) to code elements in the form of *annotations*. We have already seen one type of annotation: the use of `@Test` to indicate that a method is a unit test in JUnit.

To flag methods as tests for a unit testing framework, it would also have been possible to indicate this information in the comments, using some sort of convention. For example:

```
public class AbsTest {
  /* TEST */
  public void testAbsPositive() {
    assertEquals(5,Math.abs(5));
  }
}
```

However, code comments constitute *unstructured* information meant to be consumed by humans, not code. Using code comments to encode metadata is error prone, because there is no effective way to check that required conventions are consistently respected. Instead, Java provides a system of *annotations* that can be attached to various code locations. In Java, an *annotation type* is declared similarly to an interface, for example:

```
public @interface Test {}
```

Then, *annotation instances* can be added to the code, in the form `@Test`. The main advantage of annotations in Java is that they are typed and checked by the compiler. The `@Test` annotation used to flag unit tests in JUnit is thus a type annotation provided by the JUnit library, and its use is checked by the compiler. For example, writing `@test` (with a lowercase 't') will result in a compilation error. Java annotations support many other features (see Further Reading), but their main usage scenario is to provide a way to add structured, type-checked metadata to some code elements, that can then be read by the compiler, development environments, unit testing frameworks, and similar tools. We will see other example applications of annotations later in the book. Because they are officially part of the code, information about annotations can also be accessed through metaprogramming.[6]

5.5 Structuring Tests

Writing unit tests for non-trivial classes is often a challenging creative process, not unlike writing production code. For this reason, there is no standard formula or template for writing the code of a unit test. In fact, browsing the test suites of different open-source projects will show that different communities follow different styles and use different testing techniques. This being said, certain basic principles are generally agreed upon, including that unit tests should be *fast, independent, repeatable, focused, and readable* [7].

- **Fast.** Unit tests are intended to be run often, and in many cases within a programming-compilation-execution cycle. For this reason, whatever test suite is executed should be able to complete in the order of a few seconds. Otherwise, developers will be tempted to omit running them, and the tests will stop being useful. This means that unit tests should avoid long-running operations such as intensive device I/O and network access, and leave the testing of such functionality to tests other than unit tests. These could include, for example, *acceptance tests* or *integration tests*.
- **Independent.** Each unit test should be able to execute in isolation. This means that, for example, one test should not depend on the fact that another test executes before to leave an input object in a certain state. First, it is often desirable to execute only a single test. Second, just like code, test suites evolve, with new tests being added and (to a minimum extent) some tests being removed. Test independence facilitates test suite evolution. Finally, JUnit and similarly designed testing frameworks provide no guarantee that tests will be executed in a predictable order. In practice, this means that each test should start with a fresh initialization of the state used as part of the test.
- **Repeatable.** The execution of unit tests should produce the same result in different environments (for example, when executed on different operating systems). This means that test oracles should not depend on environment-specific properties, such as display size, CPU speed, or system fonts.

---

[6] However, only annotation instances of annotation types marked with the `@Retention-(value=RUNTIME)` meta-annotation can be accessed in this way. See Further Reading for a reference to complementary information on annotations that covers meta-annotations.

- **Focused.** Tests should exercise and verify a slice of code execution behavior that is as narrow as reasonably possible. The rationale for this principle is that the point of unit tests is to help developers identify faults. If a unit test comprises 500 lines of code and tests a whole series of complex interactions between objects, it will not be easy to determine what went wrong if it fails. In contrast, a test that checks a single input on a single method call will make it easy to home in on a problem. Some have even argued that unit tests should comprise a single assertion [7]. My opinion is that in many cases this is too strict and can lead to inefficiencies. However, tests should ideally focus on testing *only one aspect* of *one unit under test*. If that unit under test is a method, we can refer to it as the *focal method* for the test.
- **Readable.** The structure and coding style of the test should make it easy to identify all the components of the test (unit under test, input data, oracle), as well as the rationale for the test. Are we testing the initialization of an object? A special case? A particular combination of values? Choosing an appropriate name for the test can often help in clarifying its rationale.

For example, let us write some unit tests for a method canMoveTo of a hypothetical class FoundationPile that could be part of the design of the Solitaire example application. The method should return true only if it is possible to move the input pCard to the top of the pile that an instance of the class represents. According to the rules of the game, this is only possible if the pile is empty and the input card is an ace, or if the input card is of the same suit as the top of the pile, and of a rank immediately above the top of the pile (e.g., you can only put a Three of Clubs on top of a Two of Clubs).

```
public class FoundationPile {
  public boolean isEmpty()  { ... }
  public Card peek()        { ... }
  public Card pop()         { ... }
  public void push(Card pCard) { ... }

  public boolean canMoveTo(Card pCard) {
    assert pCard != null;
    if( isEmpty() ) {
      return pCard.getRank() == Rank.ACE;
    }
    else
    {
      return pCard.getSuit() == peek().getSuit() &&
        pCard.getRank().ordinal() ==
          peek().getRank().ordinal()+1;
    }
  }
}
```

As our first test, we will keep things small and only test for the case where the pile is empty:

```
public class TestFoundationPile {
  @Test
  public void testCanMoveTo_Empty() {
    FoundationPile emptyPile = new FoundationPile();
    Card aceOfClubs = Card.get(Rank.ACE, Suit.CLUBS);
    Card threeOfClubs = Card.get(Rank.THREE, Suit.CLUBS);
    assertTrue(emptyPile.canMoveTo(aceOfClubs));
    assertFalse(emptyPile.canMoveTo(threeOfClubs));
  }
}
```

This test respects our five desired properties. It will execute with lightning speed, be independent from any other test that could exist, and is not affected by any environment properties. It is also focused, not only on a single method, but also on a specific input combination for the method. Finally, many properties of this test add to its readability. First, the *name of the test* encodes both the focal method and the input of interest. Second, the *names of the variables* describe their content. Finally, the assertion statements are self-evident. Reading the last line of the test, for example, we see that calling `canMoveTo` with a Three of Clubs on an empty pile will return false, which is correct.

One issue with this test, however, is its *coverage*. The test only verifies a single path through the method, so many possible executions of the method remain untested. This issue will be further discussed in Section 5.9. For now, let us try to fix it by writing an additional test in the same class

```
@Test
public void testCanMoveTo_NotEmptyAndSameSuit() {
  Card aceOfClubs = Card.get(Rank.ACE, Suit.CLUBS);
  Card twoOfClubs = Card.get(Rank.TWO, Suit.CLUBS);
  Card threeOfClubs = Card.get(Rank.THREE, Suit.CLUBS);
  FoundationPile pileWithOneCard = new FoundationPile();
  pileWithOneCard.push(aceOfClubs);
  assertTrue(pileWithOneCard.canMoveTo(twoOfClubs));
  assertFalse(pileWithOneCard.canMoveTo(threeOfClubs));
}
```

This test improves the test suite by adding to the coverage. However, we already note a lot of redundant code between the two tests, namely, the code to create an instance of `FoundationPile`, and the code to create cards. If we had, say, 20 tests, this would look suboptimal. In test classes that group multiple test methods, it will often be convenient to define a number of default objects or values to be used as receiver objects, explicit parameters, and/or oracles. This practice avoids the duplication of setup code in each test method, which constitutes DUPLICATED CODE†. Baseline objects used for testing are often referred to as a *test fixture*, and declared as fields of a test class. However, for the reasons discussed above, and in particular because JUnit provides no ordering guarantee of any test execution, it is crucial to preserve test independence. This implies that no test method should rely on the fixture being left in a given state by another test. Conveniently, unit testing frameworks can help avoid this problem. By default, JUnit 5 will instantiate a fresh version of the test class before running every test method in the class. For this reason, the values of

the fields of the test class will contain their initial value when any test executes.[7]
Of course, immutable objects do not need to be reinitialized, so they can be stored
as static fields of the class. The code below shows an improved version of our test
class TestFoundationPile, which now uses a test fixture.

```
public class TestFoundationPile
{
  private static final Card ACE_CLUBS =
    Card.get(Rank.ACE, Suit.CLUBS);
  private static final Card TWO_CLUBS =
    Card.get(Rank.TWO, Suit.CLUBS);
  private static final Card THREE_CLUBS =
    Card.get(Rank.THREE, Suit.CLUBS);

  private FoundationPile aPile = new FoundationPile();

  @Test
  public void testCanMoveTo_Empty() {
    assertTrue(aPile.canMoveTo(ACE_CLUBS));
    assertFalse(aPile.canMoveTo(THREE_CLUBS));
  }

  @Test
  public void testCanMoveTo_NotEmptyAndSameSuit() {
    aPile.push(ACE_CLUBS);
    assertTrue(aPile.canMoveTo(TWO_CLUBS));
    assertFalse(aPile.canMoveTo(THREE_CLUBS));
  }
}
```

This code not only avoids duplication, but also increases the readability of the tests
by decluttering them. The first test in particular is very readable, while the second
only needs to add one line of test-specific initialization. The only regression in test
readability is due to the fact that by using a field to refer to the pile, we lose our flexibility to name the pile with a variable name that describes its state. In this context
this is a small price to pay for the benefit of using the fixture. Although it would always be possible to alias the aPile field into an appropriately named variable (e.g.,
emptyPile), it is not clear that this would necessarily improve readability, because
aliasing can also hinder code comprehension.

Code Exploration: Solitaire · TestFoundations

Testing an aggregate class in practice.

Most of the examples in this chapter are simplified versions adapted
from the actual testing code of the Solitaire project. In Solitaire, class
TestFoundations provides a complete example of test code for a collec-

---

[7] As an alternative, it is possible to reuse an instance of the test class for multiple tests, but to
nominate a method of the test class to execute before any test method, and initialize all the required
structures afresh. These features are available in JUnit via different annotations.

tion of stack-like structures. Instead of a FoundationPile class with four instances, the design involves a single Foundations class that stores the four piles in one object and indexes each pile using the enumerated type FoundationPile. The rest is very similar to the example in the chapter. Test class TestFoundations includes four tests for canMoveTo that achieve complete branch coverage. Because the class under test, Foundations, makes heavy use of design by contract, there is no need for testing exception handling behavior.

5.6 Tests and Exceptional Conditions

An important point when writing unit tests is that what we are testing is that the unit under test does what it is expected to. This means that when using design by contract, it does not make sense to test code with input that does not respect the method's preconditions, because the resulting behavior is unspecified. For example, let us consider a version of method peek of class FoundationPile (introduced in the previous section) which returns the top of the pile.

```
class FoundationPile {
  boolean isEmpty() { ... }
  /*
   * @return The card on top of the pile.
   * @pre !isEmpty()
   */
  Card peek() { ... }
}
```

The documented precondition implies that the method cannot be expected to fulfill its contract (to return the top card) if the precondition is not met. Thus, if we call the method on an empty pile, there is no expectation to test. The situation is different, however, when raising exceptions is explicitly part of the interface. Let us consider the following slight variant of method peek():

```
class FoundationPile {
  boolean isEmpty() { ... }
  /*
   * @return The card on top of the pile.
   * @throws EmptyStackException if isEmpty()
   */
  Card peek() {
    if( isEmpty() ) {
      throw new EmptyStackException();
    }
    ...
  }
}
```

In this case, calling `peek` on an empty pile *should* result in an `EmptyStackExcep-tion`. This is part of the specified, expected behavior. If no exception is raised when called on an empty pile, then the `peek()` method does not do what is expected, and this means it is faulty. We should have a test to detect this potential fault.

With JUnit 5 the standard way to check that a method call raises the expected exception is to use the `assertThrows` assert method. This method takes as argument an instance of class `Class` that represents the expected exception type, and an instance of a subtype of the library interface `Executable` that executes the code expected to cause the exception. This programming idiom thus requires the use of a function object, as described in Section 3.4.

```
@Test
public void testPeek_Empty() {
  assertThrows(EmptyStackException.class, new Executable() {
    public void execute() throws Throwable {
      aPile.peek();
    }
  });
}
```

In this example, I used an anonymous class to define the behavior of method `execute`, which in this case calls `peek` on an empty pile. The reason this seemingly complicated setup is required is that we need our exception-causing code to execute *within* the execution of `assertThrows`. For this reason, we pass in a function object of type `Executable`. When `assertThrows` executes, it calls `execute()` on its second argument, which normally triggers the exception.

In practice, lambda expressions are typically used with `assertThrows`. Lambda expressions were briefly introduced in Section 3.4, and will be covered in detail in Chapter 9. With a lambda expression, the use of `assertThrows` is much more compact:

```
@Test
public void testPeek_Empty_LambdaExpression() {
  assertThrows(EmptyStackException.class, () -> aPile.peek());
}
```

Code Exploration: JetUML · TestDiagramType

Testing exception handling behavior.

Class `TestDiagramType` contains examples of the use of `assertThrows`. According to the specification of method `fromName`, if the user attempts to retrieve an invalid diagram type, the test will check that an `IllegalArgumentException` is raised as expected. Looking at the implementation of method `fromName`, one would notice that it is robust enough to handle a null input in exactly the same way as an invalid non-null input. Why write two distinct tests, then? I made this decision to clarify the behavior for null inputs and to guard against future modifications that could alter this behavior.

5.7 Encapsulation and Unit Testing

A design issue that often comes up when testing is that to write the test we want, we need some functionality that is not part of the interface of the class being tested. For example, let us consider that the interface to class `FoundationPile` (see Section 5.5) does not include a method to return the number of cards in the pile (e.g., `size()`). Presumably, because `FoundationPile` does not have a `size()` method, and following the principle of information hiding, we can assume that no part of the production code needs this information. However, it would be very convenient for testing to check that, for example, the size of the pile changes as we push cards onto it or pop cards from it. Would it not make sense, then, to add a `size()` method to the interface of our target class? Although experts might disagree, my personal recommendation is to design production code to have the best and tightest encapsulation possible, and let the testing code work around whatever constraints this may impose. A typical solution when an interface does not include a method that would be convenient for testing, is to provide the desired functionality in the form of a *helper method* in the testing class instead. For example:

```java
public class TestFoundationPile {
  private FoundationPile aPile = new FoundationPile();

  private int size() {
    List<Card> temp = new ArrayList<>();
    int size = 0;

    while( !aPile.isEmpty() ) {
      size++;
      temp.add(aPile.pop());
    }

    while( !temp.isEmpty() ) {
      aPile.push(temp.remove(temp.size() - 1));
    }

    return size;
  }
}
```

There are often many ways to obtain the information we need without polluting the interface of the target class. In cases where the information is difficult to obtain using methods of the class's interface, metaprogramming is a recourse (see Section 5.4).

A related question when writing tests is, how can we test private methods? There are different possible avenues for answering that question, and again experts disagree about which one is best:

- Private methods are internal elements of other, accessible methods, and therefore are not really units that should be tested. Following this logic, the code in private methods should be tested indirectly through the execution of the accessible methods that call them;

- The `private` access modifier is a tool to help us structure the project code, and tests can ignore it.

Although I understand the rationale of the first approach, I personally consider that the second option can also be a reasonable strategy. There are often situations where a neat little method can be restricted to a class's scope, but it would still be valuable to test it in isolation. Situations where private methods should probably *not* be tested separately are when their parameters or return type encode detailed information about the internal structure of the class, or make narrow assumptions about the internal implementation of the class.

In cases where it is judged desirable to test a private method, we need to bypass the method's access restriction. This can be done using metaprogramming. For sake of discussion, let us assume that class `FoundationPile` also has a method:

```
private Optional<Card> getPreviousCard(Card pCard) { ... }
```

that we would like to test separately. This is reasonable, because it returns an `Optional<Card>` (see Section 4.5) and takes as input a single `Card`, two basic elements in our design. In our test code, we will thus create a helper method that calls this private method using metaprogramming.

```
public class TestFoundationPile {
   private FoundationPile aPile = new FoundationPile();

   private Optional<Card> getPreviousCard(Card pCard) {
      try {
         Method method = FoundationPile.class.
            getDeclaredMethod("getPreviousCard", Card.class);
         method.setAccessible(true);
         return (Optional<Card>) method.invoke(aPile, pCard);
      } catch( ReflectiveOperationException exception ) {
         fail();
         return Optional.empty();
      }
   }

   @Test
   public void testGetPreviousCard_empty() {
      assertFalse(getPreviousCard(Card.get(Rank.ACE, Suit.CLUBS)).
         isPresent());
   }
}
```

In the test class, we define a helper method that launches the execution of the unit under test (`getPreviousCard(Card)`) on an instance of `aPile`, which forms part of the test fixture. With this helper method, the code of the test looks pretty normal. However, there is one big difference. Here, the call to `getPreviousCard` is *not* a call to the unit under tests. Instead, the call is to a helper method (of the same name) that uses metaprogramming to call the unit under test while bypassing the access restriction of the `private` keyword.

Code Exploration: Solitaire · TestTableau

Using metaprogramming to access private structures.

The private method `getPreviousCard(Card)` discussed in this section is actually located in class `Tableau`. This class represents the seven piles of cards that fan downwards in a game of Solitaire. The rest of the code is the same. Class `TestTableau` provides a working implementation of an invocation of `getPreviousCard` using metaprogramming, along with examples of tests that access the private method in this way.

5.8 Testing with Stubs

The key to unit testing is to test small parts of the code *in isolation*. In some cases, however, factors can make it difficult to test a piece of code in isolation, for example, when the part we want to test:

- triggers the execution of a large chunk of other code;
- includes sections whose behavior depends on the environment (e.g., system fonts);
- involves non-deterministic behavior (e.g., randomness).

Such a case is illustrated in the following design, which is a simplified version of the Solitaire example application. The `GameModel` class has a `tryToAutoPlay()` method that triggers the computation of the next move by dynamically delegating the task to a strategy, which could be any of a number of options (see Figure 5.5). Here we would like to write a unit test for the `GameModel.tryToAutoPlay(...)` method.

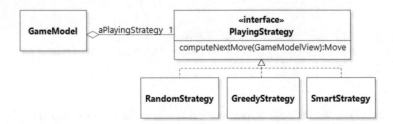

Fig. 5.5 Playing strategy in `GameModel`

In this task we face at least four problems:

- Calling the `tryToAutoPlay` method on an instance of `GameModel` will delegate the call to `computeNextMove` on a strategy object, which will involve the execution of presumably complex behavior to realize the strategy. This does not align well with the concept of unit testing, where we want to test small pieces of code in isolation.

- The implementation of the strategy may involve some randomness.
- We do not know which strategy would be used by the game engine. Presumably we need to determine an oracle for the results.
- It is unclear how is this different from testing the strategies individually.

The way out of this conundrum is the realization that the responsibility of GameModel#tryToAutoPlay(...) is not to compute the next move, but rather to delegate this to a strategy. So, to write a unit test that tests that the UUT does what it is expected to do, we only need to verify that it properly relays the request to compute a move to a strategy. This can be achieved with the writing of a *stub*.

A stub is a greatly simplified version of an object that mimics its behavior sufficiently to support the testing of a UUT that uses this object. Using stubs is heavily dependent on types and polymorphism. Continuing with our tryToAutoPlay situation, we just want to test that the method calls a strategy method, so we will define a dummy strategy in the test class:

```
public class TestGameModel {
  static class StubStrategy implements PlayingStrategy {
    private boolean aExecuted = false;

    public boolean hasExecuted() {
      return aExecuted; }

    public Move computeNextMove(GameModelView pModelView) {
      aExecuted = true;
      return new NullMove();
    }
  }
}
```

This strategy does nothing except remember that its computeNextMove method has been called, and returns a dummy Move object called NullMove (an application of the NULL OBJECT pattern). We can then use an instance of this stub instead of a real strategy in the rest of the test. To inject the stub into the game model, we can rely on metaprogramming:

```
@Test
public void testTryToAutoPlay() {
  Field strategyField =
    GameModel.class.getDeclaredField("aPlayingStrategy");
  strategyField.setAccessible(true);
  StubStrategy strategy = new StubStrategy();
  GameModel model = GameModel.instance();
  strategyField.set(model, strategy);
  ...
}
```

at which point completing the test is just a matter of calling the UUT tryToAuto-Play and verifying that it did properly call the strategy:

```
@Test
public void testTryToAutoPlay() {
  ...
  model.tryToAutoPlay();
  assertTrue(strategy.hasExecuted());
}
```

The use of stubs in unit testing can get very sophisticated, and frameworks exist to support this task if necessary.

5.9 Test Coverage

Up to now this chapter covered how to define and structure unit tests from a practical standpoint, but avoided the question of what inputs to provide to the unit under test. Despite the example of exhaustive testing in Section 5.1, it should be clear that for the vast majority of UUTs it is not even physically possible to exhaustively test the input space. For example, as discussed in Section 4.2, the number of different arrangements of cards that an instance of class Deck can take is astronomical (2.2×10^{68}). Even with a cutting-edge CPU, testing any of the methods of class Deck for all possible inputs (i.e., possible states of the implicit parameter) would take an amount of time greater than many times the age of the universe. This is quite incompatible with the requirement that unit tests execute *quickly* (see Section 5.5).

Clearly we need to select some input out of all the possibilities. This is a problem known as *test case selection*, where *test case* can be considered to be a set of input values for an assumed UUT. For example, an instance of Deck with a single Ace of Clubs in the deck is a test case of the method Deck.draw(). The basic challenge of the test case selection problem is to test *efficiently*, meaning to find a minimal set of test cases that provides us a maximal amount of testing for our code. Unfortunately, while it is fairly intuitive what a minimal number of test cases is, there is no natural or even agreed-upon definition of what an *amount of testing* is. However, there is a large body of research results and practical experience on the topic of test case selection: enough for many books (see Further Reading for a recommendation). In this section, I only summarize the key theoretical tenets and practical insights necessary to get started with test case selection. There are two basic ways to approach the selection of test cases:

- **Functional (or black-box) testing** tries to cover as much of the *specified* behavior of a UUT as possible, based on some external specification of what the UUT should do. For the Deck.draw() method, this specification is that the method should result in the top card of the deck being removed and returned. There are many advantages to black-box testing, including that it is not necessary to access the code of the UUT, that tests can reveal problems with the specification, and that tests can reveal missing logic.
- **Structural (or white-box) testing** tries to cover as much of the *implemented* behavior of the UUT as possible, based on an analysis of the source code of the

UUT. An example is provided below. The main advantage of white-box testing is that it can reveal problems caused by low-level implementation details that are invisible at the level of the specification.

Coverage of functional testing techniques is outside of the scope of this book, so the remainder of this section provides a review of the main concepts of structural testing. Let us consider again the implementation of the canMoveTo method of class FoundationPile (see Section 5.5, the assert statement was removed to simplify the discussion).

```
boolean canMoveTo(Card pCard) {
  if( isEmpty() ) {
    return pCard.getRank() == Rank.ACE;
  }
  else {
    return pCard.getSuit() == peek().getSuit() &&
      pCard.getRank().ordinal() ==
        peek().getRank().ordinal()+1;
  }
}
```

Here, we can intuitively see that the code structure can be partitioned into different pieces that might be good to test. First, there is the case where the pile is empty (the true part of the if statement), and the case where it is not empty (the else block). But then, each of these pieces can also be partitioned into different subpieces, for example to cover the case where the cards are in the correct sequence, but of different suits. In the general case, things can get hairy, and it is easy to get lost without a systematic way to understand the code.

One common method for determining what to test is based on the concept of *coverage*. A *test coverage metric* is a number (typically a percentage) that determines how much of the code executes when we run our tests. Test coverage metrics can be computed by code coverage tools that keep track of the code that gets executed when we run unit tests. This sounds simple, but the catch is that there are different definitions of what we can mean by *code*, in the context of testing. Each definition is a different way to compute *how much testing* is done. Certain software development organizations may have well-defined *test adequacy criteria* whereby test suites must meet certain coverage thresholds, but in many other cases, the insights provided by coverage metrics are used more generally to help determine where to invest future testing efforts. The following are three well-known coverage metrics (there are many others, see Further Reading).

Statement Coverage

Let us start with the simplest coverage metric: *statement coverage*. Statement coverage is the number of statements executed by a test or test suite, divided by the number of statements in the code of interest. The following test:

```
@Test
public void testCanMoveTo_Empty() {
  assertTrue(aPile.canMoveTo(ACE_CLUBS));
  assertFalse(aPile.canMoveTo(THREE_CLUBS));
}
```

achieves $2/3 = 67\%$ coverage, because the conditional statement predicate and the single statement in the `true` branch are executed, and the single statement in the `false` branch is not. The logic behind statement coverage is that if a fault is present in a statement that is never executed, the tests are not going to help find it. Although this logic may seem appealing, statement coverage is actually a poor coverage metric. A first reason is that it depends heavily on the detailed structure of the code. We could rewrite the `canMoveTo` method as follows, and achieve 100% test coverage with exactly the same tests.

```
boolean canMoveTo(Card pCard) {
  boolean result = pCard.getSuit() == peek().getSuit() &&
      pCard.getRank().ordinal() ==
        peek().getRank().ordinal()+1;
  if( isEmpty() ) {
    result = pCard.getRank() == Rank.ACE;
  }
  return result;
}
```

The second reason is that not all statements are created equally, and there can be quite a bit that goes on in a statement, especially if this statement involves a compound Boolean expression (as is the case of the first statement in the last example).

Branch Coverage

Branch coverage is the number of program *branches* (decision points) executed by the test(s) divided by the total number of branches in the code of interest. In this context, a branch is one outcome of a condition. Branch coverage is a stronger metric than statement coverage in the sense that for the same coverage result, more of the possible program executions will have been tested. Unfortunately, the concept of branch coverage is ambiguous, due to the different possible interpretations of the term *branch*. In the code of `canMoveTo`, there are only two branches if we only consider the single `if` statement. However, both the `true` and the `false` branches lead to statements that consist of Boolean expressions, which are themselves another type of branch. To be consistent with popular coverage analysis tools, I adopt the definition that Boolean expressions within statements also introduce branches. Although more complex to determine, this definition is also more useful. With this definition, the original code of `canMoveTo` exhibits eight branches: the `if`, the first `return` statement, the first comparison in the second return statement, and the second comparison in the second return statement. Each of these branches has a `true` and `false` outcome. The only test written so far thus has only $3/8 = 37.5\%$ branch coverage. If we add the other test shown in Section 5.5 to the test suite:

```
@Test
public void testCanMoveTo_NotEmptyAndSameSuit() {
  aPile.push(ACE_CLUBS);
  assertTrue(aPile.canMoveTo(TWO_CLUBS));
  assertFalse(aPile.canMoveTo(THREE_CLUBS));
}
```

we get $7/8 = 87.5\%$. This is pretty good, but our systematic coverage analysis points out that we are actually missing one branch, which corresponds to the case where the pile is not empty, and the card at the top of the pile and the card passed as argument are of different suits. Branch coverage is one of the most useful test coverage criteria. It is well supported by testing tools and relatively straightforward to interpret, and also *subsumes* statement coverage, meaning that achieving complete branch coverage always implies complete statement coverage.

Path Coverage

There are other coverage metrics stronger than branch coverage. For example, one could, in principle, compute a *path coverage* metric as the number of execution paths actually executed over all possible execution paths in the code of interest. Path coverage subsumes almost all other coverage metrics, and is a very close approximation of the entire behavior that is possible to test. Unfortunately, in many cases, the number of paths through a piece of code will be unbounded, so it will not be possible to compute this metric. For this reason, path coverage is considered a theoretical metric, useful for reasoning about test coverage in the abstract, but without any serious hope of general practical applicability. Interestingly, the number of paths in the code of canMoveTo is actually only five, so, less than the number of branches! The path coverage of the two-test test suite above can thus be computed, at $4/5 = 80\%$. Because the structure of the code is without loops, this is not overly surprising. However, as soon as loops enter the picture, reasoning about paths becomes troublesome.

Insights

This chapter described techniques to structure and implement unit tests for a project, and argued that unit tests can provide valuable feedback on the design of production code. The following insights assume you have decided to adopt unit testing and are using a unit testing framework.

- Every unit test includes the execution of unit under test (UUT), some input data passed to the UUT, an oracle that describes what the result of executing the UUT should be, and one or more assertions that compare the result of the execution with the oracle;

- Design your unit tests so that they are focused, that is, that they isolate and test a small and well-defined amount of behavior;
- Design your unit tests to run fast, be independent from each other, and be repeatable in any computing environment;
- Design your unit tests to be readable: consider using the name of the test and local variables to add clarity about what you are testing and to describe the oracle;
- Organize your test suite cleanly, with a clear mapping between tests and the code units they test. Consider separate source code directories with a parallel package structure for production and test code;
- Metaprogramming is a powerful language feature that allows you to write code to analyze other code. However, it must be used with care in production code, because it is prone to run-time errors;
- Type annotations can provide metadata about certain program elements, which can then be accessed through metaprogramming;
- Use test fixtures to structure your testing code cleanly. Remember that any data used by unit tests must be initialized before every test, since tests are not guaranteed to be executed in any specific order;
- Do not test for unspecified behavior, and in particular for input that does not respect a method's preconditions;
- Exceptions that can be raised are often an explicit part of a method's interface, in which case the raising of exceptions constitutes behavior that can be tested;
- Do not weaken the interface of a class only to provide additional state inspection methods for your tests. Instead, write helper methods in the test class to obtain this information. Consider using metaprogramming for the trickier cases;
- To isolate the behavior of stateful objects that refer to many other objects, consider using stubs to abstract the behavior of the component objects;
- Use test coverage metrics to reason about how much of the program's behavior you are testing. Favor branch coverage over statement coverage;
- Remember that passing tests do not guarantee that the code is correct.

Further Reading

The book *Software Testing and Analysis* by Pezzè and Young [13] provides a comprehensive treatment of testing, including the definition of many test coverage metrics. The Java Tutorial [10] provides a good introduction to annotations and reflection (Java's version of metaprogramming). Documentation on how to use JUnit is available on the JUnit website.

Chapter 6
Composition

Concepts and Principles: Aggregation, composition, delegation, law of Demeter, polymorphic copying, sequence diagram;
Patterns and Antipatterns: GOD CLASS†, MESSAGE CHAIN† COMPOSITE, DECORATOR, PROTOTYPE, COMMAND

Large software systems are assembled from smaller parts. In object-oriented design, parts are connected through two main mechanisms: composition and inheritance. Composition means that one object holds a reference to another object and delegates some functionality to it. Although this sounds straightforward, unprincipled composition can lead to a mess of spaghetti code. In this chapter I give a quick refresher on the mechanism of polymorphism and how it can be used to elegantly compose objects together by following some well-known design patterns. The second way of assembling systems is through inheritance, which is more complex and is covered in Chapter 7.

Design Context

This chapter draws its code examples from various problems related to the modeling of card games. The design problems address requirements at different levels of abstraction, from the management of low-level structures to represent a card source, to high-level structures that can represent the entire state of a card game. To support a discussion of a variety of potential design alternatives, the examples are not limited to the context of a Solitaire application, but also consider other usage scenarios. For the examples that do target the Solitaire application specifically, knowledge of the game terminology will be useful: see Appendix C for definitions of the main game concepts and terms and an overview of a game in progress.

© Springer Nature Switzerland AG 2022
M. P. Robillard, *Introduction to Software Design with Java*,
https://doi.org/10.1007/978-3-030-97899-0_6

6.1 Composition and Aggregation

A general strategy for managing complexity in software design is to define larger abstractions in terms of smaller ones. This is an example of the general *divide and conquer* problem-solving strategy. In software design, if we want to organize our code, data, and run-time computation by separating it in different parts (classes, methods, objects, etc.), we need a way to specify how the separate pieces interact together to form a working software application.

One way to assemble different pieces of code, data, or computation, is through object *composition*. For an object to be composed of other objects means that one object stores a reference to one or more other objects. Composition is a way to provide a solution to two common software design situations.

In a first situation, we have one abstraction whose intrinsic *representation* is that of a collection of other abstractions. For example, in the problem domain a deck of cards is conceptually a sequence of playing cards, so in a piece of software that must handle a deck of cards, it would make a lot sense for a `Deck` instance to be composed of a number of `Card` instances. In this situation, object composition corresponds exactly to our notion of composition from the problem domain: one object is *essentially* composed of other objects. As another example, a string (an instance of `String`) is essentially a collection of characters (values of type `char`). One term often used to refer to the object that is composed of other objects is the *aggregate*, whereas the objects being aggregated are the *elements*. So, in our example, class `Deck` is an aggregate of `Card` elements.

A second situation in which composition is helpful is to break down a class that would otherwise be too big and complex. In object-oriented development it is easy to follow the path of least resistance and add more of the data and functionality needed to solve a problem into a single class. This is the path of least resistance because, as members of the class share private access to each other, no design effort is required to organize the code. However, this opportunistic approach often leads to a GOD CLASS†, that is, an unmanageable class that knows everything and does everything. God classes are a problem because they violate practically every major principle of good design. To avoid god classes and similar design degradation, we can use composition to support a mechanism of *delegation*. The idea of delegation is that the aggregate object delegates some services to the objects that serve a role of specialized service to the aggregate. This looser form of composition is also known as *aggregation*.

One important property of composition is that it is *transitive*. An object that is composed of other objects can, itself, be one component or delegate of another *parent* object. Ultimately, many structures in object-oriented programs are *object graphs* that group simpler component and delegate objects into progressively more and more complex aggregates.

When designing a class, it does not hurt to be conscious of whether we are using composition for the purpose of representation or delegation. However, the purposes are not mutually exclusive, so it is necessary to be comfortable with the gray area where elements can be thought of as either components (i.e., essential parts of the aggregate object) or delegates (i.e., service providers for the aggregate object).

Let us make this discussion more concrete by studying the CameModel class of the Solitaire example application. Figure 6.1 shows a simplified class diagram of the GameModel. The diagram shows how class GameModel is an aggregate of one Deck, one CardStack (the discard pile), one Foundations, and one Tableau. A first thing to observe is that in this version of the code, instead of having a Deck class aggregate Card objects using the List library type, I used composition to define a dedicated type CardStack that provides a narrow interface dedicated to handling stacks of cards. The following is a partial implementation:

```
public class CardStack implements Iterable<Card> {
  private final List<Card> aCards = new ArrayList<>();

  public void push(Card pCard) {
    assert pCard != null && !aCards.contains(pCard);
    aCards.add(pCard);
  }

  public Card pop() {
    assert !isEmpty();
    return aCards.remove(aCards.size()-1);
  }

  public Card peek() {
    assert !isEmpty();
    return aCards.get(aCards.size()-1);
  }

  public void clear() {
    aCards.clear();
  }

  public boolean isEmpty() {
    return aCards.size() == 0;
  }

  public Iterator<Card> iterator() {
    return aCards.iterator();
  }
}
```

Technically, a game of Solitaire is just 13 piles of cards. It would definitely have been possible to design the game by referring to 13 instances of CardStack in GameModel and implement all the game algorithms in the GameModel class. However, this class would not have been pretty. Instead, the design makes use of classes Foundations and Tableau. As shown in the diagram, these two classes aggregate instances of CardStack. Following the principle of separation of concerns, we can now move a lot of computation to these classes, and delegate to them when necessary.

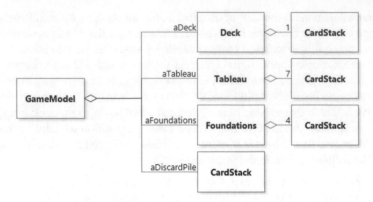

Fig. 6.1 Class diagram of the `GameModel`. Composition relations are represented using the white diamond decoration. The diamond is on the side of the aggregate. Normally, in a class diagram, model elements that represent a given class are not repeated. In this diagram I took the liberty of repeating `CardStack` for clarity. All `CardStack` elements, however, represent the *same* class.

For example, class `GameModel` needs a method `isVisibleInTableau(Card)` to determine whether a card is face up or down in the game tableau. In the design of diagram 6.1, this request is delegated to class `Tableau`:

```
public boolean isVisibleInTableau(Card pCard) {
   return aTableau.contains(pCard) && aTableau.isVisible(pCard);
}
```

In a class diagram, object composition is represented with an edge decorated with a diamond on the side of the class whose instances hold the reference to the instances of the other class. The UML notation technically allows the distinction between two types of composition: *aggregation* (white diamond) and *composition* (black diamond). As argued above, the difference between these can be murky, and experts disagree on how to choose between aggregation, composition, or plain association in UML diagrams. I get around the issue by avoiding using the distinction. Because composition is often understood to be a stronger form of aggregation, I exclusively use the white diamond annotation for all types of aggregation/composition (see Section 3.3).

Although it is technically possible to compose objects in arbitrary ways simply by defining fields and passing object references around, unprincipled use of object composition can easily degenerate into overly-complex code. This chapter covers different ways to keep a certain amount of organization in the use of composition through the use of design patterns. The overarching goal of this chapter, however, is to foster a general skill in using composition according to a well-defined design plan with a clear underlying rationale.

Code Exploration: Solitaire · GameModel

An aggregate object with delegation.

The design of the Solitaire project is consistent with the diagram of Figure 6.1. Some methods of class `GameModel` simply delegate the call to their aggregated objects. Examples include `getScore()`, `getSubStack(...)`, `getTableauPile`, and `isVisibleInTableau(...)`.

6.2 The COMPOSITE Design Pattern

As a first principled use of composition, we will consider the situation where we would like to have groups of objects behave like a single object. Let us say that we are working on a card game that takes as input a source of cards. In Section 3.1, I showed how we can use interfaces to decouple the behavior of a source of cards from its implementation using interface types. The code below repeats the definition of the `CardSource` interface for convenience.

```
public interface CardSource {

  /**
   * Removes a card from the source and returns it.
   *
   * @return The card that was removed from the source.
   * @pre !isEmpty()
   */
  Card draw();

  /**
   * @return True if there is no card in the source.
   */
  boolean isEmpty();
}
```

By relying on this interface and the polymorphism it supports, we can write loosely coupled code that can draw cards from any kind of source. The types of card sources we can support with this interface are only limited by our imagination (and actual usage scenarios in card games). For example, we could have a card source that consists of multiple decks of cards, a card source that contains only the four aces, or only face cards, etc. Or any combinations of these schemes (e.g., one deck and four extra aces).

One way to support all these options is to write one class for each option, with each class declaring to implement the `CardSource` interface:

```
public class Deck implements CardSource { ... }
public class MultiDeck implements CardSource { ... }
public class FourAces implements CardSource { ... }
```

```
public class FaceCards implements CardSource { ... }
public class DeckAndFourAces implements CardSource { ... }
```

The main feature of this design decision is that the set of possible implementations of `CardSource` is specified statically (in the source code), as opposed to dynamically (when the code runs). Three major limitations of this static structure are:

- The number of possible structures of interest can be very large. As illustrated by the fifth definition, `DeckAndFourAces`, supporting all possible configurations leads to a *combinatorial explosion* of class definitions.
- Each option requires a class definition, even if it is used very rarely. This clutters the code unnecessarily, because most implementations would probably look very similar.
- In running code, it is very difficult to accommodate the situation where a type of card source configuration is needed that was not anticipated before launching the application.

The above limitations are derived from the static nature of the design. A general solution is to support an open-ended number of configurations by relying on object composition as opposed to class definition. The fundamental idea to support this approach is to define a class that represents multiple `CardSources` while still behaving like a single one. This core idea is captured as the COMPOSITE design pattern. Figure 6.2 shows a class diagram of the COMPOSITE applied to the `CardSource` context.

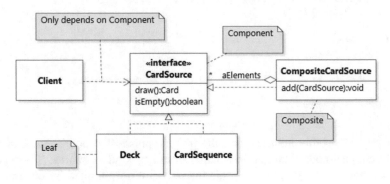

Fig. 6.2 Application of COMPOSITE to `CardSource`

The diagram shows the application of the pattern, and the roles of each element in the solution template are indicated in notes. In this pattern, the three main roles are *component*, *composite*, and *leaf*. The composite element has two important features:

- It aggregates a number of different objects of the component type (`CardSource` in our case). Using the component interface type is important, as it allows the composite to compose any other kind of elements, including other composites. In our application, a composite CardSource can aggregate any kind of CardSource: instances of Deck, CardSequence, or anything else that implements CardSource.

- It implements the component interface. This is what allows composite objects to be treated by the rest of the code in exactly the same way as leaf elements.

The diagram also captures the important insight that for the COMPOSITE to be effective, client code should depend primarily on the component type, and not manipulate concrete types directly.

An example of object graph created through a COMPOSITE design is illustrated by the object diagram of Figure 6.3.

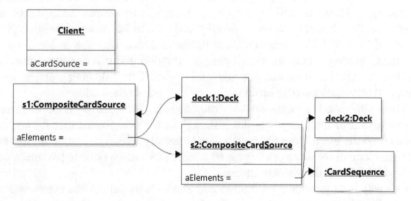

Fig. 6.3 Object diagram representing a sample composite CardSource

When applying the COMPOSITE as part of a design, the implementation of the methods of the component interface will generally involve an iteration through all the aggregated elements. As a simple example, in the above design the implementation of method CompositeCardSource.isEmpty() would be:

```
public boolean isEmpty() {
  for( CardSource source : aElements ) {
    if( !source.isEmpty() ) {
      return false; }
  }
  return true;
}
```

In the case of method draw, the behavior is a bit special. Instead of delegating the method call to all elements, we only need to iterate until we can find one card to draw.

```
public Card draw() {
  assert !isEmpty();
  for( CardSource source : aElements ) {
    if( !source.isEmpty() ) {
      return source.draw();
    }
  }
  assert false;
  return null;
}
```

Because `CompositeCardSource.draw()` is an implementation of the interface `CardSource.draw()`, it has the same preconditions as the interface method. Thus, it does not need to deal with the case where a call is made to `draw` from an empty card source, even if this is a composite. In the first line of the method, we assert that `!isEmpty()`. Here, the call to `isEmpty()` would be to method `isEmpty` of class `CompositeCardSource`, so the following code could be assumed to always find a method to draw.[1] This assumption is further encoded with the `assert false;` statement, which encodes the developer's assumption that if the precondition is respected, the execution should not reach this point. The following `return null;` statement serves no purpose besides making the code compilable.

When applying the COMPOSITE, an important implementation issue to consider is how to add to the composite the instances of the component that it composes. In other words, in our case we need a way to specify which `CardSource` instances form the elements of a `CompositeCardSource`. This can be done in two main ways, each with its strengths and weaknesses.

One way is to provide a method to add elements as part of the composite's interface. This is the method illustrated in Figure 6.2. In turn, this strategy leads to a second design question, which is whether to include the `add` method in the component or not. The more common solution is to not include it in the component, but there may be some situations where it makes more sense to include it on the interface of the component so that the component and all its children have the same interface (see Further Reading).

The second way to initialize composite objects is through their constructor. For example, we could pass a list of card sources as input:

```
public CompositeCardSource implements CardSource {
  private final List<CardSource> aElements;

  public CompositeCardSource(List<CardSource> pCardSources) {
    aElements = new ArrayList<>(pCardSources);
  }
}
```

Here we use the copy constructor to avoid leaking a reference to the private collection structure (see Section 2.5). Another option would be to use Java's *varargs* mechanism to list each card source individually (see Further Reading):

---

[1] This assumes a single-threaded system. Concurrent programming is outside the scope of this book.

```
public CompositeCardSource(CardSource... pCardSources)
```

The main reason for adopting the "add method" strategy is if we need to modify the state of the composite at run time. However, this comes at a cost in terms of design structure and code understandability, because we need to deal with a more complex life-cycle for the composite object and have to manage the difference between the interface of the component (which does not have the `add` method) and the one of the composite (which does). If run-time modification of the composite is not necessary, then it is likely a better option to initialize the composite once and leave it as is. In the context of the `CardSource` example, it would not result in an immutable composite (we still draw cards), but in other contexts immutability may be an additional advantage.

Some practical aspects related to using the pattern are independent from the structure of the pattern itself. These include:

- The location of the creation of the composite in client code;
- The logic required to preserve the integrity of the object graph induced by this design.

Because these concerns are context-dependent, their solution will depend on the specific design problem at hand. However, it is important to be aware that simply creating a well-designed composite class is not sufficient to have a correct application of the COMPOSITE. For example, with the design of Figure 6.2, it could be possible to write code that results in the object graph of Figure 6.4. However, this outcome is very likely undesirable, because the shared deck instance between `source1` and `source2` and the self-reference in `source2` would lead to unmanageable behavior.

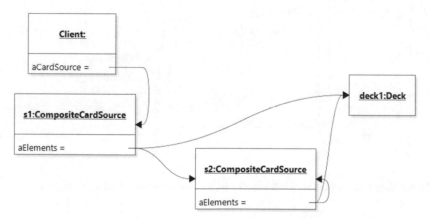

Fig. 6.4 Object diagram showing an abused design for a composite `CardSource`

6.3 Sequence Diagrams

The use of composition in software design implies design decisions that have to do with how objects collaborate with each other. This means that the impact of composition-related design decisions is reflected on how objects end up calling each other.[2] We can contrast this to more static design decisions, which have to do with how classes depend on each other. For example, an important consequence of the use of the COMPOSITE for CardSource is that to determine if a CompositeCardSource is empty, we need to call isEmpty() on some, and possibly all, of its elements.

It can sometimes be helpful to model certain design decisions related to object call sequences. With the UML, this is accomplished through *sequence diagrams*. Just like object diagrams and state diagrams, sequence diagrams model the dynamic perspective on a software system. Like object diagrams and as opposed to state diagrams, sequence diagrams represent a specific execution of the code. They are the closest representation to what one would see when stepping through the execution of the code in a debugger, for example.

To introduce sequence diagrams, and bring home the point that the COMPOSITE pattern is really a way to organize how objects interact, Figure 6.5 shows a sequence diagram that models a call to isEmpty() on an instance of CompositeCardSource.

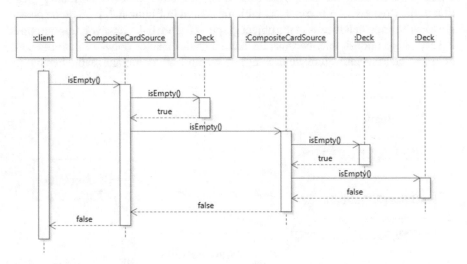

Fig. 6.5 Sequence diagram for a call to isEmpty() on a CompositeCardSource

Each rectangle at the top of the diagram represents an object. An object in a sequence diagram is also referred to as *implicit parameter*, because it is the object upon which a method is called. Consistently with other UML diagrams that repre-

---

[2] Objects *calling each other* is a linguistic shortcut. The precise, but more cumbersome, phrasing would be *code of a method with a given implicit argument calling methods with other objects as implicit arguments*.

sent the system at run time, the object names are underlined and follow the convention `name:type` as necessary. Here I did not specify a type for the client because it does not matter, and did not specify a name for any of the other objects because it does not matter either.

In the diagram, we observe the recursive descent through an instance of `CompositeCardSource`. This information cannot be captured in a class diagram, because the notation does not support the specification of the behavior of the different methods, even at an abstract level. This diagram complements the class diagram of Figure 6.2 by showing a dynamic aspect of the design that is invisible on the class diagram.

The dashed vertical line emanating from an object represents the object's *life line*. The life line represents the time (running from top to bottom) when the object exists, that is, between its creation and the time it is ready to be garbage-collected. When objects are placed at the top of the diagram, they are assumed to exist at the beginning of the scenario being modeled. The diagram thus shows an interaction between a client object and an instance of `CompositeCardSource` and all its component objects, all of which were created before the modeled interaction began. How these objects were created is an example of details left unspecified by a particular diagram.

When representing the type of an object in a sequence diagram, there is some flexibility in terms of what type to represent in the object's type hierarchy. We can use the concrete type of the object or one of its supertypes. As usual when modeling, we use what is the most informative. Here the `CompositeCardSource` and `Deck` objects are represented using their concrete type because the only other option is `CardSource`, which makes the information in the diagram less self-explanatory.

Messages between objects typically correspond to method calls. Messages are represented using a directed arrow from the caller object to the called object. By *called object* I mean the object that is the implicit parameter of the method call. Messages are typically labeled with the method that is called, optionally with some label representing arguments, when useful. When creating a sequence diagram that represents an execution of Java code, it is likely to be a modeling error if a message incoming on an object does not correspond to a method of the object's interface. Constructor calls are modeled as special messages with the label `<<create>>`.

Messages between objects induce an *activation box*, which is the thicker white box overlaid on the life line. The activation box represents the time when a method of the corresponding object is on the execution stack (but not necessarily at the top of the execution stack).

It is also possible to model the return of control out of a method back to the caller. This is represented with a dashed directed arrow. Return edges are optional. I personally only use them to aid understanding when there are complex sequences of messages, or to give a name to the value that is returned to make the rest of the diagram more self-explanatory. Here, for example, I included return edges to provide the rationale for subsequent calls in the sequence (given that the execution terminates as soon as `isEmpty()` returns `false`).

To explore some of the additional modeling features of sequence diagrams and their potential, let us model the use of an iterator in the ITERATOR pattern (see Section 3.6). Figure 6.6 shows the class diagram of the specific application of ITERATOR I model with a sequence diagram.

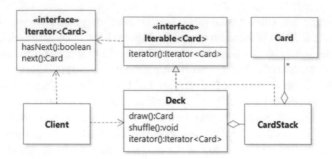

Fig. 6.6 Class diagram of the iterable `Deck`

This diagram shows a version of the `Deck` class that relies on a collection type `Stack` to store cards. Both the `Deck` and the `Stack` are iterable. The client code, represented as class `Client`, can refer to instances of class `Deck` as well as the iterators they return.

Let us look at what happens when the client code makes a call to `Deck.itera-tor()`. Figure 6.7 is the sequence diagram that models a specific execution of `Deck.iterator()` within client code. The names of model elements are provided as notes on the diagram.

The `iterator()` message to a `Deck` instance leads to the call being *delegated* to the `Stack` object. The `Stack` object is responsible for creating the iterator. It is also possible to show the creation of an instance by placing it lower in the diagram, as in the case here for the `Iterator` object. The label *iterator* is used on the return edge from both `iterator()` calls to show (indirectly) that it is the same object being propagated back to the client. In this diagram I also included a return edge from the `next()` method and labeled it *nextCard* to show that the returned object is the one being supplied to the subsequent self-call (a method called on an object from within a method already executing with this object as implicit parameter).

In terms of representing types, here the `Deck` object is represented using its concrete type, but the label `deck:Iterable<Card>` would have been a valid option as well. For the `Iterator` object I used the interface supertype because in practice the concrete type of this object is anonymous and does not really matter.

The distinction between models and complete source code applies to sequence diagrams as well. First, a sequence diagram models a specific execution, not all executions. In the above example, a different execution could have received `false` from `hasNext()` and not called `next()`, or called `next()` twice, etc. These options are not represented, because they are different scenarios. Second, sequence diagrams will naturally omit some details of the execution of the code. We use sequence diagrams to show how objects interact to convey a specific idea. Although the UML supports the specification of looping and conditional statements within a method,

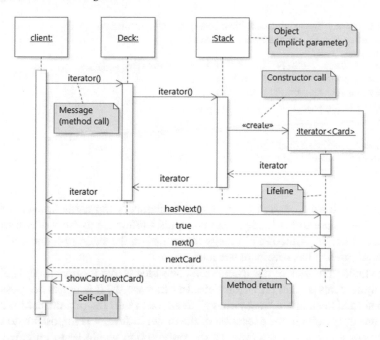

Fig. 6.7 Sequence diagram of an iteration through a `Deck` object

these are typically not included in UML sketches and I do not use this notation in the book. Asynchronous calls (which are shown using a half arrow head), are also not covered. Insignificant calls (e.g., to library methods) are typically omitted from sequence diagrams in sketches.

6.4 The DECORATOR Design Pattern

In some cases we would like to optionally have objects of a given type to exhibit special behavior, or have certain extra features. In the example of a `CardSource`, we could imagine that in some cases we might want to print a description of each card drawn on the console or in a file (a process called *logging*). As another example, we might want to keep a reference to every card drawn from a certain source (i.e., *memorizing* the drawn cards). One strategy for meeting this requirement is to enhance the static structure of the design to accommodate the new features. In other words, we can provide additional functionality by writing more classes that have that functionality. Let us consider two possible design solutions for doing this.

Our first solution, which I will call the *specialized class* solution, will be to design one class for each type of feature we want to support. For example, to have a `CardSource` that logs cards drawn, we could define our own special version of `Deck`:

```
public class LoggingDeck implements CardSource {
  private final CardStack aCards = ...

  public Card draw() {
    Card card = aCards.pop();
    System.out.println(card);
    return card;
  }

  public boolean isEmpty() {
    return aCards.isEmpty();
  }
}
```

Similarly, to have a version of `Deck` that remembers the cards drawn, we could create a new class `MemorizingDeck` that stores a reference to every drawn card in a separate structure. Although a strategy that relies on the static structure could work in simple cases, it has several drawbacks.

The main drawback of the specialized class idea is that it offers no flexibility for toggling features on and off at run time. In other words, it is not easily possible to turn a normal deck into a "memorizing" deck, or to start logging the cards drawn at some arbitrary point in the execution of the code. In Java, it is impossible to change the type of an object at run time, so the only option would be to initialize a new object and copy the state of the old object into a new object which has the desired features. Such a scheme is not very elegant. However, turning features on or off might be necessary if the user interface allows the player to turn these features on or off during game play.

We can consider a second solution that can accommodate run-time adjustments in the features of an object. I will call this solution the *multi-mode class* solution. With this solution, we provide all possible features within one class, and include a flag value to represent the *mode* the object of the class is in. The resulting code would look like this:

```
public class MultiModeDeck implements CardSource {
  enum Mode {
    SIMPLE, LOGGING, MEMORIZING, LOGGING_MEMORIZING
  }
  private Mode aMode = Mode.SIMPLE;

  public void setMode(Mode pMode) { ... }

  public Card draw() {
    if( aMode == Mode.SIMPLE ) { ... }
    else if( aMode == Mode.LOGGING ) { ... }
    ...
  }
}
```

Although the multi-mode class solution does allow one to toggle features on and off at run time, it contravenes the important principles presented in Chapter 4 by inducing elaborate state spaces for objects that should otherwise be fairly simple. It also violates the principle of separation of concerns by tangling the behavior of different features within one class, or even a single method. In the extreme, it can turn a class intended to represent a simple concept into a GOD CLASS†. As a consequence of its complexity, the multi-mode class solution also suffers from a lack of extensibility. To add a new feature, we need to add yet more code and branching behavior to account for new modes. With, say, ten features, it is easy to imagine how the code would become a nightmare of case switches and an instance of SWITCH STATEMENT†. As is often the case in the presence of a potential combinatorial explosion, the key is to move from a solution that relies on defining new classes to a solution that relies on combining objects together.

The DECORATOR design pattern offers just that solution. The context for using the pattern is a design problem where we want to *decorate* some objects with additional features, while being able to treat the decorated objects like any other object of the undecorated type. Figure 6.8 shows an application of the solution template of DECORATOR to the CardSource scenario. The diagram shows the roles played by different elements as notes.

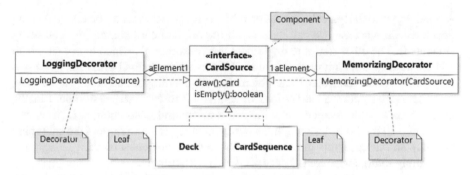

Fig. 6.8 Class diagram of a sample application of DECORATOR

In terms of solution template, the DECORATOR looks very much like the COMPOSITE, except that instead of a composite class we have some decorator classes. Indeed, the design constraints of the decorator class are similar as those of the composite class:

- A decorator aggregates one object of the component interface type (CardSource in the example). Using the component interface type is important, as it allows the decorator to decorate any other kind of components, including other decorators (and composites).
- It implements the component interface. This is what allows decorator objects to be treated by the rest of the code in exactly the same way as leaf elements.

The main question to resolve when applying the DECORATOR is what the methods of the decorator class should do. In a classic use of the DECORATOR, the implementation of the interface's methods that implement the decoration involves two steps, illustrated in the code below:

```
public class MemorizingDecorator implements CardSource {
  private final CardSource aElement;
  private final List<Card> aDrawnCards = new ArrayList<>();

  public MemorizingDecorator(CardSource pCardSource) {
    aElement = pCardSource;
  }

  public boolean isEmpty() {
    return aElement.isEmpty();
  }

  public Card draw() {
    // 1. Delegate the original request to the decorated object
    Card card = aElement.draw();
    // 2. Implement the decoration
    aDrawnCards.add(card);
    return card;
  }
}
```

One step is to delegate the execution of the original behavior to the element being decorated. In our case, we call `draw()` on the original card source (the one being decorated). The other step is to implement the "decoration", which in our case is to add the card to some internal structure. There is no prescribed order for these two steps, although in some case the problem domain may impose an order. In our case, it is necessary to draw a card before we can add it to the internal storage. Finally, although only some methods may involve a behavioral decoration, it is necessary to re-route all methods declared in the component interface to respect the subtyping contract. In our case, this means that we have to implement a method `isEmpty()` that simply returns whether the decorated element is empty.

With the DECORATOR, we can easily combine decorations. Because a decorator aggregates a component, combining features becomes as simple as decorating a decorated object. The sequence diagram of Figure 6.9 illustrates the delegation sequence when using a DECORATOR where we decorated a `Deck` with a `MemorizingDecorator`, and then again with a `LoggingDecorator`, so that the final behavior of `draw()` will be to memorize, log, and return the next card in the card source.

An important constraint when using the DECORATOR is that for the design to work, decorations must be independent and strictly additive. The main benefit of the DECORATOR is to support attaching features in a flexible way, sometimes in unanticipated configurations. For this reason, use of the pattern should not require client code to respect elaborate combination rules. As for being additive, this means that the DECORATOR pattern should not be used to *remove* features from objects. The main reason for this constraint is that it would violate a fundamental principle of object-oriented design introduced in Chapter 7.

When implementing the DECORATOR design pattern in Java, it is a good idea to specify as `final` the field that stores a reference to the decorated object, and to

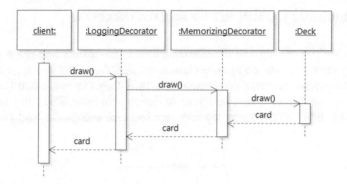

Fig. 6.9 Sequence diagram modeling a call to `draw` on a decorated `Deck`

initialize it in the constructor. A common expectation when using the DECORATOR is that a decorator object will decorate the same object throughout its lifetime.

Finally, an important consequence of decorating objects using the DECORATOR is that decorated objects *gain a different identity*. In other words, because a decorator is itself an object that wraps another object, a decorated object is not the same as the undecorated object. Figure 6.10 illustrates this change in identity for a simple `CardSource` decoration. In this diagram, we see that the client code holds a reference to a `Deck` instance we call `deck` in a variable `source1`, and a reference to a decorated version of `deck` in `source2`. Although `source1` and `source2` conceptually refer to the *same* card source, the decorated version does not have the same identity as the undecorated version. In other words, `source1` != `source2`. This issue of identity change could be a problem in a system where object comparison relies on identity instead of equality. In this case, introducing the DECORATOR pattern could break the design. See Section 4.7 to review the implications of object identity.

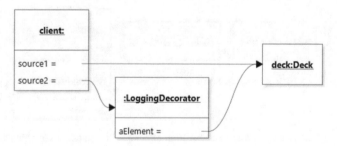

Fig. 6.10 Object diagram of a decorated `Deck`

6.5 Combining COMPOSITE and DECORATOR

Although the DECORATOR and COMPOSITE patterns are distinct and often presented separately, decorator and composite classes can easily co-exist in a type hierarchy. If they implement the same component interface, they can work hand-in-hand in supporting composition-based solutions to design problems. The class diagram of Figure 6.11 shows a type hierarchy with one leaf, one composite, and two decorators.

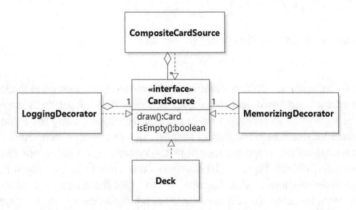

Fig. 6.11 Combining the COMPOSITE and DECORATOR in the same class hierarchy

The object diagram of Figure 6.12 shows a sample object graph that can be induced by this type hierarchy. The diagram shows examples of both a decorated composite and a composite of a decorated object.

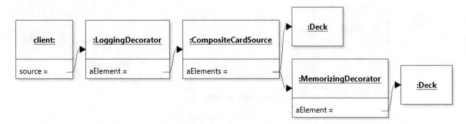

Fig. 6.12 Object diagram showing a combination of composite and decorator objects

Although, in this chapter, I developed the running example of various design options for a card game, it is good to know about the classic scenario supported by the COMPOSITE and DECORATOR patterns. A design context that is a particularly good fit for these patterns is the development of some drawing feature (e.g., for a drawing tool or slideshow presentation application). In this scenario, the component type is a

Figure with a draw() method. Leaf classes are concrete figures, such as rectangles, ellipses, text boxes, etc. Figure 6.13 shows a class diagram of the domain elements and corresponding design structures.

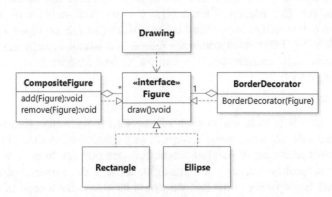

Fig. 6.13 Class diagram of the COMPOSITE and DECORATOR patterns applied to the context of a drawing editor

In this design, the CompositeFigure very naturally supports the end-user feature of *grouping* figures into an aggregate figure. A group can then be considered a single figure element, which can then be grouped with other figures and groups, etc. As for the DECORATOR, it allows decorating figures, literally. The example provided on the diagram is that of a decorator that adds a border to the decorated figure, whatever it is. This classic application of the COMPOSITE and DECORATOR patterns is good to know about, because they also provide the conceptually cleanest illustration of the behavior that must be realized by their implementation of the component interface. Specifically, the draw() method of the composite is simply an invocation of the draw() method of all the figures it contains:

```
public void draw() {
  for( Figure figure : aFigures ) {
    figure.draw();
  }
}
```

For the DECORATOR, the implementation of the draw method would be a sequence of one delegation followed by a decoration.

```
public void draw() {
  aFigure.draw();
  // Additional code to draw the border
}
```

6.6 Polymorphic Copying

We are now starting to work with designs that involve various combinations of objects in elaborate object graphs. The use of such dynamic structures has various implications for other aspects of the design. One implication is for object identity (see Section 6.4). Another implication is for designs that rely on object copying.

In Section 2.7, I discussed situations where it is useful to copy some objects, and introduced copy constructors, which allow a client to make a copy of an object passed as argument:

```
Deck deckCopy = new Deck(deck);
```

Copy constructors work fine in many situations, but their main limitation is that a constructor call requires a static reference to a specific class (here, class `Deck`). In designs that make use of polymorphism, this can turn out to be a problem. Let us consider a situation where we are managing a list of `CardSource` objects. If we want to make a deep copy of the list, we would have to make a copy of every card source in the list:

```
List<CardSource> sources = ...;
List<CardSource> copy = new ArrayList<>();
for( CardSource source : sources ) {
  copy.add(/* ??? */);
}
```

Because `CardSource` is an interface type that must be subtyped and we do not necessarily know the concrete types of the objects in the list `aSources`, we do not know what copy constructor to call. One clumsy solution would be to use a branching statement such as this:

```
CardSource copy = null;
if( source.getClass() == Deck.class ) {
  copy = new Deck((Deck) source);
} else if( source.getClass() == CardSequence.class ) {
  copy = new CardSequence((CardSequence) source);
} else if( source.getClass() == CompositeCardSource.class ) {
  copy = new CompositeCardSource((CompositeCardSource) source);
}
...
```

Solutions of this nature are not recommended because they essentially void the benefits of polymorphism, namely, to be able to work with instances of `CardSource` no matter what their actual concrete type is. Moreover, this code is also an example of SWITCH STATEMENT† which completely destroys the extensibility of the design, as it would break as soon as a new subtype of `CardSource` is introduced. Finally, it would be a mess to implement because some `CardSource` classes are wrappers around other card sources. Specifically, because `CompositeCardSource` can aggregate any kind of card source, a copy constructor for this class would also need a branching statement like the above. In the presence of polymorphism, the use of copy constructors is essentially unworkable.

Instead, what we need is a mechanism that provides us with *polymorphic copying* of objects. Specifically, we want to be able to make copies of objects without knowing the concrete type of the object. [3]

As usual, to support polymorphic behavior in a design, we need to provide a specification of this behavior. This is no different for copying objects, and for this purpose we will add a method `copy()` to our `CardSource` interface:

```
public interface CardSource {
  ...

  /**
   * @return An object that is an exact deep copy
   * (distinct object graph) of this card source.
   */
  CardSource copy();
}
```

The impact of this addition is that all concrete subtypes of `CardSource` are now required to supply a `copy()` operation. Figure 6.14 presents some of the different cases we have seen so far in previous sections, with their elements that are relevant to copying. In this design, we will assume that the `Deck` class is implemented using the class `CardStack` introduced in Section 6.1. In this scenario, `CardStack` also has a copy constructor.

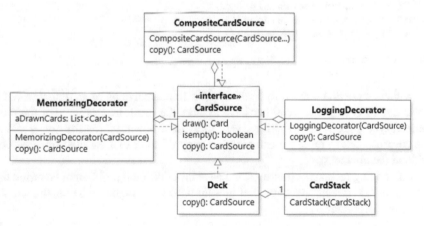

Fig. 6.14 Polymorphic copy requires all implementing classes of a type to supply a `copy()` operation

Implementing `copy()` for non-recursive structures is the most straightforward. In our case, class `Deck` is the only non-recursive structure in the design context, so we will start with this class:

---

[3] Polymorphic copying is also known as *cloning*. However, in Java, cloning also refers to a specific way to implement polymorphic copying using the library method `Object#clone()`. Cloning with `Object#clone()` is mainly relevant in the presence of inheritance, and will be covered in Chapter 7.

```
public class Deck implements CardSource {
  private CardStack aCards = new CardStack();
  ...
  public Deck copy() {
    Deck copy = new Deck();
    copy.aCards = new CardStack(aCards);
    return copy;
  }
}
```

Because the state of Deck is entirely encapsulated by its aggregated CardStack, copying the deck amounts to copying its inner CardStack structure. In the example, this is done with the help of the CardStack copy constructor. Because a CardStack only aggregates immutable Card objects, the copying can stop there.

One noteworthy aspect of this implementation of copy() is that its return type is Deck, not CardSource. This feature, introduced in Java 5, is called a *covariant return type*. This means that the return type of an implementing method can be *more specific* than the return type of the corresponding interface method it implements. This is a type-safe way to avoid unnecessary downcasts. In contexts where we are directly copying an object of the subtype, we can assign the result to a variable of the subtype.

```
Deck deck = new Deck();

// Without covariant return type
CardSource copy1 = deck.copy();
Deck copy2 = (Deck) deck.copy();

// With covariant return type
Deck copy3 = deck.copy();
```

Without a covariant return type, if we wish to make a copy of an object stored in a variable of type Deck, we either have to store the result in a variable of the more general type CardSource (as for copy1), or use a downcast (as for copy2). With the covariant return type, we can assign a copy of deck to a variable of type Deck without the downcast.

For copying recursive structures, we have the additional problem of ensuring that we actually do a recursive copy. Let us start with LoggingDecorator, the simpler of the two decorators:

```
public class LoggingDecorator implements CardSource {
  private CardSource aSource;

  public LoggingDecorator( CardSource pSource ) {
    aSource = pSource;
  }
  ...
  public LoggingDecorator copy() {
    return new LoggingDecorator(aSource.copy());
  }
}
```

In the case of a decorator, our copy consists of a new decorator of a *copy* of the original decorated element. However, because decorators can decorate polymorphically any subtype of `CardSource`, we must copy the decorated element polymorphically. Fortunately, the support we need to do this is precisely the one we are implementing throughout the `CardSource` type hierarchy: method `copy()`. The implementation of `copy()` for `MemorizingDecorator` is very similar, except that we also have to copy the additional state (`aDrawnCards`):

```
public MemorizingDecorator copy() {
  MemorizingDecorator copy =
    new MemorizingDecorator(aElement.copy());
  copy.aDrawnCards = new ArrayList<>(aDrawnCards);
  return copy;
}
```

Implementing the copy operation for `CompositeCardSource` is also similar. In this case, our copy needs a list of *copies* of all the `CardSource` instances in the composite:

```
public CardSource copy() {
  CompositeCardSource copy = new CompositeCardSource();
  copy.aElements = new ArrayList<>();
  for(CardSource source : aElements) {
    copy.aElements.add(source.copy());
  }
  return copy;
}
```

6.7 The PROTOTYPE Design Pattern

The ability to copy objects polymorphically, as seen in the previous section, is a powerful feature that can be used for a variety of purposes in composition-based designs. One specialized use of polymorphic copying is to support *polymorphic instantiation*. Let us consider a simplified model for a card game where, for every new game, we need to instantiate a fresh `CardSource`:

```
public class GameModel {
  private CardSource aCardSource;

  public void newGame() {
    aCardSource = /* Instantiate a new CardSource */;
  }
}
```

The implementation of `newGame()` can be trivial if we hard-code the specific type of source to return (for example, `new Deck()`). However, what if we want to make it possible to configure `GameModel` so that it is possible to use *any* type of `CardSource`, and to change the default card source at run time? In this case, the

problems are very similar to the ones discussed in the previous section (that the use
of a SWITCH STATEMENT† structure destroys the benefits of polymorphism, etc.).

To create a card source without hard-coding its type, one option better than a
SWITCH STATEMENT† would be to use metaprogramming (see Section 5.4). For example, we could add a parameter to newGame() of type Class<T>, which specifies
the type of the card source to add. Although workable, solutions of this nature tend
to be fragile and require a lot of error handling.

Another option is to rely on a polymorphic copying mechanism and create new
instances of an object of interest by copying a *prototype object*. This idea is captured
as the PROTOTYPE design pattern. The context for using the PROTOTYPE is the need to
create objects whose type may not be known at compile time. The solution template
involves storing a reference to the prototype object and polymorphically copying
this object whenever new instances are required.

For the GameModel scenario, the application of the PROTOTYPE would look like
this:

```
public class GameModel {
  private final CardSource aCardSourcePrototype;
  private CardSource aCardSource;

  public GameModel(CardSource pCardSourcePrototype) {
    aCardSourcePrototype = pCardSourcePrototype;
    newGame();
  }

  public void newGame() {
    aCardSource = aCardSourcePrototype.copy();
  }
}
```

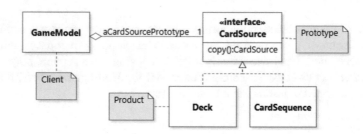

Fig. 6.15 Sample application of the PROTOTYPE, with the name of roles indicated in notes

In this solution, we use dependency injection (see Section 3.8) to inject a *card
source prototype object* into the GameModel via its constructor. Then, whenever a
fresh CardSource object is required, we make a copy of the prototype and assign
the result to aCardSource. If need be, it would also be possible to add a setter
method to change the prototype at run time.

Figure 6.15 shows a class diagram that summarizes the key aspects of the solution template, and indicates the role various elements play in the application of the

pattern. The client is a generic mention to represent any code that needs to perform polymorphic instantiation. The prototype is the abstract element (typically an interface) whose concrete prototype must be instantiated at run time. The *products* are the objects that can be created by copying the prototype.

One added benefit of the PROTOTYPE pattern is that normally the option to create objects of different types does not increase the amount of control flow (branching statements) in the client class. In a traditional, "mode-based" design, the `newGame()` method would have to check whether the object is in a specific state to create, say, `Deck` card sources as opposed to other card sources, using a control statement such as an `if` statement. With the PROTOTYPE, this branching is done through polymorphism. As the code of the `newGame()` method shows, there is no such control statement: the method just makes a copy of whatever object is the current prototype.

Code Exploration: JetUML · DiagramTabToolBar

Applying the PROTOTYPE *pattern.*

The design of the JetUML tool bar relies on the PROTOTYPE to create new nodes in a diagram. The `DiagramTabToolBar` class aggregates a number of `SelectableToolButton` instances. In turn, these instances aggregate an instance of the `Node` to create when the button is clicked. When the user presses a mouse button on the canvas, the code asks the tool bar to return the prototype associated with the button, and copies it to create the new node. Figure 6.16 shows the main participants in this interaction.

6.8 The COMMAND Design Pattern

Conceptually, a *command* is a piece of code that exercises a cohesive action: saving a file, drawing a card from a deck, etc. The way to represent a command in source code naturally aligns with the concept of a function or method, since that is an abstraction that corresponds to a piece of code that will execute. As an example, we can consider the two main state-changing functionalities of a `Deck` class: to draw a card, and to shuffle the cards. To exercise these features, we call methods:

```
deck.shuffle();
Card card = deck.draw();
```

Now that we are studying designs that make principled use of objects, we consider an alternative idea for representing commands, namely for objects to serve as *manageable units of functionality*. In sophisticated applications, there are many different contexts in which we might want to exercise a functionality such as drawing a card from the deck. For example, we might want to store a history of completed commands, so that we can undo them or replay them later. Or, we might want to accumulate commands and execute them all at once, in batch mode. Or, we might

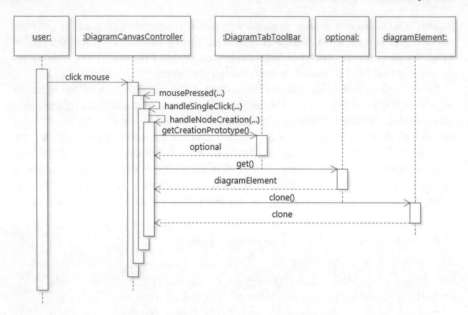

Fig. 6.16 Use of the PROTOTYPE in JetUML

want to parameterize other objects, such as graphical user interface menus, with commands. Requirements such as these point to the additional need to *manage* functionality in a principled way. The COMMAND design pattern provides a recognizable way to manage abstractions that represent commands.

The class diagram of Figure 6.17 shows a sample application of the pattern. The Command interface defines an execute method and other methods to specify the services required by the clients to manage the commands. In the example, this includes an additional undo() method, but other designs may leave it out or have other required services (such as getDescription(), to get a description of the command).

Fig. 6.17 Application of the COMMAND design pattern with the name of element roles in notes

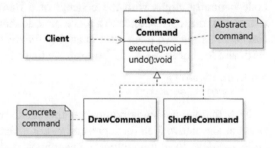

The COMMAND pattern has a simple solution template. The template involves defining commands as objects, with an interface for commands that includes a method to execute the command. Another important part of the solution template

is for the client to refer to commands through the interface. Despite the apparent simplicity of the solution template, the COMMAND pattern is not necessarily an easy one to apply, because many important design choices induced by the pattern are implementation-dependent. Let us look at some examples from our scenario.

- **Access to command target:** Command execution can modify the state of one of more objects. For example, drawing a card from a deck changes the state of the deck. The design must specify how the command gains access to the objects it must act on. Typically this is done by storing a reference to the target within the command object, but other alternatives are possible, including passing arguments to the `execute` method or using closures;
- **Data flow:** In the typical solution template for COMMAND, the interface methods have return type `void`. The design must thus include a provision for returning the result of commands that produce an output, such as drawing a card from a deck;
- **Command execution correctness:** The code responsible for executing commands must ensure that the sequence of execution is correct. For example, the design needs to specify whether commands can be executed more than once. The use of design by contract also leads to interesting implications. If commands call code with specified preconditions, the responsibility of respecting the preconditions is transferred to the code executing the command.
- **Encapsulation of target objects:** In some cases, a command object might require operations that are not available in the target object's public interface. For example, to undo the effect of calling `Deck.draw()`, it is necessary to push a card back onto the deck. In our running example class `Deck` does not have a `push` method. The design must include a solution to this issue. One possibility is to have a command factory method located in the class of the object the commands operate on. In our case, this would mean to add a `createDrawCommand()` method in class `Deck`.
- **Storing data:** Some operations supported by commands require storing some data, something that also needs to be designed as part of the pattern's application. For example, in a design context where the undoing of commands is required, the effect of executing a command may have to be cached so that it can be undone. In our case, to undo the drawing of a card from a deck, it is necessary to remember which card was drawn. This information could be stored in the command object directly, or in an external structure accessible by the command object.

To illustrate one point in the design space for each of the concerns above, the code below shows an example of how to support a command to draw cards from a deck. The key idea for this application of the pattern is to use a factory method to create commands that are instances of an anonymous class with access to fields of its outer instance (see Section 4.10). In this design, commands to operate on a `Deck` instance are obtained directly from the `Deck` instance of interest. To keep the example simple, I slightly modify the `Command` interface so that `execute()` returns an `Optional<Card>`, which allows some commands to return an instance of `Card` if applicable. The code also assumes commands are executed only once and undone in the inverse order of that in which they are executed.

```
public class Deck {
  private CardStack aCards = new CardStack();

  public Command createDrawCommand() {
    return new Command() {
      Card aDrawn = null;
      public Optional<Card> execute() {
        aDrawn = draw();
        return Optional.of(aDrawn);
      }

      public void undo() {
        aCards.push(aDrawn);
        aDrawn = null;
      }
    };
  }
}
```

With this code, a new *draw* command is created, executed, and undone as follows:

```
Deck deck = new Deck();
Command command = deck.createDrawCommand();
Card card = command.execute().get();
command.undo();
```

When `command.execute()` executes, the code in the anonymous class calls `draw()` on the instance of `Deck` stored in variable `deck`, because anonymous classes retain a reference to their outer instance. The resulting card is then stored in a field of the anonymous class, which can then be used by the `undo()` method. The `undo` method also accesses the `Deck` instance through an implicit reference to its outer instance. Because the code is defined within class `Deck`, a reference to the private member `aCards` is possible.

Independently of the specific way the pattern is applied, having command objects gives us much flexibility for managing how and when to execute the commands that operate a system.

Code Exploration: Solitaire · Move

Applying the COMMAND *pattern using inner classes.*

The Solitaire example application relies on the COMMAND pattern. The command role is taken up by the `Move` interface. The implementations of `Move` illustrate a diversity of ways that commands can be realized. Classes `CardMove` and `RevealTopMove` are private inner classes of `GameModel` so that they can refer to the private fields and methods of their outer instance, as discussed in Section 4.10. The command to represent discarding a card from the deck is very simple and thus implemented as an anonymous class instantiated as part of the initialization of a field `aDiscardMove`. An alternative option would have been to create new instances of discard move in a factory method. To me both options are almost equivalent in terms of design quality. Because it does not refer to the state of a GameModel, field NULL_MOVE is a constant and declared as static. The null move represents the situation where it is not possible to make a move in the game. This is an application of NULL OBJECT (see Section 4.5). Class CompositeMove realizes the role of the composite in the COMPOSITE pattern. In the game it is used to combine atomic moves, such as taking a card from a tableau pile and flipping the card underneath it to reveal it. Finally, one implementation of Move is a stub, used for testing (see Section 5.8).

Code Exploration: JetUML · DiagramOperation

Combining the COMMAND *and the* COMPOSITE *patterns.*

In JetUML, DiagramOperation fulfills the role of command. However, in this design, there are only two concrete command types: SimpleOperation and CompoundOperation. SimpleOperation is a wrapper for a function object that can be used to encapsulate any non-compound command using a functional-programming flavored design. I revisit this style in Chapter 9. In contrast, CompoundOperation is a typical implementation of a composite in the COMPOSITE pattern.

6.9 The Law of Demeter

When designing a piece of software using aggregation, one can often end up with long delegation chains between objects. For example, Figure 6.18 models the aggregation for card piles in the Solitaire application.

Fig. 6.18 Aggregation structure for foundation piles in Solitaire

In this design, a GameModel object holds a reference to an instance of Foundations to manage the four piles of cards of a single suit. In turn, an instance of Foundations holds references to four CardStack instances, which are specialized wrappers around List objects.

There are different ways to use such delegation chains. Figure 6.19 illustrates a hypothetical way to use the aggregation structure for adding a card to a pile.

In this design the GameModel is in charge of all the details of adding a card to a pile, and must handle every intermediate object in the delegation chain. As an

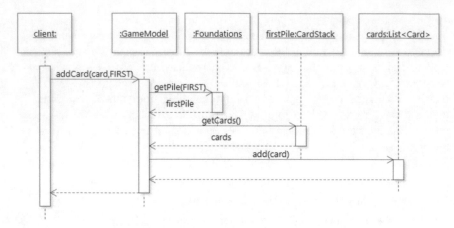

Fig. 6.19 Sample data structure access scenario for the Solitaire game design

example, in this design the implementation of `addCard` in class `GameModel` would look like this:

```
aFoundations.getPile(FIRST).getCards().add(pCard);
```

This design violates the principle of information hiding by requiring the code of the `GameModel` class to know about the precise navigation structure required to add a card to the system. Although this might be obvious in the case of a `CardStack` returning its `List<Card>`, exactly the same argument can be made for `Foundations` returning one of its `CardStack`. However, the encapsulation quality of intermediate classes in aggregation chains is easier to overlook. The intuition that designs such as this one tend to be suboptimal is captured by the MESSAGE CHAIN† antipattern. The *Law of Demeter* is a design guideline intended to help avoid the consequences of MESSAGE CHAIN†. This "law" is actually a design guideline that states that the code of a method should only access:

- The instance variables of its implicit parameter;
- The arguments passed to the method;
- Any new object created within the method;
- (If need be) globally available objects.

To respect this guideline, it becomes necessary to provide additional services in classes that occupy an intermediate position in an aggregation/delegation chain so that the clients do not need to manipulate the internal objects encapsulated by these objects. The solution in our example would be illustrated by Figure 6.20.

In this solution, objects do not return references to their internal structure, but instead provide the complete service required by the client at each step in the delegation chain.

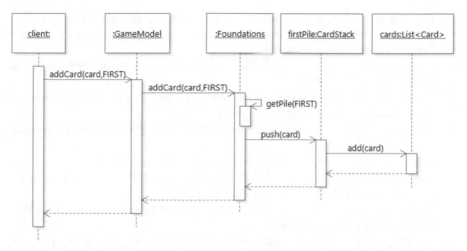

Fig. 6.20 Sample data structure access scenario for the Solitaire game design, which respects the Law of Demeter

---

Code Exploration: Solitaire · GameModel

Widening a class's interface to respect the Law of Demeter.

A study of the `GameModel` class will reveal numerous situations where I widened the interface of the class to respect the Law of Demeter. For example, method `isVisibleInTableau` has the single statement:

```
return aTableau.contains(pCard) && aTableau.isVisible(pCard);
```

As an alternative design, it would have been possible to return the tableau to the client (with something like `getTableau()`), and let the client code implement the logic directly as:

```
if( model.getTableau().contains(pCard) &&
    model.getTableau().isVisible(pCard))
```

However, this would require the client to know about the interface of `Tableau`, and violate the Law of Demeter.

Insights

This chapter presented various techniques for solving design problems by composing objects according to specific patterns.

- Large classes can be simplified by introducing classes whose objects will provide services to the initial class;

- If a design problem requires structures that change at run time or can be combined, consider building the structures by combining objects, as opposed to defining new classes for each possible structure;
- Use the COMPOSITE when you need to manipulate collections of objects the same way as single (*leaf*) objects;
- Use the DECORATOR when you need to add functionality to certain objects, while being able to use them in place of regular objects;
- The COMPOSITE and DECORATOR can be combined easily, especially if they share the same component type;
- Applying well-known object composition patterns is not sufficient to ensure the code is correct: typically, client code remains responsible for ensuring that the use of the pattern does not result in defective object graphs;
- Sequence diagrams can help communicate important arrangements of method calls between objects in a design;
- Use polymorphic copying to make copies of objects whose concrete type is not known at compile time. If the type is known at compile time, favor the simpler technique of copy constructors;
- Polymorphic copying can also be used as a way to create fresh instances of objects whose type is not known at compile time, a technique captured by the PROTOTYPE pattern;
- For designs where function objects need to be explicitly managed by client code, for example to store them or share them between code locations, the COMMAND design pattern provides a recognizable solution template;
- When applying the COMMAND pattern, be careful not to break the encapsulation of classes simply to allow command objects to operate on target objects;
- Unless there is an explicit reason not to, respect the Law of Demeter and avoid long message chains.

Further Reading

The Gang of Four book [6] has the original, detailed treatment of the COMPOSITE, DECORATOR, PROTOTYPE, and COMMAND patterns. Their descriptions of the patterns include useful complementary discussions of the implications of using the pattern. For example, the presentation of the COMPOSITE pattern includes an extended discussion of the trade-off between *transparency* and *safety* (in the type-checking sense) involved around the decision of whether to declare the child management operations in the component interface or not.

Information on variable arguments (*varargs*) can be found on the Oracle website in the list of enhancements for Java SE 5.0.

A web page with information on the Law of Demeter can be found at
`http://www.ccs.neu.edu/home/lieber/LoD.html`.

Chapter 7
Inheritance

Concepts and Principles: Abstract classes/methods, cloning, final classes/methods, inheritance, Liskov Substitution Principle, overloading, overriding;
Patterns and Antipatterns: TEMPLATE METHOD.

Inheritance is a programming language mechanism that allows us to create objects from definitions provided in multiple, inter-related classes. It is a powerful feature that offers a natural solution to many design problems related to code reuse and extensibility. At the same time, it is a complex mechanism that can all too easily be misused. This chapter provides a review of inheritance and presents the major design rules and patterns involving it.

Design Context

The examples in this chapter discuss the design of two type hierarchies: card sources and moves. The card source hierarchy follows the examples of the previous chapters where instances of objects that are subtypes of a CardSource interface are used to provide card instances to be used in card games. The second context is the design of a hierarchy of subtypes of an interface Move which, together, realize an application of the COMMAND design pattern as seen in Section 6.8.

© Springer Nature Switzerland AG 2022
M. P. Robillard, *Introduction to Software Design with Java*,
https://doi.org/10.1007/978-3-030-97899-0_7

7.1 The Case for Inheritance

So far we have seen many situations where we can leverage polymorphism to realize various design features. Polymorphism helps make a design extensible by decoupling client code from the concrete implementation of a required functionality.
The class diagram of Figure 7.1 exemplifies this benefit by showing a GameModel
that depends only on a general CardSource service whose concrete realization can
be one of at least three options: a typical Deck of cards, a MemorizingDeck that
remembers each card drawn, and a CircularDeck that places drawn cards back at
the bottom of the deck.

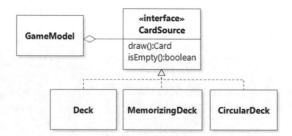

Fig. 7.1 Polymorphic reference to a CardSource service

This design is extensible because in principle the GameModel can work with any
card source. As discussed in Chapter 3, in Java polymorphism relies intrinsically
on the language's subtyping mechanism. The key to supporting various options for
a CardSource is the fact that the different concrete implementations of the service
are subtypes of the CardSouce interface type.

Although the design illustrated is clean from the point of view of polymorphism,
it has one major weakness from the point of view of the implementation of the various card source alternatives. This weakness would become apparent as soon as we
would start to implement the class hierarchy of Figure 7.1. The issue is that the
services defined by the CardSource interface are similar, and likely to be implemented in similar ways.[1] Figure 7.2 shows a slightly different variant of the class
diagram that emphasizes the implementation of the concrete CardSources instead
of the polymorphism. As is now more evident from the diagram, all three implementations of CardSource hold a reference to a CardStack delegate. Moreover:

- In all cases, the implementation of method isEmpty() is a delegation to aCards-
  .isEmpty()
- In all cases, the implementation of method draw() pops a card from aCards: the
  only difference between the three options is small variants for the remainder of

---

[1] This assumes a standard implementation, and not an application of the DECORATOR, which
would be challenging in the case of CircularDeck because of the requirement to use a service
(adding cards to the source) that is not defined on the component interface.

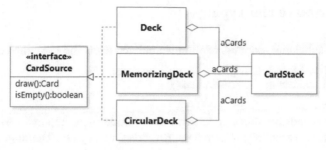

Fig. 7.2 Implementations of the `CardSource` service

the implementation of `draw` (e.g., to insert the card in the deck in the `CardStack` of `CircularDeck`).

So here we can say that the design induces DUPLICATED CODE†, also known as *code clones*. There is an extensive literature on the topic of duplicated code, but the bottom line is that it is a good idea to avoid it.

Problems of redundancies such as the one illustrated here can be improved by re-organizing the design. One mechanism of object-oriented programming languages that is especially effective for supporting code reuse (and thus avoiding DUPLICATED CODE†) is *inheritance*. Inheritance directly supports code reuse and extensibility because it allows us to define some classes in terms of other classes. The key idea of inheritance is to define a new class (the *subclass*) in terms of how it adds to (or *extends*) an existing *base class* (also called the *superclass*). Inheritance avoids re-peating declarations of class members because the declarations of the base class will automatically be taken into account when creating instances of the subclass.

In class diagrams, inheritance is denoted by a solid line with a white triangle pointing from the subclass to the superclass. Figure 7.3 illustrates a variant of our design where `MemorizingDeck` and `CircularDeck` are defined as subclasses of the `Deck` base class.

Fig. 7.3 Inheritance-based design for `CardSource`

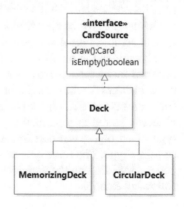

7.2 Inheritance and Typing

In Java the subclass-superclass relation is declared using the extends keyword:

```
public class MemorizingDeck extends Deck {
  private CardStack aDrawnCards;
}
```

To understand the effect of inheritance in code, it is important to remember that a class is essentially a template for creating objects. Defining a subclass MemorizingDeck as an extension of a superclass Deck means that when objects of the subclass are instantiated, the objects will be created by using the declaration of the subclass *and* of the declaration of the superclass. The result will be a single object. The run-time type of this object will be the type specified in the new operation. However, just as for interface implementation, inheritance introduces a suptyping relation. For this reason, an object can always be assigned to a variable of its superclass (in addition to its implementing interfaces).

```
Deck deck = new MemorizingDeck();
CardSource source = deck;
```

In the code above, a new object of run-time type MemorizingDeck is created and assigned to a variable named deck of compile-time type Deck. This is legal because MemorizingDeck is a subtype of Deck. The second line of the code example shows another relation between variables and values of different, yet related, types. The code declares a variable of type CardSource and assigns the value deck to it. The compile-time type of deck is Deck, which is a subtype of CardSource. For this reason, the compiler allows the assignment. At run time, it will turn out that the concrete type of deck is MemorizingDeck. However, because MemorizingDeck is a subtype of both Deck and CardSource, there is no problem.

In this chapter, the distinction between compile-time type and run-time type will become increasingly important. In our case, when an instance of MemorizingDeck is assigned to a variable of type Deck, it does not *become* a simple deck or *lose* any of its subclass-specific fields. In Java, once an object is created, its run-time type remains unchanged. All the variable reassignments accomplish in the code above is to change the type of the variable that holds a reference to the object. The run-time type of an object is the most specific type of an object when it is instantiated. It is the type mentioned in the new operation, and the one that is represented by the object returned by method getClass() (see Section 5.4). The run-time type of an object never changes for the duration of the object's lifetime. In contrast, the compile-time (or static) type of an object is the type of the *variable* in which a reference to the object is stored at a particular point in the code. In a correct program the static type of an object can correspond to its run-time type, or to any supertype of its run-time type. The static type of an object can be different at different points in the code, depending on the variables in which an object is stored. Let us consider the following example:

```
public static boolean isMemorizing(Deck pDeck) {
  return pDeck instanceof MemorizingDeck;
}

public static void main(String[] args) {
  Deck deck = new MemorizingDeck();
  MemorizingDeck memorizingDeck = (MemorizingDeck) deck;
  boolean isMemorizing1 = isMemorizing(deck); // true
  boolean isMemorizing2 = isMemorizing(memorizingDeck); // true
}
```

At the first line of the `main` method an object is created that is of run-time type `MemorizingDeck` and assigned to a variable of type `Deck`. As stated above, the run-time type of this object remains `MemorizingDeck` throughout the execution of the code. However, at the following line the static type of the variable that stores the original object is `MemorizingDeck`, and within the body of method `isMemorizingDeck` it is `Deck` (a formal parameter is a kind of variable, so the type of a parameter acts like a type of variable). Because the run-time type of the object never changes, the value stored in both `isMemorizing1` and `isMemorizing2` is `true`.

Downcasting

To make the code above compile, it is necessary to use a *cast* operation (`Memoriz-ingDeck`). In brief, a cast operation is necessary to enable unsafe type conversion operations. An example of an unsafe conversion between primitive types is to convert a value of type `long` into a value of type `int` (which may cause an overflow). Similarly, because a reference to a `Deck` is not guaranteed to refer to an instance of `MemorizingDeck` at run time, it is necessary to flag the risky conversion using a cast operator, a process known as *downcasting*.[2] When using inheritance, subclasses typically provide services in addition to what is available in the base class. For example, a class `MemorizingDeck` would probably include the definition of a service to obtain the list of cards drawn from the deck:

```
public class MemorizingDeck extends Deck {
  public Iterator<Card> getDrawnCards() { ... }
}
```

Because of the typing rules discussed in Chapter 3, it is only possible to call methods that are applicable for a given static type. So if we assign a reference to an object of run-time type `MemorizingDeck` to a variable of type `Deck`, then we will get a compilation error if we try to access a method of the subclass:

```
Deck deck = new MemorizingDeck();
deck.getDrawnCards();
```

---

[2] The direction implied in the term is a consequence of the convention that in type hierarchies, the top of the hierarchy is usually considered to be the root of the hierarchy

This makes a lot of sense. The code above would be type unsafe. Because references to an instance of any subtype of Deck can be stored in variable Deck, there is no guarantee that, at run time, the object in the variable will actually define a getDrawnCards() method. If, based on our knowledge of the code, we are sure that the object will always be of type MemorizingDeck, we can downcast the variable from a supertype down to a subtype:

```
MemorizingDeck memorizingDeck = (MemorizingDeck) deck;
Iterator<Card> drawnCards = memorizingDeck.getDrawnCards();
```

Downcasting involves some risks because a downcast implicitly encodes an assumption that the run-time type of the object referred to in the variable is of the same type as (or a subtype of) the type of the variable. In a way the code above would be like writing:

```
assert deck instanceof MemorizingDeck;
```

If the assumption is wrong, most likely due to a programmer error, then the execution of the code cannot proceed, and the downcast will raise a ClassCast-Exception. For this reason, downcasting code will often be protected by control structures to assert the run-time type of an object, such as:

```
if( deck instanceof MemorizingDeck ) {
  return ((MemorizingDeck)deck).getDrawnCards();
}
```

Singly-Rooted Class Hierarchy

Java supports *single inheritance*, which means that a given class can only declare to inherit from a single class. This is in contrast to languages such as C++, which support *multiple inheritance*. However, because the superclass of a class can also be defined to inherit from a superclass, classes can have, in effect, more than one superclass. In fact, classes in Java are organized into a *single-rooted class hierarchy*. If a class does not declare to extend any class, by default it extends the library class Object. Class Object constitutes the root of any class hierarchy in Java code. The complete class hierarchy for variants of Deck thus includes class Object, as illustrated in Figure 7.4. Because the subtyping relation is transitive, objects of class MemorizingDeck can be stored in variables of type Object.

7.3 Inheriting Fields

With inheritance, the subclass inherits the declarations of the superclass. The consequences of inheriting field declarations are quite different from those of method declarations, so I discuss them separately.

Fig. 7.4 Complete class hierarchy for Deck

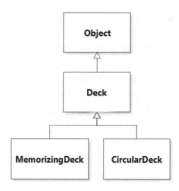

Field declarations define the structure of information stored by the instantiated object. When creating a new object, this object will have a field for each field declaration in the class named in the new operation, and each of its superclasses, transitively. Given the following class hierarchy:

```
public class Deck implements CardSource {
  private final CardStack aCards = new CardStack();
  ...
}

public class MemorizingDeck extends Deck {
  private final CardStack aDrawnCards = new CardStack();
  ...
}
```

objects created with the statement new MemorizingDeck(); will have two fields: aCards and aDrawnCards. It does not matter that the fields are private. Accessibility is a static concept, meaning that it is only relevant for the source code. The fact that the code in class MemorizingDeck cannot access (or *see*) the field declared in its superclass does not change anything about the fact that this field is part of the object. For the fields to be accessible to subclasses, it is possible to set their access modifier to protected instead of private, or to access their value through a getter method. Type members declared to be protected are only accessible within methods of the same class, classes in the same package, and subclasses in any package. To respect the principles of encapsulation presented in Chapter 2, the accessibility of fields should however be minimized. This means that, unless widening a field's visibility to protected provides a clear advantage, a field should be declared private, even if its value is required by subclasses. I revisit this point in Section 7.4.[3]

The inheritance of fields creates an interesting problem of data initialization. When an object can be initialized with default values, the process is simple. In

---

[3] The Java Language Specification (JLS) considers that private fields are not "inherited". This is a matter of terminology, because objects of subclasses do include the private fields declared in their parent classes. When learning object-oriented design, mixing the concepts of visibility and inheritance can be confusing, so I do not retain the terminology of the JLS. In this book, the concepts of field inheritance and visibility are kept consistently distinct.

our case, if we assign the default values using the field initialization statement as in the above statements (i.e., = new CardStack();), and rely on the default (i.e., parameterless) constructors, we can expect that creating a new instance of class MemorizingDeck will result in an instance with two fields of type CardStack, each referring to an empty instance of CardStack.[4]

However, it is often the case that object initialization requires input data. For example, what happens if we want to make it possible to initialize a deck with a set of cards supplied by the client code? For example:

```
Card[] cards = {Card.get(Rank.ACE, Suit.CLUBS),
                Card.get(Rank.ACE, Suit.SPADES)};
MemorizingDeck deck = new MemorizingDeck(cards);
```

In such situations it becomes important to pay attention to the order in which the fields of an object are initialized. The general principle in Java is that the fields of an object are initialized *top down*, from the field declarations of the most general superclass down to the most specific class (the one named in the new operation). In our example, aCards would be initialized, then aDrawnCards. This order is achieved by the fact that the first instruction of any constructor is to call a constructor, generally of its superclass, and so on.[5] For this reason, the order of constructor calls is *bottom up*. In our running example, declaring:

```
public class MemorizingDeck extends Deck {
   private final CardStack aDrawnCards = new CardStack();

   public MemorizingDeck(Card[] pCards) {
     /* Automatically calls super() */
     ...
   }
}
```

means that the default constructor of Deck is called and terminates before the code of the MemorizingDeck constructor executes. It is also possible to invoke the constructor of the superclass explicitly, using the super(...) call. However, if used, this call must be the first statement of a constructor. Although it illustrates how constructor calls are chained, the example above does not quite do what we want, because it ignores the input cards. With the initialization mechanism we have seen so far, however, it becomes possible to pass input values up to initialize fields declared in a superclass. In our case we want to store the input cards into the aCards field defined by the Deck superclass. We would accomplish this as follows:

---

[4] If no constructor is declared for a class, a default constructor with no parameter is invisibly made available to client code. Declaring any non-default constructor in a class disables the automatic generation of a default constructor.

[5] If the superclass declares a constructor with no parameter, this call does not need to be explicit. It is also possible for the first instruction of a constructor to be a call to another constructor of the same class, using the statement this(...). Eventually, however, construction has to execute the constructor of the superclass.

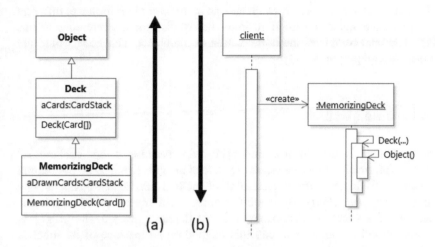

Fig. 7.5 Order of constructor call (a) and object construction (b). The calls to the constructors of a superclass are self-calls

```
public class Deck {
  private final CardStack aCards = new CardStack();

  public Deck(){} // Relies on the field initialization

  public Deck(Card[] pCards) {
    for( Card card : pCards) {
      aCards.push(card); }
  }
}

public class MemorizingDeck extends Deck {
  private final CardStack aDrawnCards = new CardStack();

  public MemorizingDeck(Card[] pCards) {
    super(pCards);
  }
}
```

Here the only statement of the MemorizingDeck constructor is an *explicit* call to the constructor of the superclass. This call passes in the initialization data. Once the super call terminates, the execution of the constructor of the same class continues with the initialization of the aDrawnCards field.

Calling the constructor of the superclass with super(...) is very different from calling the constructor of the superclass with a new statement. In the latter case, two different objects are created. The code:

```
public MemorizingDeck(Card[] pCards) {
  new Deck(pCards);
}
```

calls the constructor of `Deck`, which creates an *additional* `Deck` instance, different from the instance under construction, immediately discards the reference to this instance, and then completes the initialization of the object. This code would not serve many useful purposes.

7.4 Inheriting Methods

Inheriting methods is different from inheriting fields because method declarations do not store information that represents the state of an object, and so do not require any initialization. Instead, the implications of method inheritance center around the question of *applicability*. By default, methods of a superclass are applicable to instances of a subclass. For example, if we define a method `shuffle()` in class `Deck`, it will be possible to call this method on an instance of its subclass `MemorizingDeck`:

```
MemorizingDeck memorizingDeck = new MemorizingDeck();
memorizingDeck.shuffle();
```

This "feature" is nothing special, as it is only a consequence of what a method represents and the rules of the type system. Here it is worth remembering that an instance (i.e., non-static) method is just a different way to express a function that takes an object of its declaring class as its first argument. For example, the method `shuffle()` in `Deck`:

```
public class Deck implements CardSource {
    private CardStack aCards = new CardStack();

    public void shuffle() {
        // The 'this' keyword is optional in this case. It is used
        // here to contrast with the alternative below.
        this.aCards.clear();
        this.initialize();
    }

    private void initialize() {
        /* Adds all 52 cards to aCard in random order */
    }
}
```

is more or less equivalent to the static method:

```
public static void shuffle(Deck pThis) {
    pThis.aCards.clear();
    pThis.initialize();
}
```

In the first case the function is invoked by specifying the target object *before* the call: `memorizingDeck.shuffle()`. In this case we refer to the `memorizingDeck` parameter as the *implicit parameter*. A reference to this parameter is accessible through the `this` keyword within the method.[6] In the second case, the function is invoked by specifying the target object as an *explicit* parameter, so, after the call: `shuffle(memorizingDeck)`. In this case to clear any ambiguity it is usually necessary to specify the type of the class where the method is located, so `Deck.shuffle(memorizingDeck)`. What this example illustrates is that methods of a superclass are automatically applicable to instances of a subclass because instances of a subclass can be assigned to a variable of any supertype. In our example, because it is legal to assign a reference to a `MemorizingDeck` to a parameter of type `Deck`, the `shuffle()` method is applicable to instances of any subclass of `Deck`.

In some cases, a method inherited from a superclass does not do quite what we want. In our running example, this would be the case for method `draw()`, which in the `Deck` base class just draws a card from the deck:

```
public class Deck implements CardSource {
  private CardStack aCards = new CardStack();

  public Card draw() {
    return aCards.pop();
  }
}
```

Here using `Deck`'s version of method `draw()` on instances of `MemorizingDeck` through inheritance does not do what we need, because that method does not memorize anything. In such cases, we need to *redefine*, or *override*, the behavior of the inherited method by supplying an implementation in the subclass that only applies to instances of the subclasses. For method `draw()` we would want:

```
public class MemorizingDeck extends Deck {
  private CardStack aDrawnCards = new CardStack();

  public Card draw() {
    Card card = aCards.pop();
    aDrawCards.push(card);
    return card;
  }
}
```

Unfortunately, this code will not compile because the code of method `draw()` in `MemorizingDeck` refers to private field `aCards` of class `Deck`. Because private fields are only accessible within the class where they are declared, this field is not visible in other classes, including subclasses. One possible workaround is to define `Deck.aCards` as `protected` instead. A `protected` access modifier for a field allows subclasses to manipulate some structure of the superclass when overriding methods. Unfortunately, increasing the visibility of `aCards` from `private` to `protected` has a corresponding negative impact on encapsulation, because now it is possible to refer to the field, and thus mutate the object it refers to, from many different classes instead of just one. To circumvent this issue, we can resort to other alternatives, including the use of *super calls*, introduced below.

---

[6] Use of the `this` keyword is optional, as it can be implied if absent.

Overriding inherited methods has a major consequence on the design of an object-oriented application, because it introduces the possibility that multiple method implementations apply to an object that is the target of a method invocation. For example, in the code:

```
Card card = new MemorizingDeck().draw();
```

both `Deck#draw()` and `MemorizingDeck#draw()` are applicable and can thus legally be used. Which one is used? For the program to work, the programming environment (the Java Virtual Machine) must follow a consistent *method selection algorithm*.

For overridden methods, the selection algorithm is relatively intuitive: when multiple implementations are applicable, the run-time environment selects the *most specific one* based on the *run-time type of the implicit parameter*. As previously defined, the run-time type of an object is the actual class that was instantiated: the class name that follows the `new` keyword, or the class type represented by the object returned by a call to `Object.getClass()`. Because the selection of an overridden method relies on run-time information, the selection procedure is often referred to as *dynamic dispatch*, or *dynamic binding*. It is important to remember that type information for variables is ignored for dynamic dispatch. So, in this example:

```
Deck deck = new MemorizingDeck();
Card card = deck.draw();
```

the method `MemorizingDeck#draw()` would be selected, even though the static (compile-time) type of variable holding the target object is `Deck`.

In some cases, it can be necessary to bypass the dynamic binding mechanism and link to a specific, statically-predictable method implementation. In Java, however, for instance methods it is only possible to do so by referring to the implementation of the method that is being directly overridden. This exception to the usual dynamic binding mechanism is intended to support the common case where a method is overridden to provide behavior *in addition* to what the inherited method does. To illustrate this case, let us return to the issue of overriding method `draw()` in class `MemorizingDeck`. This time, we will do it without declaring `Deck.aCards` to be `protected`.

The key insight we use to accomplish this is to observe that to draw a card from `aCards`, we can also use `Deck`'s own `draw()` method. So what we want would be like this:

```
public class MemorizingDeck extends Deck {
  private CardStack aDrawnCards = new CardStack();

  public Card draw() {
    Card card = draw(); // Problematic
    aDrawCards.push(card);
    return card;
  }
}
```

Here, the naive intention is that by calling `draw()` inside `MemorizingDeck#-draw()`, we can execute the code of `Deck#draw()` and thus draw a card from aCards. Unfortunately this does not work precisely because of the dynamic binding mechanism described above. Because the call to draw() within MemorizingDeck#-draw() will be dispatched on the same object, the same method implementation will be selected, endlessly. The result will be a *stack overflow* error, because the method will recursively call itself without a termination condition.

What we really want, instead, is to refer *specifically* to Deck#draw() within MemorizingDeck#draw(). In other words, we want to *statically* bind the method call draw() to the implementation located in Deck. In Java, to refer to the specific implementation of a method located in the superclass *from within a subclass*, we use the keyword super followed by the method call.

```
public class MemorizingDeck extends Deck {
  public Card draw() {
    Card card = super.draw();
    aDrawCards.push(card);
    return card;
  }
}
```

This mechanism is referred to as a *super call*. Its effect is to statically bind the method call to the first overridden implementation of the method found by going up the class hierarchy. The implementation does not need to be in the immediate superclass, but there needs to be at least one inherited method that can be selected in this way.

Annotating Overridden Methods

For a method to effectively override another one, it needs to have the same signature as the one it overrides.[7] This requirement for matching method signatures opens the door to errors with mystifying consequences.

For example, let us say we want to override the equals and hashCode methods for class Deck, as discussed in Section 4.7, and we proceed as follows:

```
public class Deck implements CardSource {
  public boolean equals(Object) { ... }
  public int hashcode() { ... }
}
```

With these definitions we would expect that instances of Deck could be stored in collections such as a HashSet without problem, given that we are properly overriding hashCode() to ensure equal instances of Deck have the same hash code. Except that we are not. Actually the name of the method declared in Deck is hashcode() and not hashCode(). Although we expect Object#hashCode() to be overridden, the hard-to-see, one-character difference in the name means that the method is, in

---

[7] Technically, it could have a *subsignature* as defined in Section 8.4.2 of the Java Language Specification. However, this subtlety is outside the scope of this book, so for simplicity we can consider that the match in terms of method names, parameter types, and declared exceptions, must be exact.

fact, not overridden. Unless we notice the name difference, the bugs this problem would cause could be very hard to explain.

To avoid situations like these, where we expect a method to be overridden when it is not, we can use Java's `@Override` annotation (see Section 5.4 for a review of annotation types). The goal of this annotation is to allow programmers to formally state their intent to override a method. The compiler can then check this intent against reality and warn of any mismatches. In practice, if a method annotated with `@Override` does not actually override anything, a compilation error is raised. The case for using `@Override` annotations is very compelling, and personally I use them systematically.[8]

7.5 Overloading Methods

As we saw above, overriding methods allows programmers to declare different versions of the same method, so that the most appropriate method will be selected based on the run-time type of the implicit parameter. Java and many other programming languages support another mechanism for specifying different implementations of the same method, this time by selecting the method based on the types of the *explicit* parameters. This mechanism is known as *overloading*. A typical example of overloading can be found in math libraries such as `java.lang.Math`, which provide basic functions such as `abs` (absolute value) for arguments of different primitive types, such as `int` and `double`. Another typical application of overloading is for constructors. For example, Section 7.3 discusses a scenario where two constructors for `MemorizingDeck` are provided, one that takes no argument, and one that takes an array of `Card` instances.

The main thing to know about overloading is that the selection of a specific overloaded method or constructor is based on the number and *static* types of the *explicit* arguments. The selection procedure is to find all *applicable* methods and to select the *most specific* one. Let us consider the following version of `MemorizingDeck`, which overloads the constructor with three different versions:

```java
public class MemorizingDeck extends Deck {
  private CardStack aDrawnCards = new CardStack();

  public MemorizingDeck() {
    /* Version 1: Does nothing besides the initialization */
  }

  public MemorizingDeck(CardSource pSource) {
    /* Version 2: Copies all cards of pSource into
     * this object */
  }
```

---

[8] For conciseness, overriding annotations are, however, not included in the code examples in the chapters.

```
public MemorizingDeck(MemorizingDeck pSource) {
  /* Version 3: Copies all cards and drawn cards of pSource
   * into this object */
}
}
```

If we call a constructor for MemorizingDeck, three versions of the constructor are available to fulfill the task. In some cases, which version is selected can be trivially deduced. For instance, if we call the constructor and supply no argument, clearly, Version 1 will be selected. However, things can get tricky when the types of over-loaded versions are related to each other within a type hierarchy. The following code illustrates the situation:

```
MemorizingDeck memorizingDeck = new MemorizingDeck();
Deck deck = memorizingDeck;

Deck newDeck1 = new MemorizingDeck(memorizingDeck);
Deck newDeck2 = new MemorizingDeck(deck);
```

Here the constructor of MemorizingDeck is invoked three times. In the first call, the parameterless constructor is selected. In the second call, the constructor used is Version 3, which might be intuitive in this example because MemorizingDeck is both the run-time type of the argument object and the static type of the variable holding a reference to it. However, it can appear surprising that for newDeck2, it is Version 2 of the constructor that is used. That is because in this case the static type of the argument passed to the constructor is Deck. Because Deck is a subtype of CardSource but *not* a subtype of MemorizingDeck, the only applicable overload is Version 2. If we change the type of deck from Deck to MemorizingDeck, then Version 3 is the one that will be selected. Note that the types of variables newDeck1 and newDeck2 play no role whatsoever in the selection algorithm for overloaded methods and constructors.

Although overloading provides a convenient way to organize related alterna-tives of a given specification, the use of this mechanism can also lead to hard-to-understand code. This is especially the case when the types of the parameters of overloaded versions of a method or constructor are related within a type hierarchy, as illustrated above. For this reason I recommend avoiding overloading methods ex-cept for widely used idioms (such as constructor overloading or library methods that support different primitive types). In many designs, the same properties can be ob-tained without overloading (namely, by giving different names to the methods that take different types of arguments).

7.6 Polymorphic Copying with Inheritance

In the presence of inheritance, the guideline to minimize the visibility of fields can conflict with our ability to implement polymorphic copying (see Section 6.6). To make an exact copy of an object, it is necessary to have detailed information about the complete state of the object so as to be able to replicate it faithfully. For sake of illustration, let us assume that we are implementing polymorphic copying for the class hierarchy shown in Figure 7.6.

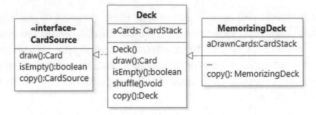

Fig. 7.6 Implementing polymorphic copying with inheritance

The implementation of method `copy()` in class `Deck` causes no problem, as we have seen in Section 6.6:

```
public Deck copy() {
  Deck deck = new Deck();
  deck.aCards = new CardStack(aCards);
  return deck;
}
```

In the presence of inheritance, however, it will be important to systematically override the `copy()` method, because inheriting it will lead to faulty code. The following example shows a faulty usage of an inherited version of method `copy()`:

```
Deck deck = new MemorizingDeck();
Deck copy = deck.copy(); // Error
```

In this case, because there is no available implementation of `MemorizingDeck#-copy`, the most specific applicable method for the call to `copy()` is `Deck#copy`. However, this method returns an object of type `Deck` as a copy of an object of type `MemorizingDeck`. This behavior will violate one of the main constraints for object equality, namely that the objects be of the same type (see Section 4.7). To correctly support polymorphic copying, it is thus imperative that we override `copy()` in all leaf classes of the `CardSource` type hierarchy. Unfortunately, this leads to another problem. Let us attempt an implementation of method `copy()` for class `MemorizingDeck`:

```
public MemorizingDeck copy() {
  MemorizingDeck deck = new MemorizingDeck();
  deck.aCards = new CardStack(aCards); // Compilation error
  deck.aDrawnCards = new CardStack(aDrawnCards);
  return deck;
}
```

This code will not compile because `aCards` is a private field of class `Deck`, and thus not visible within class `MemorizingDeck`. One option is to change the visibility of the field to `protected`. However, widening the accessibility of a field in a superclass is not a general solution, because in many design contexts we may be inheriting from a class that we cannot change (for example, a library class). Second, by widening the scope of a field in a superclass, we are weakening the encapsulation in the overall design, just to support copying.

Java provides a mechanism, called *cloning*, to get around this limitation. This cloning mechanism revolves around the overriding of the protected clone() method of class Object. Unfortunately, the Java cloning mechanism suffers from a variety of design flaws which render it "fragile, dangerous", and complex to use [1]. For this reason, it should only be used to support polymorphic copying with inheritance when no better alternative is available. Because the Java cloning mechanism is described at length in existing references (see Further Reading), I only summarize its main underpinnings here.

To clone an object, it is necessary to override Object#clone() as a public method, and make a super call to clone() from within the method. For example, to support cloning for class Deck, we would write (within class Deck):

```
public Deck clone() {
  // NOT Deck clone = new Deck();
  Deck clone = (Deck) super.clone();
  ...
}
```

The statement super.clone() calls the clone() method in the superclass, which here means method Object#clone(). This method is special: it uses metaprogramming features (see Section 5.4) to make a field-by-field shallow copy of the current object and returns the copy. This is unusual because, although the method is implemented in the library class Object, it still returns a new instance of class Deck.

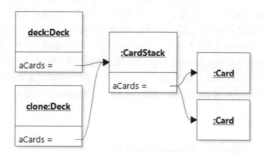

Fig. 7.7 Object graph resulting from an incomplete implementation of clone()

Whenever an object aggregates other mutable objects, the shallow copy performed via Object#clone() will likely be insufficient. For example, in the code above, the execution of the clone() method results in a shared reference to the value of the field aCards, as illustrated in Figure 7.7. Because this outcome would break encapsulation and most likely be incorrect, the clone() method must also make a new copy of the CardStack, this time using a copy constructor:

```
public Deck clone() {
  Deck clone = (Deck) super.clone();
  clone.aCards = new CardStack(aCards);
  return clone;
}
```

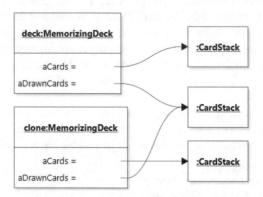

Fig. 7.8 Object graph resulting from an inherited implementation of `clone()`

Because of the requirement to deep-copy certain structures, inheriting `clone()` still carries the risk of error, even if the class of the returned object is the correct one. In our current scenario, calling the inherited method `Deck#clone()` on an object of type `MemorizingDeck` would lead to the structure illustrated in Figure 7.8. As we can see, the use of `Object#clone()` leads to an object of the correct class being created, but the absence of a specialized version of `clone()` for `MemorizingDeck` means that the `aDrawnCards` field is only shallow-copied.

In an attempt to mitigate all the risks of misusing `Object#clone`, the designers of the cloning mechanism imposed a number of additional constraints for classes that implement cloning. One such constraint is the need to implement interface `Cloneable` and deal with some unintuitive exception-handling requirements. Readers interested in using cloning in their design are encouraged to study the technical documentation carefully before proceeding (see Further Reading).

7.7 Inheritance Versus Composition

Inheritance provides an alternative to composition as a design approach to deal with situations where some objects are *extended* versions of other objects. To explore some of the differences between the two, let us consider the composition vs. inheritance alternatives for meeting the requirements for a `MemorizingDeck`.

With composition, we can define a class `MemorizingDeck` that implements `CardSource` but *aggregates* a simple deck. The methods of `MemorizingDeck` will then *delegate* their call to methods on the `Deck` object.

```
public class MemorizingDeck implements CardSource {

  private final CardStack aDrawCards = new CardStack();
  private final Deck aDeck = new Deck();

  public boolean isEmpty() {
    return aDeck.isEmpty();
  }

  public void shuffle() {
    aDeck.shuffle();
    aDrawnCards.clear();
  }

  public Card draw() {
    Card card = aDeck.draw();
    aDrawnCard.push(card);
    return card;
  }
}
```

In contrast, with inheritance, the cards in the deck are not stored in a separate deck, but rather referred to from a field *inherited* from the superclass. In terms of methods, shuffle(), isEmpty(), and draw() are also inherited from the superclass, so they do not all need to be redefined to delegate the call, as in composition. In our example we only need to override shuffle() and draw() to account for the memorization. Method isEmpty() can be directly inherited and still do what we want. In the code of the overridden methods, the delegation to another object is replaced by a super call, which executes on the *same* object.

```
public class MemorizingDeck extends Deck {
  private final CardStack aDrawCards = new CardStack();

  public void shuffle() {
    super.shuffle();
    aDrawnCards.clear(); // Error
  }

  public Card draw() {
    Card card = super.draw();
    aDrawnCard.push(card);
    return card;
  }
}
```

This last implementation, however, illustrates how designing with inheritance can be tricky. With the code above, attempting to create a new MemorizingDeck() will throw a NullPointerException from within method shuffle(). How is this possible, given that the field is immediately initialized with a reference to a CardStack object? The explanation has to do with the order of field initialization, as described in Section 7.3. When the constructor of MemorizingDeck is called, the first instruction to execute is to call the constructor of `Deck`.[9] At this point, `aDrawnCards` is not yet initialized, and thus refers to `null`. Then the constructor of `Deck` executes, which calls method `shuffle()`. However, because this method is now overridden in `MemorizingDeck`, it is that implementation that gets selected. This method executes *without the fields declared in* `MemorizingDeck` *having been initialized.* After the super call returns, the attempt to call a method on `aDrawnCards` will trigger the `NullPointerException`. One solution is to add a null check around the call.

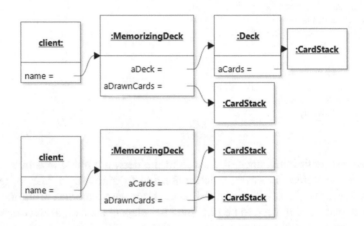

Fig. 7.9 Two implementations for `MemorizingDeck`: composition-based (top), and inheritance-based (bottom)

Overall, the main difference between the composition- and inheritance-based solutions is the number of `Deck` objects involved (see Figure 7.9). The composition-based approach provides a solution that requires coordinating the work of two `Deck` objects: a basic `Deck` object and a *wrapper* (or *decorator*) object `MemorizingDeck`. Thus, as discussed in Section 6.4, the identity of the object that provides the full `MemorizingDeck` set of features is different from that of the other object that provides the basic card-handling services of the deck. In contrast, the use of a `MemorizingDeck` subclass creates a *single* `MemorizingDeck` object that contains all the required fields.

In many situations, it will be possible to realize a design solution using either inheritance or composition. Which option to choose will ultimately depend on the context. Composition-based reuse generally provides more run-time flexibility. This option should therefore be favored in design contexts that require many possible configurations, or the opportunity to change configurations at run time. At the same time, composition-based solutions provide fewer options for detailed access to the internal state of a well-encapsulated object. In contrast, inheritance-based reuse solutions tend to be better in design contexts that require a lot of compile-time con-

---

[9] Because the declaration of the constructor is left out, this is not visible in the code. However, a default (parameterless) constructor gets generated which calls the default constructor of `Deck`.

figuration, because a class hierarchy can easily be designed to provide privileged access to the internal structure of a class to subclasses (as opposed to aggregate and other client classes). Inheritance also supports finer-grained polymorphism. With inheritance, it is possible to store a reference to an instance of `MemorizingDeck` in a variable of type `Deck`. This is not possible in the composition-based solution because `MemorizingDeck` is not a subtype of `Deck`.

7.8 Abstract Classes

There are often situations where locating common class members into a single superclass leads to a class declaration that it would not make sense to instantiate. As a running example for this section and the next, I continue to develop the concept of command objects as introduced in Section 6.8. Let us assume that for a card game application we decide to apply the COMMAND pattern and use the following definition of the command interface.

```
public interface Move {
  void perform();
  void undo();
}
```

A *move* represents a possible action in the game. Calling `perform()` on any subtype of `Move` performs the move, and calling `undo()` undoes the move. The class diagram of Figure 7.10 shows a hypothetical application of the COMMAND pattern. Following a common naming convention, classes that implement the interface include the name of the interface as a suffix (for example, `DiscardMove` represents the move that discards a card from the deck).

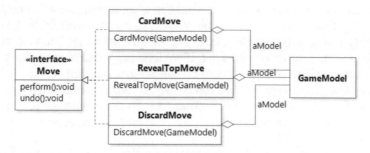

Fig. 7.10 Abstract and concrete commands

At a glance the diagram reveals a redundancy: each concrete command class stores an aggregation to an instance of `GameModel`, which the implementation of `perform()` and `undo()` will rely on when executing the respective commands. In terms of source code, this would look very similar: a field of type `GameModel` (called `aModel` in the diagram). As pointed out in Section 7.1, avoiding CODE DUPLICATION† is an important motivation for inheritance, so we should *pull up* the field aModel into a common superclass. However, there is a big difference between the Deck class example of Section 7.1 and the command example discussed here. With a Deck base class and various subclasses that specialize it, *it makes sense to instantiate the base class*. If we want an instance of a Deck with no frills, we do new Deck() and we have what we want. In the case of commands, what would be the base class? One option is to arbitrarily select one concrete command and use it as the base class, as illustrated by the diagram of Figure 7.11.

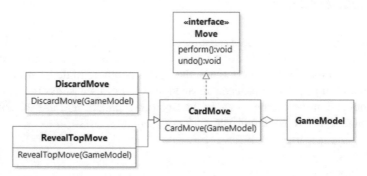

Fig. 7.11 Abuse of inheritance: the members of the base class end up being completely redefined instead of specialized

Although this could work, it is not good design. An important principle of inheritance is that a subclass should be a *natural subtype* of the base class that *extends* the behavior of the base class. In our case, a DiscardMove is not really a specialized version of a CardMove, they are just two different moves. First, CardMove may define non-interface methods that make no sense for users of its subclass (e.g., getDestination() to get the destination when moving a card). Second, this idea is risky, because DiscardMove and RevealTopMove automatically inherit the perform() and undo() methods of class CardMove, which need to be overridden to implement the actual move we want. If we forget to implement one (undo() for example), then calling perform() will do one thing, and calling undo() will undo something else! These types of bugs can be hard to catch. I return to the issue of design ideas that abuse inheritance in Section 7.11. To use inheritance properly, here we need to create an entirely new base class, and have all actual commands inherit it, as shows in Figure 7.12.

Now we avoid the hack of having subclasses that morph their superclass into something entirely different. However, at the same time we have a problematic situation: what is a DefaultMove, really? What would the implementation of perform() and undo() do? Here, even using some sort of default behavior seems questionable, because that would bring us back to the idea of using a base class that is not conceptually a base for anything. A key realization to move forward is that our new base class represents a purely abstract concept that needs to be refined to gain concreteness. This design situation is directly supported by the *abstract class* feature

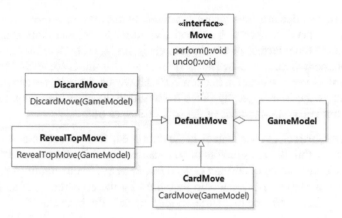

Fig. 7.12 Inheritance with additional base class

of a programming language. Technically, an abstract class represents a correct but *incomplete* set of class member declarations.

In Java, a class can be declared abstract by including the keyword `abstract` in its declaration. It is also a common practice to prefix the identifier of an abstract class with the word `Abstract`. Hence, in our design the `DefaultMove` should be called `AbstractMove`, and its definition would look like this:

```
public abstract AbstractMove implements Move {
  private final GameModel aModel;

  protected AbstractMove(GameModel pModel) {
    aModel = pModel;
  }
  ...
}
```

Declaring a class to be abstract has three main consequences:

- The class cannot be instantiated, which is checked by the compiler. This is a good thing because abstract classes should represent abstract concepts that it makes no sense to instantiate. Another typical example, besides abstract commands, would be something like an `AbstractFigure` in a drawing editor. Unlike concrete figures (rectangles, ellipses), an abstract figure has no geometric representation, so in most designs something like that would be likely to end up as an abstract class.
- The class no longer needs to supply an implementation for all the methods in the interface(s) it declares to implement. This relaxing of the interface contract is type-safe because the class cannot be instantiated. However, any concrete (that is, non-abstract) class will need to have implementations for all required methods. What this means in our case is that, even though `AbstractMove` declares to implement `Move`, we do not have to supply an implementation for `perform()` and `undo()` in the abstract class. However, this assumes that non-abstract subclasses of `AbstractMove` will supply this missing implementation.

- The class can declare new *abstract methods* using the same `abstract` keyword, this time placed in front of a method signature. In practice, this means adding methods to the interface of the abstract class, and thereby forcing the subclasses to implement these methods. The usage scenario for this is somewhat specialized, and I will cover it in detail in Section 7.10. However, for now, we can just say that abstract methods are typically called from within the class hierarchy: by methods of the base class, by methods of the subclasses, or both.

Because abstract classes cannot be instantiated, their constructor can only be called from within the constructors of subclasses. For this reason it makes sense to declare the constructors of abstract classes `protected`. In our running example, the constructor of `AbstractMove` would be called by the constructor of subclasses to pass the required reference to the `GameModel` up into the base class:

```
public class CardMove extends AbstractMove {
   public CardMove(GameModel pModel) {
      super(pModel);
   }
}
```

Code Exploration: JetUML · Edge class hierarchy

A multi-level type hierarchy with interface and abstract class.

JetUML defines a class hierarchy rooted at interface `Edge` (itself a subinterface of the more general `DiagramElement`). There is a lot going on in the `Edge` hierarchy. This discussion will focus on how I used subclasses to progressively extend the data stored by edge objects.

The immediate implementation type for interface `Edge` is `AbstractEdge`. This class already inherits from another abstract class `AbstractDiagram-Element`. Class `AbstractDiagramElement` groups declarations that apply to both nodes and edges, whereas its subclass `AbstractEdge` adds fields that are only relevant to edges. These fields include a reference to the start and end node for the edge and the diagram in which the edge is located. The separation between `AbstractDiagramElement` and `AbstractEdge` illustrates how it can be useful to have multiple abstract classes in a type hierarchy.

Among the different subclasses of `AbstractEdge`, let us focus on `SingleLabelEdge`. This class is also abstract. It adds one field that corresponds to a label on the edge. Thus, `SingleLabelEdge` can be subclassed by any class intended to represent a UML edge that has at least one label. For example, `ReturnEdge` (which represents a return edge in a sequence diagram) is a concrete subclass because return edges only need one label. However, some edges require three labels. `ThreeLabelEdge` is a fourth abstract class down the `Edge` class hierarchy that adds two more label fields, for a total of three. The classes that represent actual edges are the leaves of the class hierarchy, and their names map to the names of UML edges (aggregation, generalization, etc.). These classes are declared to be final.

7.9 Revisiting the DECORATOR Design Pattern

In Section 6.4, we saw how we can use the DECORATOR pattern to add features, or *decorations*, to an object at run time. The key idea of the DECORATOR is to define these decorations using wrapper classes and composition as opposed to subclasses. Figure 7.13 reproduces Figure 6.8, which shows a class diagram of the sample application of DECORATOR to the CardSource design context.

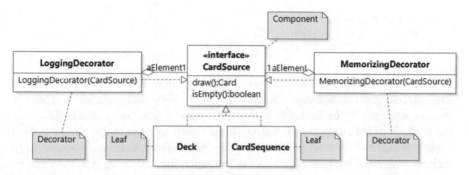

Fig. 7.13 Class diagram of a sample application of DECORATOR

When a design involves multiple decorator types, as in this example, each decorator class will need to aggregate an object to be decorated. This introduces the kind of redundancy that inheritance was designed to avoid. Thus, we can use inheritance to *pull up* the aElement field into an abstract decorator base class, and define concrete decorator subclasses that then only need to deal with the specific decoration. This solution, shown in Figure 7.14, is a good illustration of a design that combines ideas of composition (as seen in Chapter 6) and inheritance. Specifically, a decorator object is of a subtype that *inherits* the aElement field, which is then used to *aggregate* the instance of CardSource that is being decorated.

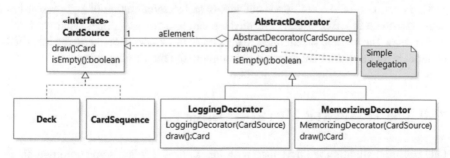

Fig. 7.14 Class diagram of a sample application of DECORATOR that uses inheritance

With this design, the AbstractDecorator includes default delegation to the decorated element.

```
public abstract class AbstractDecorator implements CardSource {
  private final CardSource aElement;

  protected AbstractDecorator(CardSource pElement) {
    aElement = pElement;
  }

  public Card draw() {
    return aElement.draw();
  }

  public boolean isEmpty() {
    return aElement.isEmpty();
  }
}
```

It is worth noting that the `aElement` field is private. This means that concrete decorator classes will not have access to it. This level of encapsulation is workable because normally in the DECORATOR, decorated elements are only accessed through the methods of the component interface. In this case, subclasses can simply use the implementation of the interface methods they inherit from `AbstractDecorator` to interact with the decorated object. As an example, the following is a basic implementation of a `LoggingDecorator` that outputs a description of the cards drawn to the console.

```
public class LoggingDecorator extends AbstractDecorator {
  public LoggingDecorator(CardSource pElement) {
    super(pElement);
  }

  public Card draw() {
    Card card = super.draw();
    System.out.println(card);
    return card;
  }
}
```

Class `LoggingDecorator` does not supply an implementation of `isEmpty()` because the one it inherits, which delegates the call to `aElement`, does what we want. As for `draw`, the method is redefined to do a basic draw operation using the inherited method, print the card, then return it to complete the require behavior.

7.10 The TEMPLATE METHOD Design Pattern

One potential situation we may face with inheritance is when some common algorithm applies to objects of a certain base type, but a part of the algorithm varies from subclass to subclass. To illustrate this situation, let us go back to the design context of creating and managing moves in the Solitaire application, as discussed above in Section 7.8 and illustrated in Figure 7.12 (with `DefaultMove` renamed to

AbstractMove). In this context we also assume that aModel's access modifier is protected.

Let us assume that calling method perform() on moves *of any type* should accomplish three actions: *1)* Add the move to an undo stack, possibly located in the GameModel;[10] *2)* Perform the actual move; *3)* Log the move by writing out a description of what happened. This algorithm can be described with the following code, which could be in any concrete subclass of AbstractMove:

```
public void perform() {
  aModel.pushMove(this);
  /* Actually perform the move */
  log();
}
```

In this code, the first statement of method perform() pushes the current move object onto a command stack located in the game model. The block comment corresponds to the actual implementation of the move, which would vary from move to move. The final statement implements some logging of the move, for example by printing the name of the command class to the console. Let us assume the same approach is used for undo(), with moves being popped instead of pushed. Because parts of the code are in common, it will benefit from being pulled up to the AbstractMove superclass for two main reasons:

* So that it can be reused by all concrete Move subclasses, thereby avoiding DUPLI-CATED CODE†;
* So that the design is robust to errors caused by inconsistently re-implementing common behavior. Specifically, we want to prevent the possibility that a developer could later declare a new concrete subclass of Move and supply it with an implementation of method perform() that does not do steps 1 and 3, for example.

Because the implementation of perform() needs information from subclasses to actually perform the move, it cannot be completely implemented in the superclass.[11] The solution to this problem is to put all the common code in the superclass, and to define some *hooks* to allow subclasses to provide specialized functionality where needed. This technique is called the TEMPLATE METHOD design pattern. The name relates to the fact that the common method in the superclass is a *template*, that gets *instantiated* differently for each subclass. The steps in the algorithm are defined

---

[10] This is not necessarily the best idea from a separation of concerns standpoint, but I use this example for simplicity.

[11] Although, technically, it would be possible to have a SWITCH STATEMENT† in perform() that checks the concrete type of the object using instanceof or getClass() and executes the appropriate code for all commands, this would introduce a dependency cycle between the base class and its subclasses, and destroy the benefits of polymorphism. A bad idea of epic proportions.

as non-private[12] methods in the superclass. The code below further illustrates the solution template for the TEMPLATE METHOD:

```
public abstract class AbstractMove implements Move {
  protected final GameModel aModel;

  protected AbstractMove(GameModel pModel) {
    aModel = pModel;
  }

  public final void perform() {
    aModel.pushMove(this);
    execute();
    log();
  }

  protected abstract void execute();

  private void log() {
    System.out.println(getClass().getName());
  }
}
```

In this code example, the implementation of method `perform()` introduces two new concepts related to inheritance: *final* methods (and classes) and *abstract method declarations* in classes.

Final Methods and Classes

In Java, declaring a method to be `final` means that the method cannot be overridden by subclasses. The main purpose for declaring a method to be `final` is to clarify our intent that a method is not meant to be overridden. One important reason for preventing overriding is to ensure that a given constraint is respected. Final methods are exactly what is needed for the TEMPLATE METHOD, because we want to ensure that the template is respected for all subclasses. By declaring the `perform()` method to be `final`, subclasses cannot override it with an implementation that would omit the call to `pushMove` or `log()`.

The use of the `final` keyword with methods has an effect that is different from the use of the same keyword with fields and local variables (see Section 4.6). The use of `final` with fields limits how we can assign values to variables, and does not involve inheritance, dynamic dispatch, or overriding.

The `final` keyword can also be used with classes. In this case, the behavior is consistent with the meaning it has for methods: classes declared to be `final` cannot be inherited. Inheritance in effect broadens the interface of a class by allowing

---

[12] The step methods can have default, public, or protected visibility depending on the design context. However, they cannot be private because private methods cannot be overridden. This constraint makes sense because private methods are technically not visible outside of their class, and overriding requires method signature matching across classes.

extensions by other classes. As demonstrated in Figure 7.11 and as will be further discussed in the next section, inheritance is a powerful mechanism that can easily be misused. A good principle to follow with inheritance is "design for inheritance or else prohibit it" [1, Item 19]. In other words, inheritance should be used to support specific extension scenarios (as the one illustrated in this section), or not used at all. Because, by default, it is possible to inherit from a class, the mechanism needs to be explicitly disabled to prohibit its use. Generally, stating that a class cannot be inherited tends to make a design more robust because it prevents unanticipated effects caused by inheritance. In our current example, we could decide to make immediate subclasses of `AbstractMove` `final` to make it clear that the class hierarchy should not be extended through inheritance beyond a single level of concrete move subclasses.

Although run-time performance is not a primary concern discussed in this book, it is also worth noting that declaring classes and methods to be final can also have some positive implications for the execution speed of a program, because the absence of dynamic dispatch for final classes means that code can be optimized to run faster.

Abstract Methods

In the implementation of the `perform()` template method in `AbstractMove`, the second step is to perform the actual move. Within class `AbstractMove`, this step is meaningless given that an abstract move does not represent any concrete move we could perform. For this reason, we need to leave out the actual execution of the move. However, we cannot leave this step out *entirely*, because as part of our template we do need to specify that executing the move needs to happen, and needs to happen specifically after the move is pushed to the move stack and before the move execution is logged. In our design we thus specify that this computation needs to happen by calling a method. However, because in Java all methods that are called need to be declared, we must add a new method declaration. In this example I called it `execute()`, because we cannot give it the same name as the template method (this would result in a recursive call). Because we do not have any implementation for `execute()`, we can defer the implementation to the subclasses. This is allowed because `AbstractMove` is declared to be `abstract`, so there is no issue if the class's interface is not fully implemented. Although it sometimes makes sense to declare abstract methods to be public, here I declare `execute()` to be protected because the only classes that need to see this method are the subclasses of `AbstractMove` that must supply an implementation for it.

Summary of the Pattern

The declaration of class AbstractMove, above, illustrates the key ideas of the solution for TEMPLATE METHOD. The following points are also important to remember about the use of the pattern:

- The method with the common algorithm in the abstract superclass is the *template method*; it calls the concrete and abstract *step methods*;
- If, in a given context, it is important that the algorithm embodied by the template method be fixed, it could be a good idea to declare the template method final, so it cannot be overridden (and thus changed) in subclasses;
- It is important that the abstract step method has a different signature from the template method for this design to work. Otherwise, the template method would recursively call itself, quite possibly leading to a stack overflow; following the advice of Section 7.5 about avoiding unnecessary overloading, I would recommend actually using a different name in all cases.
- The most likely access modifier for the abstract step methods is protected, because in general there will likely not be any reason for client code to call individual steps that are intended to be internal parts of a complete algorithm. Client code would normally be calling the template method;
- The steps that need to be customized by subclasses do not necessarily need to be abstract. In some cases, it will make sense to have a reasonable default behavior that could be implemented in the superclass. In this case it might not be necessary to make the superclass abstract. In our example, there is a default implementation of log() that can be overridden by subclasses. In a different context, it might make more sense to declare this method abstract as well.

When first learning to use inheritance, the calling protocol between code in the super- and subclasses can be confusing because, although it is distributed over multiple classes, the method calls are actually dispatched to the *same target object*. The sequence diagram in Figure 7.15 illustrates a call to perform() on a DiscardMove instance. As can be seen, although it is implemented in subclasses, the call to the abstract step method is a self-call.

7.11 Proper Use of Inheritance

Inheritance is both a code reuse and an extensibility mechanism. This means that a subclass inherits the declarations of its superclass, but also becomes a subtype of its superclass (and its superclass's superclass, and so on). To avoid major design flaws, inheritance should only be used for *extending* the behavior of a superclass. As such, it is bad design to use inheritance to restrict the behavior of the superclass, or to use inheritance when the subclass is not a proper subtype of the superclass.

Fig. 7.15 Call sequence in
the TEMPLATE METHOD

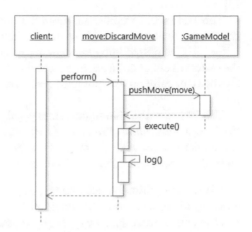

Restricting What Clients of Base Classes Can Do

As an example of a design idea to limit what a superclass can do using our running
example of a deck of cards, let us say that in some design context we need to have
decks of cards that cannot be shuffled. Given that we already have a class (Deck)
that defines everything we need to instantiate a deck, can we simply subclass Deck
to "deactivate" the shuffling? We could try this in different ways. For example:

```java
public class UnshufflableDeck extends Deck {
  public void shuffle() {
    /* Do nothing */
  }
}
```

or,

```java
public class UnshufflableDeck extends Deck {
  public void shuffle() {
    throw new OperationNotSupportedException();
  }
}
```

Actually, both versions are a bad design decision because they conflict directly
with the use of polymorphism, which supports calling operations on an object independently of the concrete type of the object. Let us consider the following hypothetical calling context:

```java
private Optional<Card> shuffleAndDraw(Deck pDeck) {
  pDeck.shuffle();
  if( !pDeck.isEmpty() ) {
    return Optional.of(pDeck.draw());
  }
  else {
    return Optional.empty();
  }
}
```

This code will compile and, given the interface documentation of Deck, should do exactly what we want. However if, when the code executes, the run-time type of the instance passed into shuffleAndDraw happens to be an UnshufflableDeck, the code will either not work as expected (first variant, the deck silently does not get shuffled), or raise an exception (second variant). There is clearly something amiss here.

The intuition that inheritance should only be used for extension is captured by the *Liskov Substitution Principle* (LSP). The LSP essentially states that subclasses should not restrict what clients of the superclass can do with an instance. Specifically, this means that methods of the subclass:

- Cannot have stricter preconditions;
- Cannot have less strict postconditions;
- Cannot take more specific types as parameters;
- Cannot make the method less accessible (e.g., from public to protected);
- Cannot throw more checked exceptions;
- Cannot have a less specific return type.

This list seems like a lot of things to remember when designing object-oriented software, but the whole point of the principle is that once we have assimilated its logic, we no longer need to remember specific elements in the list. In addition, all situations except for the first two points are prevented by the compiler. Nevertheless, at first some of these points can seem counter-intuitive, so let us consider concrete scenarios.

Remembering our interface CardSource, which has method isEmpty() and a method draw() with the precondition !isEmpty(), we can design a new subclass of Deck that draws the highest of the two top cards on the deck, and replaces the lowest one back on top of the deck.

```
public class Deck implements CardSource {
   protected final CardStack aCards = new CardStack();

   public Card draw() { return aCards.pop(); }

   public boolean isEmpty() { return aCards.isEmpty(); }
}

public class DrawBestDeck extends Deck {
   public Card draw() {
      Card card1 = aCards.pop();
      Card card2 = aCards.pop();
      Card high = // identify highest card between card1 and card2
      Card low = // identify lowest card  between card1 and card2
      aCards.push(low);
      return high;
   }
}
```

This code looks relatively simple, which can be a symptom of good design. There is a catch, however: for this solution to work, the deck needs to have at least two cards in it. How can we deal with this? One solution is to rework the code of the draw override to handle both cases:

```
public Card draw() {
  Card card1 = aCards.pop();
  if( isEmpty() ) {
    return card1;
  }
  Card card2 = aCards.pop();
  ...
}
```

However, this code is not as elegant as the first version, it is more onerous to test, etc. Given that we know about design by contract (see Section 2.9), why not simply declare the precondition that, to call draw() on an instance of DrawBestDeck, there needs to be at least two cards in the deck?

```
public class DrawBestDeck extends Deck {
  public int size() {
    return aCards.size();
  }

  public Card draw() {
    assert size() >=2;
    ...
  }
}
```

This makes the precondition stricter (i.e., less tolerant), and thus violates the LSP. This is because the mere presence of the subclass makes code like this unsafe for cases where a deck has only one card.

```
if( deck.size() >=1 ) {
  return deck.draw();
}
```

Actually, in our specific example, the idea is bad for an additional, if less funda-mental, reason. Because the inteface CardSource does not have a size() method, it is not possible to check the precondition polymorphically. To check that a call to draw() respects all preconditions, it would thus be necessary to do:

```
Deck deck = ...
Optional<Card> result = Optional.empty();
if( deck instanceof DrawBestDeck &&
    ((DrawBestDeck)deck).size() >= 2 ||
      !deck.isEmpty() ) {
  result = Optional.of(deck.draw());
}
```

Ultimately, we solved nothing by trying to make the overridden version of draw() simpler, because the size check just migrated to the client, acquiring some additional complexity in the process.

Similarly, the LSP is the reason why Java does not allow overriding methods to take more specific types as parameters or have less specific types as return types. Let us say we add a method `init(Deck)` to the interface of `Deck` that re-initializes the target instance to contain exactly the cards in the argument. If we have a `MemorizingDeck` in our class hierarchy, we might be tempted to override `init` in `MemorizingDeck` to initialize both the cards and the drawn cards, as illustrated in Figure 7.16.

Fig. 7.16 Invalid attempt at method overriding that does not respect the LSP

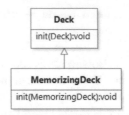

Although this code will compile, it will actually create an *overloaded* version of `init` as opposed to an *overridden* version, as perhaps expected. This is extremely confusing. The systematic use of the `@Override` annotation (see Section 7.4) would help flag this as a problem, but otherwise, the code would lead to very mysterious executions, given that the result of both calls to `init` would be different in the code below:

```
MemorizingDeck deck = new MemorizingDeck();
MemorizingDeck memorizingDeck = new MemorizingDeck();
Deck mDeck = memorizingDeck;
deck.init(memorizingDeck); // Calls MemorizingDeck.init
deck.init(mDeck); // Calls Deck.init
```

The reason for this seemingly strange behavior is again to ensure the design respects the LSP. If clients of the base class `Deck` can call `init` and pass in instances of *any* subtype of `Deck`, then it would be limiting what they can do to require the clients to only pass certain subtypes to `init` (like `MemorizingDeck`).

The case of return types inverses the logic: if a method returns an object of a certain type, it should be possible to assign it to a variable of that type. If subclasses can redefine methods to return more general types, then it would no longer be possible to complete the assignment. For example, let us say that in a (bad) design, a developer adds a version of `Deck` that contains a joker card, and that objects that represent jokers are not subtypes of `Card`, but merely subtypes of the `Object` root type. Then calls like this:

```
Card card = deck.draw();
```

would become problematic if some versions of method `draw()` can return objects that are not subtypes of `Card`.

The classic example of a violation of the LSP is the so-called Circle–Ellipse problem, wherein a class to represent a circle is defined by inheriting from an `Ellipse` class and preventing clients from creating any ellipse instance that does not have equal proportions. This violates the LSP because clients that use an `Ellipse` base class can set the height to be different from the width, and introducing a `Circle` subclass would eliminate this possibility:

```
Ellipse ellipse = getEllipse();
// Not possible if ellipse is an instance of Circle
ellipse.setWidthAndHeight(100, 200);
```

How to avoid the Circle–Ellipse problem in practice will, as usual, depend on the context. In some cases, it may not be necessary to have a type `Circle` in the first place. For example, in a drawing editor, user interface features could be responsible for assisting users in creating ellipses that happen to be circles, while still storing these as instances of `Ellipse` internally. In cases where a type `Circle` can be useful, it might make sense to have different `Circle` and `Ellipse` classes that are siblings in the type hierarchy, etc.

Subclasses That Are Not Proper Subtypes

Inheritance accomplishes two things (see Section 7.2):

- It reuses the class member declarations of the base class as part of the definition of the subclass;
- In introduces a subtype–supertype relation between the subclass and the super-class.

To use inheritance properly, it has to make sense for the subclass to need *both* of these features. A common abuse of inheritance is to employ it only for reuse, and overlook the fact that subtyping does not make sense:

> Inheritance is appropriate only in circumstances where the subclass really is a *subtype* of the superclass. In other words, a class *B* should extend a class *A* only if an "is-a" relationship exists between the two classes. [1, p. 92]

Some well-known acknowledged violations of this principle include the library type `Stack` (which inappropriately inherits from `Vector`), and `Properties` (which inappropriately inherits from `Hashtable`). When subtyping is not appropriate, composition should be used.

Code Exploration: JetUML · NodeViewer class hierarchy

Calling methods within the class hierarchy.

The `Edge` class hierarchy discussed earlier provides a rich illustration of field inheritance. In contrast, the `NodeViewer` hierarchy provides many interesting examples of method inheritance. In JetUML, *viewers* are objects that specialize in handling the position and look of diagram objects. The methods of the `NodeViewer` interface include things like `draw`, `getBounds`, `getConnectionPoint`, etc. All things that have to do with the geometry of the nodes.

Let us start our study of the `NodeViewer` hierarchy at the top, with a look at `AbstractNodeViewer`. One thing to note already is that the class does not provide an implementation for the interface methods `draw` or `getBounds()`. This is consistent with the concept of abstract classes. Here it would be meaningless to draw something that is not concrete, so we leave it out.

The implementation of method `contains()`, however, involves an interesting quirk: it calls the object's own `getBounds()` method, for which no implementation is provided in the `AbstractNodeViewer` class. This is an example where we can provide a complete implementation for one service (to see if a point is contained in a node) by relying on the existence of another service (getting the bounds for a node) whose implementation is delegated to the subclasses.

The design of classes `TypeNodeViewer` and `InterfaceNodeViewer` illustrates the extent to which inheritance supports code reuse. The viewer classes are used to depict class and interface nodes in a class diagram. The code is not simple as it must handle different geometries depending on whether the nodes have attributes or methods. At the same time, the only visual difference between types and interface nodes is that interface nodes include the `interface` UML stereotype in their name. To support code reuse, `TypeNodeViewer` defines a protected placeholder method `getNameText` to get the name of the node, with a default implementation to use the node's name as text. The subclass `InterfaceNodeViewer` then overrides this method to add the interface stereotype to the text, and inherits the complete viewing machinery from its superclass.

Insights

This chapter introduced inheritance as a mechanism to support code reuse and extensibility.

*   Use inheritance to factor out implementation that is common among subtypes of a given root type and avoid DUPLICATED CODE†;
*   UML class diagrams can describe inheritance-related design decisions effectively;
*   To the extent possible, use the services provided by a subclass through polymorphism, to avoid the error-prone practice of downcasting;
*   Even in the presence of inheritance, consider keeping your field declarations private to the extent possible, as this ensures tighter encapsulation;
*   Subclasses should be designed to complement, or specialize, the functionality provided by a base class, as opposed to redefining completely different behavior;
*   Use the `@Override` annotation to avoid hard-to-find errors when defining overriding relations between methods;

- Because it can easily lead to code that is difficult to understand, keep overloading to a minimum. Overloading is best avoided altogether when the parameter types of the different versions of a method are in a subtyping relation with each other;
- Inheritance- and composition-based approaches are often viable alternative when looking for a design solution. When exploring inheritance-based solutions, consider whether composition might not be better;
- You can use Java's cloning mechanism to implement polymorphic copying when the fields of the superclass are not accessible. However, cloning is a complex and error-prone mechanism that must be used very carefully;
- Ensure that subclasses that extend a base class can also be considered meaningful subtypes of the base class, namely that instances of the subclass are in a "is-a" relation with the base class;
- Ensure that any inheritance-based design respects the Liskov Substitution Principle. In particular, do not use inheritance to restrict the features of the base class;
- If some of the fields and methods that can be isolated through inheritance do not add up to a data structure that it makes sense to instantiate, encapsulate them in an abstract class;
- Remember that abstract classes can define abstract methods, and that methods of the abstract class can call its own abstract methods. This way you can use abstract classes to define abstract implementations of algorithms;
- Consider using the TEMPLATE METHOD pattern in cases where an algorithm applies to all subclasses of a certain base class, except for some steps of the algorithm that must vary from subclass to subclass;
- If there is no scenario for overriding a method, consider declaring it `final`. Similarly, if there is no specific reason for a class to be extensible using inheritance, consider declaring it `final`.

Further Reading

The Java Tutorial [10] has a section on interfaces and inheritance that provides complementary material on inheritance, with a focus on the programming language aspects.

In terms of design guidelines, Chapter 4 of *Effective Java* [1], titled *Classes and Interfaces* provides many items of guidance relevant to this chapter. Examples include Item 15, *Minimize the accessibility of classes and members*, Item 18, *Favor composition over inheritance* and Item 19 *Design and document for inheritance or else prohibit it*. Additional items relevant to this chapter include Item 13, *Override* `clone` *judiciously* and Item 52, *Use overloading judiciously*.

Chapter 8
Inversion of Control

Concepts and Principles: Application framework, callback, event handling, graphical user interface (GUI), inversion of control, model–view–controller (MVC) decomposition;
Patterns and Antipatterns: PAIRWISE DEPENDENCIES†, OBSERVER, VISITOR.

Inversion of control involves reversing the usual flow of control from caller code to called code to achieve separation of concerns and loose coupling. It allows us to build sophisticated applications while keeping the overall design complexity down to a manageable level. One of the main realizations of the principle takes the form of the OBSERVER pattern. This pattern is pervasive in software development, and it is realized by most graphical user interface toolkits on most software development platforms, from desktop to web to mobile applications.

Design Context

Inversion of control brings the level of discussion to a higher level of abstraction that needs to consider the design of an entire application. To be able to focus on the issue of inversion of control, this chapter introduces new design contexts. The context used as a running example for the chapter is that of a small application to allow the user to select and view a number in different formats (for example, digits vs. text). A different context, of an observable stack of cards, is introduced in Section 8.4 to provide an additional example. I return to the design of recursive card source structures seen in previous chapters to introduce the VISITOR pattern in Section 8.8.

© Springer Nature Switzerland AG 2022
M. P. Robillard, *Introduction to Software Design with Java*,
https://doi.org/10.1007/978-3-030-97899-0_8

8.1 Motivating Inversion of Control

One concrete situation that motivates inversion of control in software design is when
a number of stateful objects need to be kept consistent. An example from the programming domain itself is an integrated development environment such as Eclipse
or IntelliJ IDEA, which presents different views of the source code. In Eclipse, for
example, the Package Explorer and Outline views shows the structure of a class that
can also be viewed in the source code editor (see Figure 8.1). If a user changes the
class declaration, for example by adding a field in the source code editor, this change
is immediately reflected in all the different views. Likewise, if the user reorders the
method declarations in the Outline view, the new order of method declarations is
reflected in the source code editor. Hence, we could say that the problem we are trying to solve is one of *synchronization*,[1] where we are trying to keep different objects
consistent with each other.

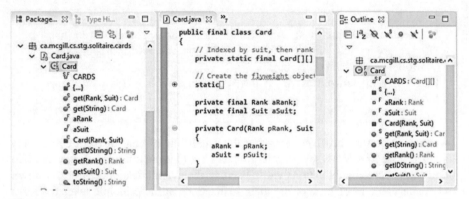

Fig. 8.1 Three different views of the source code in Eclipse

To isolate the issue of view synchronization, I distilled the design problem into
a toy application called LuckyNumber. The application allows a user to select a
number (presumed to be lucky) between 1 and 10 inclusively. The interesting part
of the application, however, is that users can select their lucky number in different
ways, for example by entering the digit(s) that represent the number, typing out the
name of the number in English, or selecting it from a slider (see Figure 8.2).

In the application, each horizontal panel allows the user to view the number in a
specific way, but also to change the number. If the number is changed in one panel,
the change is immediately reflected in all other panels. In addition to its current
features, one requirement for this application is that it can be extended to accommodate any additional type of view. For example, old-fashioned users may request the
option to select their number using Roman numerals, geeky users may want to use
binary notation, etc.

---

[1] The term *synchronization* is also used in the context of concurrent programming, a topic that is
outside the scope of this book.

Fig. 8.2 Screenshot of the
LuckyNumber application

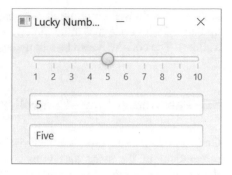

A consequence of implementing this functionality naively is to be left with complete PAIRWISE DEPENDENCIES†. With PAIRWISE DEPENDENCIES†, whenever the user changes the number in a panel, this panel directly contacts all other panels and updates their view of the number. Figure 8.3 illustrates these dependencies in a class diagram.

Fig. 8.3 Example of PAIR-
WISE DEPENDENCIES†

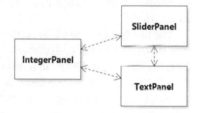

This design suffers from at least the following two related limitations:

- **High coupling**: Each panel explicitly depends on many other panels. Panels could be of different types and require different types of interactions. For example, to update the number it may be necessary to call `setDigit` on one panel and `setSliderValue` on a different panel.
- **Low Extensibility**: To add or remove a panel, it is necessary to modify all other panels. For example, to remove the slider panel, it would be necessary to modify all other panels to remove the statements that update the slider panel. Similarly, to add a Roman numeral panel, it would be necessary to change every panel to add some statements to manage the new panel, etc.

What is even worse, is that the impact of these issues increases quadratically with the number of panels, given that there are $n \cdot (n-1)$ directed edges in a complete graph with n vertices. In the initial application with three panels, we need six call dependencies to keep all panels synchronized. This may not seem like much, but if we throw in a Roman numeral panel and a binary notation panel, for a total of five, then we need 20 dependencies scattered over five components, just to keep a single number consistent. This is poor separation of concerns, because a significant amount of code will be required to manage the dependencies that is likely to end up tangled with code that more directly supports the required logic (e.g., adjusting a slider). The code will also be less understandable, harder to test, etc.

8.2 The Model–View–Controller Decomposition

One way out of using complete pairwise dependencies to synchronize multiple representations of the same data is to separate abstractions responsible for *storing data* from abstractions responsible for *viewing data*, from abstractions responsible for *changing data*. This key insight is generally known as *Model–View–Controller* (MVC) from the name of the three abstractions. The *Model* is the abstraction that keeps the unique copy of the data of interest. In our simple context, that would be the lucky number. The *View* is, not surprisingly, the abstraction that represents one view of the data. Generally in a MVC decomposition there can be more than one view of the same model. This is illustrated in the LuckyNumber application by the presence of different views for something as simple as a single integer. Finally, the *Controller* is the abstraction of the functionality necessary to change the data stored in the model.

The origin of the MVC is somewhat obscure. The idea can be traced back to the late 1970s and Xerox PARC researchers working on Smalltalk software, but there is little besides a few memos in terms of written reports on the original development of the concept. Currently, the term MVC is used fairly loosely. Some software developers refer to it as a design pattern. Others refer to it as something slightly different called an *architectural pattern* or *architectural style* (somewhat like a design pattern, but at a higher level of design abstraction). Some refer to it simply as a general concept. Finally, some web technology platforms use the terms model, view, and controller to refer to specific software components. Because I see the main benefit of the Model–View–Controller as a guideline to separate concerns, I like to think of it simply as a *decomposition* (of concerns). In this sense, it is more general than a design pattern, because it does not include a solution template that is specific enough to apply directly.

The lack of a well-defined solution template for the MVC means that there is little guidance on how to realize the idea in practice. This also means that there are innumerable ways to go about separating the model, view, and controller in a design context. For example, the model could be a single object, or a collection of objects. The view and controller could be different objects, or fused together. In the latter case, the separation of concerns would be organized along the interfaces of objects rather than the objects themselves (see Section 3.9 on the idea of interface segregation).

Such a vague concept as the MVC is not easy to grasp in itself when learning software design. Fortunately, there exists a related idea that is much more concrete, namely the OBSERVER pattern.

8.3 The OBSERVER Design Pattern

The central idea of the OBSERVER pattern is to store data of interest in a specialized object, and to allow other objects to *observe* this data. The object that stores the data of interest is called, alternatively, the *subject, model,* or *observable*, and it corresponds to the Model abstraction in the Model–View–Controller decomposition. For this reason, the *context* for the OBSERVER pattern corresponds to the motivation discussed in Section 8.1: we want a simple way to manage multiple objects that must be aware of state changes in the same data. The class diagram of Figure 8.4 illustrates how this is realized for the LuckyNumber application.

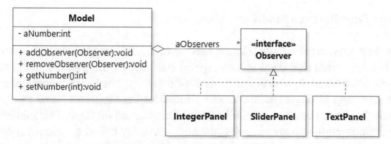

Fig. 8.4 Application of the OBSERVER to the LuckyNumber application

In this situation, the object in charge of keeping the data is an instance of `Model`, which keeps track of a single integer and allows clients to query and change this integer.

Linking Model and Observers

Where things become interesting is that the `Model` class also includes an aggregation to an `Observer` interface, with methods to add and remove `Observer` instances from its collection. This process is called *registering* and *deregistering* observers. The mechanism for managing observers can be trivially implemented, for example:

```
public class Model {
  private int aNumber = 5;
  private List<Observer> aObservers = new ArrayList<>();

  public void addObserver(Observer pObserver) {
    aObservers.add(pObserver);
  }

  public void removeObserver(Observer pObserver) {
    aObservers.remove(pObserver);
  }
}
```

Classes that define objects that need to observe the model must then declare to implement the `Observer` interface:

```
class IntegerPanel implements Observer { ... }
```

Through polymorphism, we thus achieve loose coupling between the model and its observers. Specifically:

- The model can be used without any observer;
- The model is aware that it can be observed, but its implementation does not depend on any concrete observer class;
- It is possible to register and deregister observers at run time.

Control Flow Between Model and Observers

A first key question about the relation between a model an its observers is, how do the observers learn that there is a change in the state of the model that they need to know about? The answer is that whenever there is a change in the model's state worth reporting to observers, the model should let the observers know by cycling through the list of observers and calling a certain method on them. This method has to be defined on the `Observer` interface and is usually called a *callback (method)* because of the *inversion of control* that it implies. We talk of inversion of control because, to find out information from the model, the observers do not call a method on the model, they instead *wait* for the model to *call* them (*back*). This procedure is often referred to as the Hollywood Principle ("don't call us, we'll call you"). That is also why the method that is called by the model on the observer is called a *callback*. Continuing with the movie industry metaphor, the name of the method to call back is like the phone number of the prospective actor. If the casting director determines that the actor should be auditioned, they will call the number. Likewise, if the model determines that the observers should be notified, it will call their callback method.

In the case of the LuckyNumber application, an appropriate name for the callback method would be `newNumber`, given that this is the method that will be called whenever the model needs to inform its observers that it has changed the number it is storing. We thus define this method in the `Observer` interface:

```
public interface Observer {
  void newNumber(int pNumber);
}
```

When first learning about callbacks, their logic can be a bit puzzling, especially if the name of the callback is ambiguous. In the case above, it may look like the method is intended to *set* a new number on an observer, because it would be called like this:

```
someObserver.newNumber(5);
```

However, the method name should not be mentally read as "set number to this new value", but rather as "the model has a new number, here it is". In other words, a callback is not to *tell observers what to do*, but rather to *inform* observers about some change in the model, and let them deal with it as they see fit (through the logic provided in the callback). The analogy with the movie studio still works. If an actor (the observer) gets an audition, the studio might call them and say "you have an audition", but not specify the details of how to react to this information (for example, by preparing, arranging transportation, etc.). The lesson here is that to help others understand a design, it is a good practice to name callback methods with a name that describes a state-change situation, as opposed to a command. In our case, other explicit names for the callback method would include numberChanged and newNumberAvailable.

Once we have a callback defined, within class Model, we can create a helper method, called a *notification method*[2] that will notify all observers and provide them with the number they should know about:

```
public class Model {
  private void notifyObservers() {
    for(Observer observer : aObservers) {
      observer.newNumber(aNumber);
    }
  }
}
```

To ensure that the model dutifully notifies observers whenever a state change occurs, two strategies are possible:

- A call to the notification method must be inserted in every state-changing method; in this case the method can be declared private;
- Clear documentation has to be provided to direct users of the model class to call the notification method whenever the model should inform observers. In this case the notification methods needs to be non-private.

As usual, which strategy is better depends on the context. In cases where notifications can be issued for every model change, the first method provides a simpler life cycle for the state of the model. However, in certain cases, notifying observers with every state change may lead to some performance problems. For example, if we had a model that could be initialized with a large collection of data items by adding each item one at a time, notifying observers after each individual addition may dramatically degrade the performance while providing no benefit. In situations such as this one, it may be better to change the model *silently* (without notifying the observers), and then trigger a notification once the batch operation is done. In cases where such flexibility is needed, the second strategy can provide it.

The sequence diagram of Figure 8.5 illustrates what happens when we change the number on the LuckyNumber application, using the first strategy.

Inside the state-changing method setNumber(int), we added a call to notify-Observers to loop through each observer and call the method newNumber on each. The implementation of the newNumber callback dictates how each observer reacts to the change in state. In the case of the LuckyNumber application, each observer

---

[2] In Java the notification method cannot be called simply notify(), because a legacy method with this name is already defined in class Object.

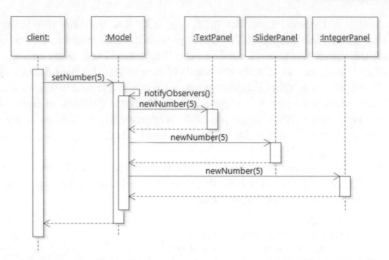

Fig. 8.5 Call sequence for the OBSERVER

deals with the callback in a different way. For example, the `IntegerPanel` sets the number of the integer in a text field; the `TextPanel` looks up the name of the integer in an array, and sets the value of the text field to that string; the `SliderPanel` positions the slider to correspond to the value, etc.

Data Flow between Model and Observers

The second key question about the relation between a model and its observers is, how do the observers access the information that they need to know about from the model? Two main strategies are available. The first strategy is to make the information of interest available through one or more parameters of the callback. This strategy is also known as the *push* data-flow strategy because the model is explicitly *pushing* data of a pre-determined structure to the observers.

Applying this strategy to our context, we could define the callback method to include a parameter that represents the number most recently stored in the model. This is the strategy that I illustrated above with the `newNumber(int)` callback.

```
public interface Observer {
  void newNumber(int pNumber);
}
```

This way, whenever a callback method is called on an observer, the implementation of the callback can obtain the value of interest from the argument bound to the parameter. For example, relevant parts of the implementation of the `IntegerPanel` would look like this:

```
public class IntegerPanel implements Observer {
  // User interface element that represents a text field
  private TextField aText = new TextField();

  ...
  public void newNumber(int pNumber) {
    aText.setText(Integer.toString(pNumber));
  }
}
```

This strategy makes one major assumption: that we know in advance what type of data from the model the observers will require. In our case, this strategy is a good fit because there is nothing but a single integer that observers could require. However, this is not the general case. For example, we could enhance the model to remember each lucky number ever selected, and the timestamp of its selection. Observers now have more data to choose from. Given the context, we could still assume that the most common case for an observer will be to show the most recent number, but more sophisticated observers might want to show the last three numbers, for example, or the amount of time a certain number remained selected.

As another example, we now assume that we want to make the `Deck` class discussed in previous chapters into an observable object. What would observers be interested in? Again, one usage scenario stands out: to show the card drawn. So we could fix this expectation with the callback:

```
public interface DeckObserver {
  void cardDrawn(Card pCard);
}
```

However, in some cases this might be too strict. Some observers might be interested in the number of cards left in the deck, or they may want to know about the top card, etc.

A more flexible strategy is instead to let observers *pull* the data they want from the model using query methods defined on the model. Appropriately, this approach is known as the *pull* data-flow strategy. To convert the design of the LuckyNumber application to use the pull strategy, we could exchange the `pNumber` parameter with one that would refer to the entire model:

```
public interface Observer {
  void newNumber(Model pModel);
}
```

That way, the data to put in the text field must be obtained from the model:

```
public class IntegerView implements Observer {
  // User interface element that represents a text field
  private TextField aText = new TextField();

  ...
  public void newNumber(Model pModel) {
    aText.setText(Integer.toString(pModel.getNumber()));
  }
}
```

Now, any data available through the methods of class `Model` also becomes available to the observers. To implement the pull data flow strategy, observers must have a reference to the model, but this reference must not necessarily be provided as an argument to the callback method. Another option is to initialize observer objects with a reference to the model (stored as a field), and refer to that field as necessary. This design is illustrated in the class diagram of Figure 8.6. That design makes it clear that the reference to the model is obtained through the constructor.

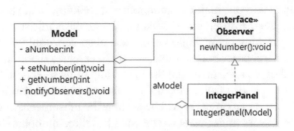

Fig. 8.6 Class diagram of LuckyNumber as a model using the pull data-flow strategy for observers

At first glance, it may look like the pull data-flow strategy introduces a circular dependency between a model and its observers, given that both depend on each other. However, the crucial difference is that, in this design, the model does not know the concrete type of its observers. Through interface segregation, the only slice of behavior that the model needs from observers is specified through their callback method. This being said, one of the main drawbacks of the pull data-flow strategy is that it does, indeed, increase the coupling between observers and model. In the design of Figure 8.6, observers can not only call `getNumber()`, they can also call `setNumber(int)`! In other words, by holding a reference to the model, observers have access to much more of the interface of the model than they need. Fortunately, we saw how to deal with this situation with the Interface Segregation Principle (ISP, see Section 3.2). To apply ISP to our design, we could create a new interface `ModelData` that only includes the getter methods for the model, and only refer to this type in the observers. Figure 8.7 illustrates this solution.

Although I presented them here separately, the push and pull strategies can be combined. For example, it is possible to specify a callback that includes a parameter for both data from the model and a reference back to the model. This design would not be very useful in our scenario, but I include its implementation for sake of illustration:

```
public interface Observer {
  void newNumber(int pNumber, ModelData pModel);
}
```

In general, supporting both strategies can help increase the reusability of the `Observer` interface at the cost of a more complex design that may include situations

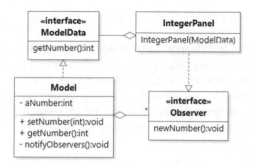

Fig. 8.7 Class diagram of the pull method with ISP

where one parameter is not used.[3] At the other extreme, for simple design contexts it may be the case that the only information that needs to flow between the model and the observers is the fact that a given callback method was invoked. In such cases, neither the push nor the pull strategy is required: receiving the callback invocation is enough information for the observers to do their job. An observer that serves as a counter of a type of event would be one example.

As a final remark regarding the flow of data between the model and its observers, it is worth noting that in the examples above, none of the callbacks return any value, and therefore have return type `void`. This is not a design decision, but a constraint of the pattern. Because the model is supposed to ignore how many observers it has, it can be tricky for observers to attempt to manage the model by returning some value. Technically, it is possible to declare the return type of callbacks to be non-void, and to aggregate the results across many invocations. For example, one could design the callback to return `true` if it somehow succeeded in responding to the callback (and `false` otherwise), and have the model apply a logical operator to the results. Such schemes represent uncommon and possibly fragile applications of the pattern. When starting out with the OBSERVER, my recommendation is to have callbacks return `void`.

Event-Based Programming

One way to think about callback methods is as *events*, with the model being the *event source* and the observers being the *event handlers*. Within this paradigm, the model generates a series of events that correspond to different state changes of interest, and other objects are in charge of reacting to these events. What events correspond to in practice are simply method calls. Thinking about observers as event handlers helps realize that we actually have a lot of flexibility when designing callbacks. In the LuckyNumber application, the design to date has involved a single callback,

---

[3] The Java library includes a pair of types, `Observable` and `Observer`, where `Observer` defines the single callback `void update(Observable, Object)`, which supports both data-flow strategies. These types are, however, deprecated since Java 9.

newNumber. However, for sake of discussion, we can imagine a situation where a Model might be used by observers that are sometimes interested only if the lucky number increased (or, conversely, decreased), or whether the number is set to its maximum or minimum value. Implementing this feature in the current design would be difficult: every observer would have to store a copy of the number, and check it against the new number to determine if it has increased or decreased, in addition to checking for maximum or minimum value. We can do things differently by adjusting the design of the callbacks to explicitly capture the events of potential interest:

```
public interface Observer {
  void increased(int pNumber);
  void decreased(int pNumber);
  void changedToMax(int pNumber);
  void changedToMin(int pNumber);
}
```

With this design, observers do not need to store a copy of the old number, and they can be notified of precisely the event they are interested in.[4] In cases where an observer does not need to react to an event, the unused callbacks can be implemented as empty (*do-nothing*) methods. In the class below, it is assumed that the events are mutually exclusive, namely that the event increased means *increased but not to the maximum value*, and similarly for decreased.

```
public class IncreaseDetector implements Observer {
  public void increased(int pNumber) {
    System.out.println("Increased to " + pNumber);
  }
  public void decreased(int pNumber) {}
  public void changedToMax(int pNumber) {}
  public void changedToMin(int pNumber) {}
}
```

If the reliance on empty methods occurs too often, it is possible to implement these empty methods in a class and inherit from it instead. Such classes are sometimes called *adapters*:

```
public class ObserverAdapter implements Observer {
  public void increased(int pNumber) {}
  public void decreased(int pNumber) {}
  public void changedToMax(int pNumber) {}
  public void changedToMin(int pNumber) {}
}
```

With an adapter, the *do-nothing* behavior becomes inherited, and observers can override only the subset of callbacks that correspond to the events they need to respond to:

---

[4] Whether we need the parameter for the changeToMax and changeToMin methods depends on the context, that is, whether the minimum and maximum values are known globally.

```
public class IncreaseDetector extends ObserverAdapter {
  public void increased(int pNumber) {
    System.out.println("Increased to " + pNumber);
  }
}
```

In the current scenario, I defined class `ObserverAdapter` to make the concept of an adapter class more explicit. However, in Java version 8 and later, the same benefit can be accomplished using default methods.

```
public interface Observer {
  default void increased(int pNumber) {}
  // etc.
}
```

The use of default methods for this purpose not only makes the code more compact, it also enables the concrete observer to inherit from a different class if necessary.

In some cases, extensive use of empty methods might point to a mismatch between the varied needs of observers and the design of the callbacks. Again, it is possible to rely on the Interface Segregation Principle to clean things up. In our situation, we could define *two* observer interfaces that correspond to more specialized event handlers. For example:

```
public interface ChangeObserver {
  void increased(int pNumber);
  void decreased(int pNumber);
}

public interface BoundsReachedObserver {
  void changedToMax(int pNumber);
  void changedToMin(int pNumber);
}
```

With two abstract observers, concrete observers can be more targeted and only register for the sets of events they need to respond to. The trade-off for more flexibility is a slightly heavier interface for the `Model` class, because it now has to support two lists of observers with their corresponding registration methods.

Summary of the Pattern

The context for using the OBSERVER is fairly rich: it involves situations where many objects should be able to observe some data, and become aware of changes to the state of this data, while minimizing the coupling between the data and the observers of that data. Given a class that represents the data (the *model*), the solution template for the pattern involves making objects of this class observable by aggregating a number of *abstract observers* (usually defined with an interface). The following are important variation points when applying the OBSERVER:

• What callbacks methods to define on an abstract observer. An abstract observer can have any number of callbacks that can correspond to different types of events;

- What data flow strategy to use to move data between the model and observers (push, pull, none, or both);
- Whether to use a single abstract observer or multiple ones. Multiple abstract observers with different combinations of callbacks give observers more flexibility to respond to certain events or not;
- How to connect observers with the model if observers need to query or control the model. Here the use of the Interface Segregation Principle is recommended;
- Whether to include a notification helper method and, if so, whether to make this method public or private. If public, clients with references to the model get to control when notifications are issued. If private, it is assumed that the method is called at appropriate places in the state-changing methods of the model.

The listing below shows the complete code of the `Model` and `Observer` type declarations for the variant that uses the push data-flow strategy.

```
public interface Observer {
  void newNumber(int pNumber);
}

public class Model {
  private List<Observer> aObservers = new ArrayList<>();
  private int aNumber = 5;

  public void addObserver(Observer pObserver) {
    aObservers.add(pObserver);
  }

  public void removeObserver(Observer pObserver) {
    aObservers.remove(pObserver);
  }

  private void notifyObservers() {
    for(Observer observer : aObservers) {
      observer.newNumber(aNumber);
    }
  }

  public void setNumber(int pNumber) {
    if( pNumber <= 0 ) {
      aNumber = 1;
    }
    else if( pNumber > 10 ) {
      aNumber = 10;
    }
    else {
      aNumber = pNumber;
    }
    notifyObservers();
  }
}
```

Code Exploration: Solitaire · GameModel

Application of the OBSERVER *with pull data flow and a single parameterless callback.*

Class `GameModel` in the Solitaire application captures the complete state of a game in progress. This class is an observable subject, as it maintains a list of `GameModelListeners` (the abstract observer). Interface `GameModelListeners` contains a single, parameterless callback: `gameStateChanged()`. Concrete observers are thus responsible for obtaining their own reference to the game model and pulling the information they need using querying methods. These querying methods are collected within interface `GameModelView`. For this application of the pattern I choose the pull data flow strategy because of the large variety of information required from the model. I chose to store a reference to the model within observers instead of passing this reference via the callback because some observers need this reference to initialize themselves.

8.4 Applying the OBSERVER Design Pattern

The design space for applying the OBSERVER is extensive. Even in a small, well-defined context, many different alternatives are possible for designing the observer and observable types. To illustrate some of the options available and their corresponding trade-offs, let us now explore different designs for an observable version of the `CardStack` class introduced in Section 6.1.

The `CardStack` class provides an implementation of the stack abstract data type specialized for `Card` objects. Figure 8.8 summarizes the definition of the class. With this design, it is only possible to find out about the state of a `CardStack` in the traditional way, by querying it via methods of its interface: `peek()`, `isEmpty`, and via its iterator. Let us now assume that other objects may want to observe instances of this class. When applying the OBSERVER, we usually wish to make the design general enough to accommodate an open-ended variety of observers. However, to make the discussion more concrete I will consider two specific observers:

- A *counter*, which reports the number of cards in the stack at any point, and detects when the last card has been popped;
- An *ace detector*, which detects whether an ace is added to the stack at any point.

Basic design with Push Data-Flow

The simplest design I can think of for making the `CardStack` observable is to introduce one abstract observer with three callbacks, one per state-changing method.

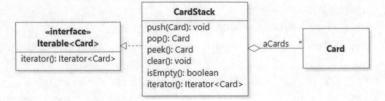

Fig. 8.8 The `CardStack` class

Figure 8.9 shows the relevant design elements, including classes for the two required concrete observers.

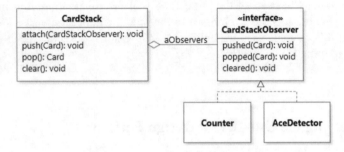

Fig. 8.9 The `CardStack` with basic observer support

In addition to the introduction of the new `CardStackObserver` interface, the required code changes include the modification of `CardStack` to manage the list of observers, as well as notify them of state changes:

```java
public class CardStack implements Iterable<Card> {
   private final List<Card> aCards = new ArrayList<>();
   private final List<CardStackObserver> aObservers =
      new ArrayList<>();

   public void attach(CardStackObserver pObserver) {
      aObservers.add(pObserver);
   }

   public void push(Card pCard) {
      assert pCard != null && !aCards.contains(pCard);
      aCards.add(pCard);
      for( CardStackObserver observer : aObservers ) {
         observer.pushed(pCard);
      }
   }
   // Likewise for pop() and clear()
}
```

As for the observers, their implementation reveals some of the limitations of this design. For the AceDetector, we are only really interested in one event, and must therefore provide two empty callback implementations:

```
public class AceDetector implements CardStackObserver {
  public void pushed(Card pCard) {
    if( pCard.getRank() == Rank.ACE ) {
      System.out.println("Ace detected!");
    }
  }

  public void popped(Card pCard) {}
  public void cleared() {}
}
```

The implementation of Counter surfaces a different problem. Because there is no way to obtain the number of cards in the stack from the information passed via the callback, it is necessary to either retain a reference to the card stack, or duplicate part of its state. For sake of discussion, I will leave the observer decoupled from the observable, and accumulate state within the observer:

```
public class Counter implements CardStackObserver {
  private int aCount = 0;

  public void pushed(Card pCard) {
    aCount++;
    System.out.println("PUSH Counter=" + aCount);
  }

  public void popped(Card pCard) {
    aCount--;
    System.out.println("POP Counter=" + aCount);
    if( aCount == 0 ) {
      System.out.println("Last card popped!");
    }
  }

  public void cleared() {
    aCount = 0;
    System.out.println("CLEAR Counter=" + aCount);
  }
}
```

In addition to replicating state, this solution suffers from the problem that it will only function correctly if the observer is attached to an empty CardStack. While this additional constraint may be acceptable in some contexts, it does make the design more brittle.

Design with Inheritance

The solution sketched above fuses the application of the observer pattern to the implementation of CardStack, thereby coupling client code with the observer machinery (the `attach` method and observer notification) even when it is not needed. An approach that yields more flexibility is to use inheritance to provide an observable extension to `CardStack`. The left side of Figure 8.10 captures this decomposition.

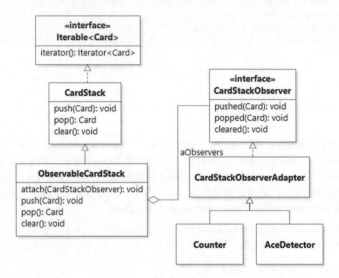

Fig. 8.10 The `ObservableCardStack` with inheritance

With this design, client code that only requires the plain `CardStack` can refer to the original version, and clients in contexts that require an observable one can instantiate the subclass instead. The `ObservableCardStack` subclass reuses all the original state-changing methods, but also overrides them to add the observer notification. For example, for `pop()`:

```
public class ObservableCardStack extends CardStack {
  ...
  public Card pop() {
    Card popped = super.pop();
    for( CardStackObserver observer : aObservers ) {
      observer.popped(popped);
    }
    return popped;
  }
}
```

While we are at it, we can also leverage inheritance to solve the problem that we may need to provide empty callback implementations in some observers (such as `AceDetector`). As illustrated on the right side of Figure 8.10, we can provide an adapter class for the `Observer` interface. The class `CardStackObserverAdapter` provides empty implementations for all callbacks. By inheriting from the adapter, observers only need to provide an implementation for the relevant callbacks.[5]

Design with Pull Data-Flow

Let us now try out an implementation with a pull data-flow strategy. With this alternative, we want to allow observers to pull (fetch) the data they need from the observable card stack, while maintaining a minimal amount of coupling between the observers and their subject. For this purpose, we will use the Interface Segregation Principle (see Section 3.9) and define a new interface that declares only the state-querying methods of `CardStack`. The new interface `CardStackView` will allow us to have objects that can query the state of a card stack, without being coupled to state-changing methods such as `push` or `pop`, or the observer registration method (`attach`). Figure 8.11 illustrates the new design variant.

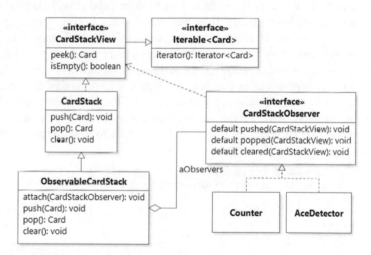

Fig. 8.11 The `ObservableCardStack` with pull-style data-flow

In this design, the callbacks now take a `CardStackView` as parameter. The impact on the observable is minimal: instead of passing a card as argument, the `ObservableCardStack` passes a reference to itself, for example in `pop()`:

---

[5] I used an explicit adapter class to emphasize the inheritance relation. In practice, it would be preferable to inherit from default methods declared in the interface as described in *Event-Based Programming*, Section 8.3.

```
public Card pop() {
  Card popped = super.pop();
  for( CardStackObserver observer : aObservers ) {
    observer.popped(this);
  }
  return popped;
}
```

The implementation of the observers is more impacted, however. The `AceDetec-tor` must now rely on `peek()` to detect an ace, since there is no longer any information available about the card that was just pushed onto the stack:

```
public void pushed(CardStackView pView) {
  if( pView.peek().getRank() == Rank.ACE ) {
    System.out.println("Ace detected!");
  }
}
```

As for the `Counter` observer, we have an interesting situation. Because the entire state of the card stack is now accessible, we no longer need to replicate the size of the stack in a field within `Counter`. However, the `CardStackView` does not provide a method `size()` that would allow us to retrieve this size conveniently. Instead, we would have to iterate every time through all the cards in the stack to get the size. Two alternatives are to either modify the `CardStack` and `CardStackView` types to include a `size()` method, or to implement a helper method within `Counter`. The trade-off is that in the first case, we widen the interface of the class, possibly for a rare usage scenario, whereas the second option may prove overly inefficient if we are dealing with large stacks. For now, I will chose to use a helper method in `Counter`:

```
public class Counter implements CardStackObserver {
  private static int size(CardStackView pView) {
    int size = 0;
    for( Card card : pView ) {
      size++;
    }
    return size;
  }

  public void popped(CardStackView pView) {
    System.out.println("POP Counter=" + size(pView));
    if( pView.isEmpty() ) {
      System.out.println("Last card popped!");
    }
  }
  ...
}
```

It is worth noticing that with this solution, the implementation of the `Counter` is no longer brittle, as the callbacks will return the correct card count independently of when the object is attached to its subject `ObservableCardStack`.

Design with Single Callback and Push/Pull Data-Flow

As our final variant, we will look at a design with only a single callback that supports both push and pull data-flow strategies. Figure 8.12 shows the changed elements in the solution. With only one callback for multiple kinds of events, the nature of the event is no longer represented by the name of the method, so I changed it to the general `actionPerformed`. We still need a way to distinguish between the kinds of events being reported, however. For this purpose, we can introduce a value that represents the event kind. This role is served by the parameter of enumerated type `Action`. To support both push and pull data-flow strategies, I combined the structures we defined above: a parameter to represent the card involved in the state change, and a parameter to refer back to the observable structure. While it makes sense to include a reference to the observable for all kinds of event, the same is not true for the value we push. For the `CLEAR` event, there is no card involved in the event. One solution to this problem is to use an `Optional` wrapper to avoid passing `null` (see Section 4.5).

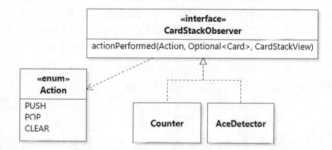

Fig. 8.12 The `ObservableCardStack` with dual push/pull-style data-flow

In terms of observer implementation, this solution is more general and flexible because we can more easily add different kinds of events. The trade-off is that the observer implementations must do additional checking to see whether the callback applies to the event. For example, for `AceDetector`:

```
public void actionPerformed(Action pAction, Optional<Card> pCard,
  CardStackView pView) {
  if( pAction == Action.PUSH &&
    pView.peek().getRank() == Rank.ACE) {
    System.out.println("Ace detected!");
  }
}
```

Unfortunately, for observers that must handle multiple events (such as `Counter`), the routing of all events through a single callback is likely to lead to a SWITCH STATEMENT† as one method needs to handle separate computations:

```
public void actionPerformed(Action pAction, Optional<Card> pCard,
  CardStackView pView) {
  switch(pAction) {
    case PUSH:
      System.out.println("PUSH Counter=" + size(pView));
      break;
    case POP:
      ...
    case CLEAR:
      ...
  }
}
```

One alternative solution is to create three different observers, one for each type. If we go down this route, we could also get rid of the `Action` type parameter and maintain three lists in the observable, one for each type of event. In this case, the registration context would be necessary to determine the type of event.

With just a simple design context, we have already explored many different ways to apply the OBSERVER. Even then, many implementation variants remain possible. For example, in some contexts it may make sense to have at most one observer per event type. When inversion of control is needed, it is thus more important to carefully consider the requirements of the design context and apply the pattern accordingly, than to try to employ a predetermined solution template.

Code Exploration: JetUML · UserPreferences

Application of the OBSERVER *with push–pull data flow, combined with the* SINGLETON.

In JetUML, `UserPreferences` is the class that stores and manages the various preferences that users can select via the application menus (for example, whether to show the grid or not). The class is both a SINGLETON and a subject in the OBSERVER pattern. The instance of the class manages two types of preferences, depending on whether they are Boolean or integer values. In this design, preferences are represented as values of enumerated types. Let us take `BooleanPreference` as an example. The method `setBoolean` stores the preference value, then notifies all the registered `BooleanPreferenceChangeHandler` objects. This design makes it possible to have completely different parts of the application react to changes in user preferences without complex chains of method calls. For example, class `DiagramCanvas` is a concrete observer of Boolean preference changes. In its callback, it checks whether the preference that changed is `showGrid` and, if so, it repaints the canvas.

8.5 Introduction to Graphical User Interface Development

In many technologies, the code that implements the Graphical User Interface (GUI) portion of an application makes heavy use of the OBSERVER. This section and the next two are an introduction to GUI development that serves the dual purpose of introducing the concept of an *application framework* and reinforcing knowledge of the OBSERVER pattern through its application in a new context. This part of the chapter is based on JavaFX, an extensive GUI framework for the Java language. However, the general concepts presented here apply to other GUI development frameworks. Conceptually, the code that makes up a GUI application is split into two parts:

- **The framework code** consists of a *component library* and an *application skeleton*. The component library is a collection of reusable types and interfaces that implement typical GUI functionality: buttons, windows, etc. The application skeleton is a GUI application that takes care of all the inevitable low-level aspects of GUI applications, and in particular monitoring events triggered by input devices and displaying objects on the screen. By itself, the application skeleton does not do anything visible: it must be extended and customized with *application code*.
- **Application code** consists of the code written by GUI developers to extend and customize the application skeleton so that it provides the required user interface functionality.

A GUI application does not execute the same way as the script-like applications we write when learning to program. In such programs, the code executes sequentially from the first statement of the application entry point (the `main` method in Java) and the flow of control is entirely dictated by the application code. With GUI frameworks, the application must be started by *launching* the framework using a special library method. The framework then starts an *event loop* that continually monitors the system for input from user interface devices. Throughout the execution of the GUI application, the framework remains in control of calling the application code. The application code, written by the GUI developers, only get executed at specific points, in response to calls by the framework. This process is thus a clear example of inversion of control. Application code does not tell the framework what to do: it waits for the framework to call it.

Figure 8.13 illustrates the essence of the relation between the LuckyNumber application and the JavaFX framework. The class diagram shows how the application code defines a `LuckyNumber` class that inherits from the framework's `Application` class. To launch the framework, the following code is used:

```
public class LuckyNumber extends Application {
  public static void main(String[] pArgs) { launch(pArgs); }

  @Override
  public void start(Stage pPrimaryStage) {
    ...
  }
}
```

Fig. 8.13 Relation between
application and framework
code for the LuckyNumber
application

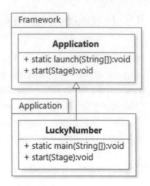

This code calls the static method `Application#launch`, which launches the
GUI framework, instantiates class `LuckyNumber` and then executes method `start()`
on this instance.[6] With this setup, class `LuckyNumber` is effectively used as the con-
nection point between the application code used to extend the GUI and the framework code in charge of running the show.

Conceptually, the application code for a GUI application can be split into two
categories: the *component graph*,[7] and the *event handling code*.

The component graph is the actual user interface and is comprised of a number
of objects that represent both visible (e.g., buttons) and invisible (e.g., regions) elements of the application. These objects are organized as a tree, with the root of
the tree being the main window or area of the GUI. In modern GUI frameworks,
constructing a component graph can be done by writing code, but also through configuration files that can be generated by GUI building tools. Ultimately, the two
approaches are equivalent because, once the code runs, the outcome is the same:
a tree of plain Java objects that form the user interface. The design of the library
classes that support the construction of a component graph makes heavy use of polymorphism and the COMPOSITE and DECORATOR patterns. In JavaFX, the component
graph for a user interface is typically instantiated in the application's `start(Stage)`
method.

Once the framework is launched and displaying the desired component graph, its
event loop will automatically map low-level system events to specific interactions
with components in the graph (for example, placing the mouse over a text box, or
clicking a button). In common GUI programming terminology, such interactions
are called *events*. Unless specific application code is provided to react to an event,
nothing will happen as a result of the framework detecting this event. For example,
clicking on a button will graphically show the button to be clicked using some user
interface cue, but then the code will simply continue executing without having any
impact on the application logic. To build interactive GUI applications, it is necessary
to *handle* events like button clicks and other user interactions. Event handling in
GUI frameworks is an application of the OBSERVER pattern, where the model is a

---

[6] Method `launch` uses metaprogramming to discover which application class to instantiate.

[7] In the documentation for JavaFX, the component graph is called the *scene graph*.

GUI component (such as a button). Handling a button click, or any similar event, then becomes a matter of defining an observer and registering it with the button. The next two sections detail how to design component graphs and handle events on GUI components.

8.6 Graphical User Interface Component Graphs

The component graph is the collection of objects that forms what we usually think of as the user interface: windows, textboxes, buttons, etc. At different stages in the development of a graphical user interface, it can be useful to think about this user interface from three different point of views, or perspectives: user experience, source code, and run time.

The User Experience Perspective

The user experience perspective corresponds to what the user experiences when interacting with the component graph. Figure 8.2, shown earlier in this chapter, shows the user experience perspective on the component graph for the LuckyNumber application. Because not every object in the component graph is necessarily visible, it is important to remember that the user experience perspective does not show the complete picture of the application. This picture is complemented by the other two perspectives.

The Source Code Perspective

The source code perspective shows the kind of information about the component graph that is readily available from the declarations of the classes of the objects that form the component graph. This information is best summarized by a class diagram. Figure 8.14 models the source code perspective on the component graph of the LuckyNumber application. Despite the application being tiny, the diagram shows that a lot of code is required to instantiate its component graph. Let us walk through this diagram.

The Scene holds a reference to the root node of the component graph, something we can deduce from the fact that it is not a subtype of Node, and no class in the diagram aggregates it. The Scene class aggregates class Parent. This may be puzzling at first, because in my logical model of the component graph, I indicated that the Scene contains a GridPane. This is an example of polymorphism in use. To allow users to build any kind of application, the Scene library class accepts any subtype of type Parent as its child object. In turn, Parent is a subtype of the general Node type that adds functionality to handle children nodes. In JavaFX, all objects that can be part of a component graph need to be a subtype of Node, either directly or, more

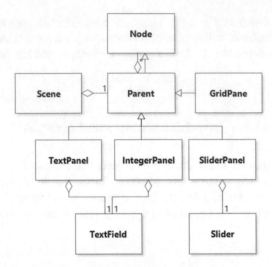

Fig. 8.14 Source code perspective on the LuckyNumber application

generally, indirectly by inheriting from other subtypes of Node. The fact that Parent nodes, which can contain children nodes, are themselves of type Node shows that the design of the GUI component hierarchy is an application of the COMPOSITE pattern.

By continuing our investigation of the diagram, we find class GridPane as a subtype of Parent. This is the reason it is possible to add a GridPane to a scene. A GridPane is a type of user interface Node that specializes in organizing its children into a grid. I used it for LuckyNumber to lay out the number views vertically on top of each other.

In the LuckyNumber application, a GridPane contains a set of Parent components. In the general case, a GridPane can contain any subtype of Node. However, in my design of the application, I created three classes that inherit from Parent: TextPanel, IntegerPanel, and SliderPanel. These classes represent the three views of the number in the Model–View–Controller decomposition. By defining these classes as subclasses of Parent, I achieve two useful properties:

- I *reuse* the *parenting* functionality of Parent to add a widget (e.g., a slider) to a Node;
- By defining my view classes as subtypes of Node, I make it possible to add them as children of a GridPane through polymorphism.

The remainder of the diagram shows how the tree would generate its leaves: the SliderPanel aggregates a Slider instance, and both the TextPanel and the IntegerPanel aggregate a TextField instance. Note that because this is a class diagram and not an object diagram, the fact that both TextPanel and IntegerPanel have an association to the TextField model element does *not* mean that their instance would refer to the *same* TextField instance!

The diagram of Figure 8.14, already somewhat involved, actually omits, for clarity, many intermediate types in the inheritance hierarchy for nodes. For example, the diagram shows `GridPane` to be a direct subclass of `Parent`. In reality, `GridPane` is a subclass of `Pane`, which itself is a subclass of `Region`, which is a subclass of `Parent`. Figure 8.15, while still an incomplete model, shows a bigger picture of the class hierarchy that can be leveraged to define component graphs in JavaFX.

The Run-time Perspective

The run-time perspective is the instantiated component graph for a graphical interface. This perspective can best be represented as an object diagram. Figure 8.16 shows the instantiated component graph for LuckyNumber.

Defining the Object Graph

In Section 8.5 I mentioned how after the framework starts it calls the `start` method of the main application class (`LuckyNumber` in our case). This `start` method is the natural integration point for extending the framework, and this is where we put the code that builds the component graph. The code below is the minimum required to get the application to create the LuckyNumber component graph. In practice, this kind of code would typically be extended with additional configuration code and organized using helper methods. The additional configuration code can be used to beautify the application, for example by adding margins around components, a title to the window, etc. The JavaFX functionality to generate component graphs from configuration files is outside the scope of this book.

```
public class LuckyNumber extends Application {
  public void start(Stage pStage) {
    Model model = new Model();

    GridPane root = new GridPane();
    root.add(new SliderPanel(model), 0, 0, 1, 1);
    root.add(new IntegerPanel(model), 0, 1, 1, 1);
    root.add(new TextPanel(model), 0, 2, 1, 1);

    pStage.setScene(new Scene(root));
    pStage.show();
  }
}
```

The first statement of method `start` is to create an instance of `Model`. This instance will play the role of the model in the OBSERVER pattern. It is related to the construction of the component graph because, as detailed later, some of the components in the graph need access to the model. The second statement creates a `GridPane`, which is an invisible component used for assisting with the layout of children components. The local variable that holds a reference to this component is

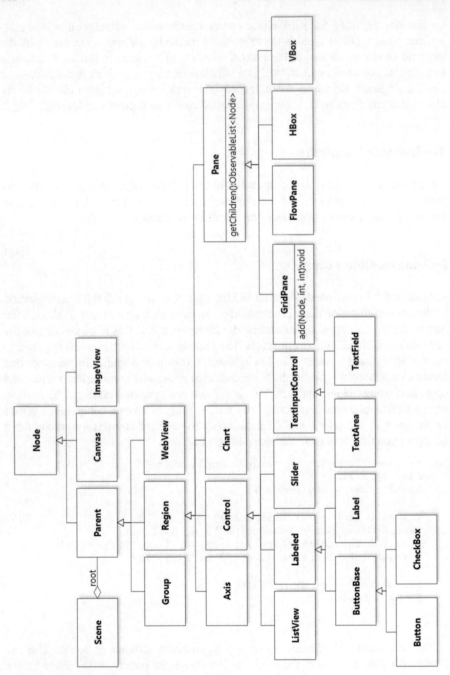

Fig. 8.15 Partial Node class hierarchy in JavaFX

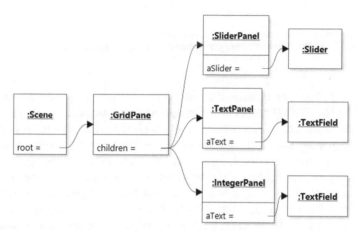

Fig. 8.16 Run-time perspective of the LuckyNumber user interface

helpfully named `root` to indicate that it is the root of the component graph. Then, three application-defined components are added to the grid. The parameters to the `add` method indicate the column and row index and span. For example, the statement:

```
root.add(new SliderPanel(model), 0, 0, 1, 1);
```

specifies to add an instance of the `SliderPanel` in the top-left cell in the grid, and span only one column and one row. Because `SliderPanel` is a subtype of `Parent`, and thus a subtype of `Node`, it can be added to the grid. Another important thing to note about the instantiation of the panel components is that their constructor takes as argument a reference to the model.

The last two statements of the method are not really related to the construction of the component graph, but are nevertheless crucial steps in the creation of the GUI. The statement with the call to `setScene` creates a `Scene` from the component graph and assigns it to the framework's `Stage`. Finally, the last statement requests that the framework display the `Stage` onto the user's display.

For additional insights on the creation of the component graph, the code below shows the relevant part of the constructor of the `IntegerPanel` (the other panels are very similar).

```
public class IntegerPanel extends Parent implements Observer {
  private TextField aText = new TextField();
  private Model aModel;

  public IntegerPanel(Model pModel) {
    aModel = pModel;
    aModel.addObserver(this);
    aText.setText(new Integer(aModel.getNumber()).toString());
    getChildren().add(aText);
    ...
  }
}
```

```
public void newNumber(int pNumber) {
  aText.setText(new Integer(pNumber).toString());
}
}
```

This code illustrates a number of insights about the design of the component graph. First, as already mentioned, the application-defined `IntegerPanel` class extends the framework-defined `Parent` class so that it can become part of the component graph. Second, an instance of `IntegerPanel` aggregates a framework-defined `TextField` component. However, the mere fact of defining an instance variable of type `TextField` inside the class does not add the `TextField` to the component graph. To do this, it is necessary for the `IntegerPanel` to add the instance of `TextField` to itself, something that is done with the call `getChildren()` `.add(aText)`. Method `getChildren()` is inherited from class `Parent`, and used to obtain the list of children of the parent user interface `Node`, to which the `TextField` instance can then be added.

The `IntegerPanel` instance also maintains a reference to the `Model`. The reason for this is that the `IntegerPanel` needs to act as a controller for the `Model`, something that will be explained in more detail in the next section. Also, it is worth noticing how the `IntegerPanel` is an observer of the `Model` instance: it declares to implement `Observer`, it registers itself as an observer upon construction (second statement of the constructor), and it supplies an implementation for the `newNumber` callback. As expected, the behavior of the callback is to set the value of the `TextField` user interface component with the most recent value in the model, obtained from the callback parameter.

As a final insight on the design of the component graph, we can note how the instance of `Model` created in method `start` (see preceding code fragment) is stored in a *local variable*. In other words, the application class `LuckyNumber` does *not* manage an instance of the model: this is only done within each panel. This design decision is to respect the guideline provided in Chapter 4, to keep the number of fields to a minimum. Without care, an application-defined user interface component can become a GOD CLASS† bloated with numerous references to stateful objects, which makes a design much harder to understand.

8.7 Event Handling

In GUI frameworks, objects in the component graph act as models in the OBSERVER. Once the framework is launched, it continually goes through a loop that monitors input events and checks whether they map to events that can be observed by the application code. This process is illustrated in Figure 8.17.

Typically, events are defined by the component library supplied by the framework. For example, the `TextField` user interface component defines an *action event*. According to its class documentation "The action handler is normally called

Fig. 8.17 The event loop in a
GUI framework

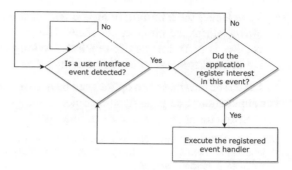

when the user types the ENTER key". This means that an instance of `TextField` can play the role of the model in the OBSERVER. Figure 8.18 shows the correspondence between the code elements and the roles in the OBSERVER pattern.

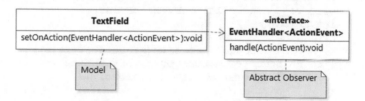

Fig. 8.18 Correspondence between `TextField` and the roles in the OBSERVER

Handling the action event on a text field is thus pretty straightforward. All we need to do is to:

- **Define a handler for the event.** This means defining a class that is a subtype of `EventHandler<ActionEvent>`. The class will be our event handler class.
- **Instantiate a handler.** This means creating an instance of the class we defined in the previous step. The instance will be our *event handler instance*, also called *event handler*, or even just *handler*.
- **Register the handler.** This means calling the registration method on the model and passing the handler as an argument. In the case of `TextField`, we need to call `setOnAction(handler)`. It is worth noticing an interesting design choice for this application of OBSERVER: it is only possible to have a single observer for a `TextField`.

Although the basic mechanism for specifying and registering event handlers is always the same, one design choice that must be resolved is where to place the definition of the handling code. For this, two main strategies are possible:

- **To define the handler as a function object** using an anonymous class or a lambda expression (see Section 3.4). This is a good choice if the code of the handler is simple and does not require storing data that is specific to the handler;

- **To delegate the handling to an element of the component graph** by declaring to implement the observer interface. This is a good choice if the code of the handler is more complex or requires knowing about many different aspects of the internal structure of the target component.

Let us see how these two options can be realized in the context of the LuckyNumber application. Using the function object strategy, we could complete the code of the constructor of `IntegerPanel` as follows:

```
public class IntegerPanel extends Parent implements Observer {
    private TextField aText = new TextField();
    private Model aModel;

    public IntegerPanel(Model pModel) {
        aModel = pModel;
        aModel.addObserver(this);
        aText.setText(new Integer(aModel.getNumber()).toString());
        getChildren().add(aText);
        aText.setOnAction(new EventHandler<ActionEvent>() {
            public void handle(ActionEvent pEvent) {
                int number = 1;
                try {
                    number = Integer.parseInt(aText.getText());
                } catch(NumberFormatException pException ) {
                    /* Just ignore. We use 1 instead. */
                }
                aModel.setNumber(number);
            }
        });
    }
}
```

With this strategy, the constructor of `IntegerPanel` creates a function object using an anonymous class and, at the same time, registers this object to become the handler of the action event on the text field. The behavior of the handler is to serve as the controller for the model.

At this point in the design of the application, we now have *two* applications of the OBSERVER at play. One subject is the `Model` being observed by all three panels, and another subject is the `IntegerPanel`'s `TextField` that is observed by the anonymous function object. Figure 8.19 captures the design. Naturally, in the finished application, we would also need an event handler for the text panel and the slider panel, which would bring the total number of applications of the OBSERVER to four.

In the case of the LuckyNumber application, one alternative to using function objects for defining handlers is to delegate the handling of GUI events to the panels themselves. In our case, this would mean declaring `IntegerPanel` to implement both `Observer` and `EventHandler<ActionEvent>`. The `Observer` interface is the same one as before, used to receive callbacks when the model (the number) is changed. The difference in this case is the addition of the `EventHandler` interface, which allows the `IntegerPanel` to respond to the event that corresponds to the *Enter* key being pressed in the panel's text field.

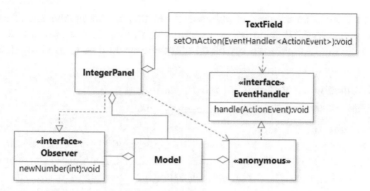

Fig. 8.19 Two applications of the OBSERVER pattern

```
public class IntegerPanel extends Parent implements Observer,
  EventHandler<ActionEvent> {
  private TextField aText = new TextField();
  private Model aModel;

  public IntegerPanel(Model pModel) {
    aModel = pModel;
    aModel.addObserver(this);
    aText.setText(new Integer(aModel.getNumber()).toString());
    getChildren().add(aText);
    aText.setOnAction(this);
  }

  public void handle(ActionEvent pEvent) {
    int number = 1;
    try {
      number = Integer.parseInt(aText.getText());
    } catch(NumberFormatException pException ) {
      /* Just ignore. We'll use 1 instead. */
    }
    aModel.setNumber(number);
  }

  public void newNumber(int pNumber) {
    aText.setText(new Integer(pNumber).toString());
  }
}
```

There are two main implications of this choice on the code. First, the `handle` method needs to be declared directly in class `IntegerPanel`. Second, the argument passed to `aText.setOnAction` is now `this`, because it is the `IntegerPanel` instance itself that is now responsible for handling the event.

Although both design options for locating the handler code are workable, for the LuckyNumber application I prefer the function object alternative. The handler code is just a few lines long, and with the function object the behavior of the handler is located with other code that initializes the text field, so everything is in one place.

Although there is an element of subjectivity to this argument, the use of function objects to specify GUI handlers is a common practice. In the absence of a good reason to do things otherwise, my recommendation would be to use it by default.

Code Exploration: Solitaire · Solitaire

Overview of the GUI design for a small application.

The GUI code for Solitaire is located in the ...solitaire.gui package. The application class is Solitaire. With the exception of the application class, CardDragHandler and CardTransfer, each remaining class in the package defines a graphical component panel that specializes in viewing a specific part of the data of the GameModel. For example, DiscardPileView is a subclass of the framework class Hbox that is also a GameModelListener. Whenever the game model changes, this component responds to the event (gameStateChanged()) and shows an image of the card at the top of the discard pile. As usual, the component graph is constructed in the application's start method. The design of the Solitaire application relies on a GUI feature called drag-and-drop. Although the design of drag-and-drop functionality was not covered explicitly in the chapter, its operation is also based on the OBSERVER pattern. The basic idea is that images of cards are objects in the component graph, and it is possible to register a handler for an event that corresponds to a drag gesture being detected on this component.

Code Exploration: JetUML · EditorFrame

Pointers into the GUI design of a full-features application.

The user interface of JetUML is not simple, but it makes use of a wide variety of GUI framework features (menus, tabs, dialog boxes, persistent properties), so studying its code should have a high return on investment for readers interested in learning GUI programming in more depth. The application class is JetUML, but most of the heavy lifting is accomplished by class EditorFrame, which is responsible for creating the top window of the application. Reading through the code of EditorFrame will expose most of the main design decisions that underlie the user interface code, including how tabs are managed, how menus are created, and how we create dialog boxes.

8.8 The VISITOR Design Pattern

Inversion of control can be useful to create loosely coupled design solutions in contexts other than applications of the OBSERVER pattern and event handling mechanisms. An additional recognized use for inversion of control is the VISITOR design pattern. The context for applying the VISITOR pattern is when we want to make it possible to support an open-ended number of operations that can be applied to an object graph, but without impacting the interface of the objects in the graph. To illustrate such a context, we will use yet another variant of the `CardSource` type hierarchy. Figure 8.20 shows a design where different types of concrete card sources have the `CardSource` interface in common, but then different individual interfaces for services other than `draw()` and `isEmpty()`;

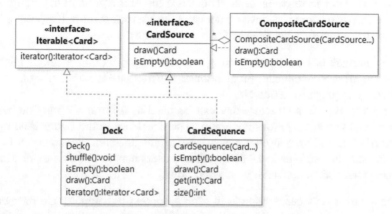

Fig. 8.20 Design context for a sample application of the VISITOR. The constructor uses the vararg construct to accept an unspecified number of cards as argument. The mechanism is also employed by the constructor of `CompositeCardSource`.

In this design, there are three different types of card sources. Although they all implement the `CardSource` interface, their commonality ends there. Class `Deck` can be shuffled and is iterable. A `CardSequence` can be initialized with a predetermined list of cards, but cannot be shuffled and is not iterable. Instead, elements in a `CardSequence` can be accessed through an integer index. For this reason, the class also includes a `size()` method. Finally, `CompositeCardSource` is an application of the COMPOSITE with a narrow interface, as it offers no services besides those of `CardSource`. In this example as well as in general, the reason classes that implement an interface have methods other than the ones in the interface is simply that each class is intended to work in a specific context where its additional methods are necessary and, to respect the Interface Segregation Principle, the only methods in the common type are those used by all contexts (see Section 3.9).

The above design will fulfill its mandate as long as the client code only requires the limited functionality it currently provides. Problems will arise, however, when we start needing additional functionality from the card sources. Examples of operations that may be necessary at some point include:

- Printing to the console a description of each of the cards in the source;
- Obtaining the number of cards in the card source;
- Removing a certain card from a card source;

- Determining if a card source contains a certain card;
- Obtaining an iterator over all the cards in the source;

Because all of the concrete card source classes share a common supertype, there is a straightforward solution to the problem of adding these operations: we can define new methods on the `CardSource` interface, one per operation, and implement them in each subclass. For example, we could make `CardSource` extend `Iterable<Card>`, and add the methods `print()`, `size()`, `remove(Card)`, and `contains(Card)` to its declaration. If such a solution is a good fit in a design context, then we can adopt it and we do not need the VISITOR pattern. However, adding methods to an interface has drawbacks and limitations:

- The interface of `CardSource` will get much bigger. Not all methods might be used in all usage contexts. As mentioned above, there is a risk of violating the Interface Segregation Principle;
- For a versatile data structure that can be used as a library, it may be hard to anticipate which operations are going to be necessary in the future. Adding operations that end up unused is a clear case of SPECULATIVE GENERALITY†. In fact, if the code is distributed as a library, future users may not be able to, or want to, change the code to add additional operations.

The VISITOR provides a solution in such a context by supporting a mechanism whereby it is possible to define an operation of interest in a separate class and inject it into the class hierarchy that needs to support it. In our case, this means we could write a separate class to implement the `contains(Card)` operation, and use this class to determine if any concrete `CardSource` contains the card of interest.

Abstract and Concrete Visitors

The cornerstone of the VISITOR pattern is an interface that describes objects that can *visit* objects of all classes of interest in an object graph. This interface is appropriately called the *abstract visitor*. An abstract visitor follows a prescribed structure: it contains one method with signature `visitElementX(ElementX pElementX)` for each different type of concrete class `ElementX` in the object structure.[8] In our case, the abstract visitor would be defined as follows:

```
public interface CardSourceVisitor {
   void visitCompositeCardSource(CompositeCardSource pSource);
   void visitDeck(Deck pDeck);
   void visitCardSequence(CardSequence pCardSequence);
}
```

---

[8] Technically, the methods can be overloaded, which leads to the more compact form `visit(ElementX pElementX)`. For the reasons discussed in Section 7.5, I recommend avoiding overloading by using the longer form.

As usual, a *concrete visitor* is an implementation of this interface. In the Visitor pattern, we implement one concrete visitor for each operation of interest. In a concrete visitor, each `visitElementX` method provides the behavior of the operation as applied to a given class. For example, a simple visitor that prints all the cards in a card source to the console would be defined as such:

```
public class PrintingVisitor implements CardSourceVisitor {

  public void visitCompositeCardSource(CompositeCardSource pSource)
  {}

  public void visitDeck(Deck pDeck) {
    for( Card card : pDeck) {
      System.out.println(card);
    }
  }

  public void visitCardSequence(CardSequence pCardSequence) {
    for( int i = 0; i < pCardSequence.size(); i++ ) {
      System.out.println(pCardSequence.get(i));
    }
  }
}
```

The first thing to notice in this code is that method `visitCompositeCardSource` does not do anything. Because composite card sources do not store cards directly (they store other card sources), we can defer the printing behavior to the actual card sources they aggregate. How this works exactly is described below. The second thing to notice is that methods `visitDeck` and `visitCardSequence` do not require `Deck` and `CardSequence` to have the same interface: they can use whatever methods are available on the concrete type to implement the required behavior.

Another interesting observation about the implementation of the concrete visitor is that it provides a way to organize code in terms of *functionality* as opposed to *data*. In a classic design, the code to implement the printing operation would be scattered throughout the three card source classes. In this design, all this code in located in a single class. One of the benefits of the Visitor is thus to allow a different style of assignment of responsibilities to classes, and thus a separation of concerns along a different criterion (functionality-centric vs. data-centric).

Integrating Operations into a Class Hierarchy

Although a concrete visitor separates a well-defined operation into its own class, it still needs to be integrated with the class hierarchy that defines the object graph on which the operation will be applied (henceforth referred to as the *class hierarchy*). This integration is accomplished by way of a method, usually called `accept`, that acts as a gateway into the object graph for visitor objects. An `accept` method takes as single argument an object of the abstract visitor type (`CardSourceVisitor` in our case). Unless there is a good reason not to, we normally define the `accept` method on the common supertype of the class hierarchy:

```
public interface CardSource {
  Card draw();
  boolean isEmpty();
  void accept(CardSourceVisitor pVisitor);
}
```

The implementation of `accept` by concrete types is where the integration really happens. This implementation follows a prescribed formula: to call the `visit` method for the type of the class that defines the `accept` method. For example, the implementation of `accept` for class `Deck` is:

```
public void accept(CardSourceVisitor pVisitor) {
  pVisitor.visitDeck(this);
}
```

and the one for class `CardSequence` is:

```
public void accept(CardSourceVisitor pVisitor) {
  pVisitor.visitCardSequence(this);
}
```

The only difference between the two implementations of `accept` is the specific `visitElementX` method that is being called. The version of `accept` for the `CompositeCardSource` class is more involved, and is discussed further below, in the section *Traversing the Object Graph*.

Figure 8.21 shows the result of applying the VISITOR to our context. The figure includes two concrete visitors to emphasize that the goal of the pattern is to support adding multiple operations to a class hierarchy.

With the `accept` method in place, executing an operation on the object graph is now a matter of creating the concrete visitor object that represents the operation, and passing this object as argument to method `accept` on the target element:

```
PrintingVisitor visitor = new PrintingVisitor();
Deck deck = new Deck();
deck.accept(visitor);
```

Figure 8.22 shows the result of calling accept on an instance of `Deck`. The client code, which holds the reference to the concrete visitor, calls `accept` on an instance of `Deck` with the visitor as argument. The `accept` method then calls back the appropriate method on the visitor. In this sequence, the `visitDeck` method qualifies as a callback method. With complex object structures, it may not always be possible to determine when a `visit` method will be called. Just like in the OBSERVER pattern, the model calls its observers back at the appropriate time, in the VISITOR, concrete elements call the visitors at the appropriate time.

Traversing the Object Graph

So far in our application of the VISITOR we have left out a critical aspect of the pattern: the traversal of the object graph. Any object graph with more than one element

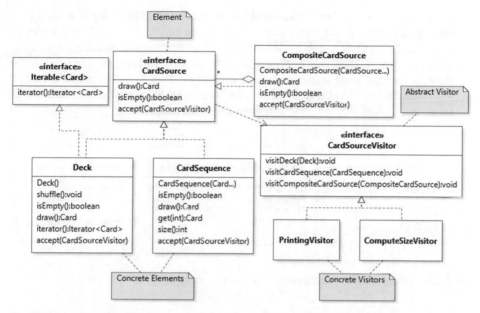

Fig. 8.21 Sample application of the VISITOR pattern with the name of the roles in notes

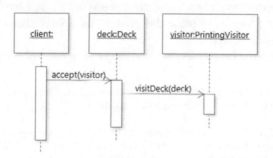

Fig. 8.22 Sequence diagram of a call to an `accept` method in an application of VISITOR

will have an aggregate node as its root. In our case this is `CompositeCardSource`, so let us look at what happens when we apply an operation to such a node. Let us say we implement `accept` for this class similarly as for `Deck` and `CardSequence`:

```java
public class CompositeCardSource implements CardSource {
  public void accept(CardSourceVisitor pVisitor) {
    pVisitor.visitCompositeCardSource(this);
  }
}
```

Then, if we call `accept` on an instance of `CompositeCardSource`, the method invokes its callback `visitCompositeCardSource`, which does nothing.

The two core ideas of the VISITOR pattern are to *1)* enable the integration of an open-ended set of operations that *2)* can be applied by traversing an object graph, often a recursive one. For the traversal aspect of the pattern to be applicable, at least one element type in the target hierarchy needs to serve as an aggregate for other types. In our case this role is played by `CompositeCardSource`. Let us consider the object graph illustrated in Figure 8.23. If we want to print the cards reachable through the `root` card source, we would need to traverse the entire graph to find all the cards. We would also need to do such a traversal to count the total number of cards in a source, remove all instances of a specific card, etc.

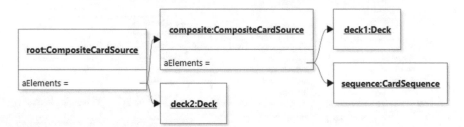

Fig. 8.23 Sample object graph generated by the `CardSource` types

There are two main ways to implement the traversal of the object graph in the VISITOR. One option is to place the traversal code in the `accept` method of aggregate types. The other option is to place this code in the `visit` methods that serve as callbacks for aggregate types.

In our case, placing the traversal code in the `accept` method is relatively straight-forward:

```
public class CompositeCardSource implements CardSource {
  private final List<CardSource> aElements;

  public void accept(CardSourceVisitor pVisitor) {
    pVisitor.visitCompositeCardSource(this);
    for( CardSource source : aElements ) {
      source.accept(pVisitor); }
  }
}
```

Because the traversal code is implemented within the class of the aggregate, it can refer to the private field that stores the aggregation (`aElements`). This access to private structures is one major motivation for implementing the traversal code within the `accept` method. I discuss additional advantages and disadvantages of this choice below. Figure 8.24 shows the beginning of the call sequence that results from calling `accept` on the `root` target node of Figure 8.23. From this figure it becomes easier to visualize the concrete visitor as an implementation of callback methods: some independent code traverses an object structure and calls the `visitElementX` call-backs as appropriate, and methods of the visitor object respond to these visitation notifications. The fact that the traversal code is implemented in `accept` is visible by the fact that some calls to `accept` originate from the activation bar of a different `accept` invocation.

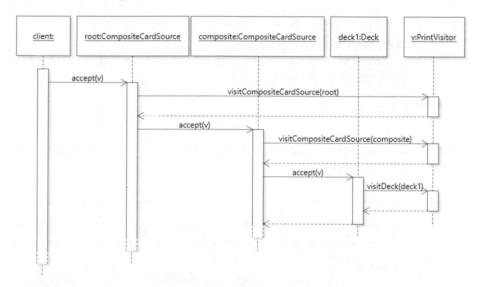

Fig. 8.24 Partial call sequence resulting from a call to `root.accept` on the object graph of Figure 8.23 when the traversal code is implemented in the `accept` method

The second option for implementing the traversal code is to put it in the visit method that corresponds to the element types that are aggregates. In our case this means, as before, `CompositeCardSource`. Unfortunately, in our context it is not possible to implement this option directly, because the aggregate class offers no public access to the `CardSource` objects it aggregates. Because the code of the `visit` methods is in a separate class, we need a way to access the objects stored by the private field `aElements`. To make this work we make `CompositeCardSource` iterable over the `CardSource` instances it aggregates. However, this requirement to decrease the level of encapsulation of the class is a disadvantage of this design decision.

```
public class CompositeCardSource implements CardSource,
   Iterable<CardSource> {
   private final List<CardSource> aElements;

   public Iterator<CardSource> iterator() {
     return aElements.iterator();
   }
   ...
}
```

With this additional service available on `CompositeCardSource`, we can now re-move the traversal code from the `accept` method and update the code of `visit-CompositeCardSource` in our concrete visitor:

```
public class PrintVisitor implements CardSourceVisitor {
  public void visitCompositeCardSource(
    CompositeCardSource pCompositeCardSource) {
    for( CardSource source : pCompositeCardSource ) {
      source.accept(this);
    }
  }
  ...
}
```

Figure 8.25 shows the corresponding call sequence on the root of the object graph illustrated in Figure 8.23.

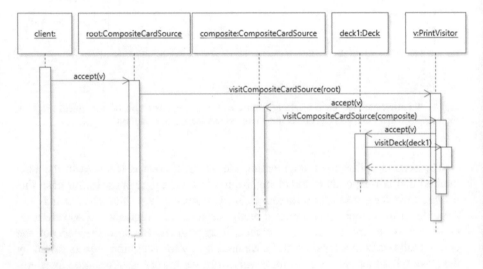

Fig. 8.25 Partial call sequence resulting from a call to `root.accept` on the object graph of Figure 8.23 when the traversal code is implemented in the `visit` method

As we have seen above, the main advantage of placing the traversal code in the `accept` method is that it can help achieve stronger encapsulation because the internal structures can be accessed without being part of the class's interface. The main disadvantage of placing the traversal code in the `accept` method, however, is that the traversal order is fixed in the sense that it cannot be adapted by different visitors. In our simple example, the traversal order did not really matter. But let us say that in our print visitor we care about the order in which the cards are printed. The code for the `accept` method, above, implements a pre-order traversal (visit the node, then the children). Some operations, however, might require a post-order traversal (visit the children, then the node). If the traversal code is implemented in `accept`, concrete visitors cannot change it. In a nutshell, if encapsulation of target elements is more important, it is better to place the traversal code in the `accept` method. If the ability to change the traversal order is more important, then it is better to place the traversal code in the `visit` method.

Using Inheritance in the Pattern

The question of where to place the traversal code brings up the issue of code DUPLI-CATED CODE† again. If we place the traversal code in the `visit` methods, and have more than one concrete visitor class, every class is bound to repeat the traversal code in its `visit` method. A common solution to alleviate this issue is to define an `abstract` visitor class to hold default traversal code.[9] In our case, the following would be a good implementation of an `abstract` visitor class:

```
public abstract class AbstractCardSourceVisitor
   implements CardSourceVisitor {
   public void visitCompositeCardSource(
     CompositeCardSource pCompositeCardSource) {
     for( CardSource source : pCompositeCardSource ) {
       source.accept(this);
     }
   }

   public void visitDeck(Deck pDeck) {}
   public void visitCardSequence(CardSequence pCardSequence) {}
}
```

There are two important things to observe about this implementation. First, I retained the interface. Because most concrete visitors would be implemented as subclasses of `AbstractCardSourceVisitor`, one can wonder, why not just use this abstract class to serve in the role of abstract visitor, and get rid of the interface? The general reason is that interfaces promote more flexibility in a design. For example, one concrete drawback of using an abstract class is that, because Java only supports single inheritance, defining the abstract visitor as an abstract class prevents classes that already inherit from another class to serve as concrete visitors.

The second notable detail in the above code is that the `visit` methods for classes `Deck` and `CardSequence` are implemented as empty placeholders. Given that `AbstractCardSourceVisitor` is declared `abstract`, we do not need these declarations. However, providing empty implementations for visit methods allows the abstract visitor class to serve as an adapter. In more realistic applications of the pattern, the element type hierarchy can have dozens of different types, with a corresponding high number of `visit` methods. With empty implementations, concrete visitors only need to override the methods that correspond to types they are interested in visiting.

As an example, the following declaration creates an anonymous visitor class that prints the number of cards in every `CardSequence` in a card source structure, and ignores the rest. Because the class inherits the traversal code, card sequences aggregated within composite card sources will also be reached.

---

[9] Here it is important to distinguish between an `abstract` visitor *class* and an abstract *visitor*, which is usually an interface.

```
CardSourceVisitor visitor = new AbstractCardSourceVisitor() {
   public void visitCardSequence(CardSequence pSequence) {
      System.out.println(pSequence.size() + " cards");
   }
};
```

As a more elaborate example, the following implements a visitor that prints a representation of the object graph that includes the nesting depth of a card source type:

```
public class StructurePrinterVisitor
   extends AbstractCardSourceVisitor {
   private int aTab = 0;

   private String tab() {
      StringBuilder result = new StringBuilder();
      for( int i = 0; i < aTab; i++ ) {
         result.append(" ");
      }
      return result.toString();
   }

   public void visitCompositeCardSource(
      CompositeCardSource pCompositeCardSource) {
      System.out.println(tab() + "Composite");
      aTab++;
      super.visitCompositeCardSource(pCompositeCardSource);
      aTab--;
   }

   public void visitDeck(Deck pDeck) {
      System.out.println(tab() + "Deck");
   }

   public void visitCardSequence(CardSequence pCardSequence) {
      System.out.println(tab() + "CardSequence");
   }
}
```

The result of using this visitor on the object graph of Figure 8.23 would be:

```
Composite
   Deck
   Composite
   Deck
   CardSequence
```

This example introduces two new aspects to our discussion so far. First, the visitor is *stateful*, as it stores data. Specifically, the class defines a field aTab that stores the depth of the element currently being visited. Depth increases when visiting the elements aggregated by a composite card source. Correspondingly, the second notable aspect in the code above is the *reuse of the traversal code through a super call*. Here, the pre-order traversal implemented in the abstract visitor class is what we need. However, additional code is required when visiting a composite card source.

To make this possible, `visitCompositeCardSource` is overridden to manage the indentation level, and a super call is made to trigger the traversal code at the appropriate point.

Supporting Data Flow in Visitor Structures

So far our examples of concrete visitors have carefully avoided the issue of data flow, because the `PrintVisitor` neither requires input nor produces output. Most realistic operations, however, do involve some data flow. For example, a visitor to compute the total number of cards in a card source must be able to return this number. As another example, an operation to determine if a certain card is contained in a card source must receive the card of interest as input. When operations are implemented in traditional methods, this kind of data flow is not an issue: input is passed in as argument to a method, and output can be returned to the calling context through return statements. In the VISITOR pattern, this is more complex. To support a general and extensible mechanism for defining operations on an object graph, the pattern requires that no assumption be made about the nature of the input and output of operations.

Data flow for VISITOR-based operations is thus implemented differently, by storing data within a visitor object. Input values can be provided when constructing a new visitor object and made accessible to the visit methods. Output values can be stored internally by `visit` methods during the traversal of the object graph, and made accessible to client code through a getter method.[10] Let us consider each case in turn, starting with output values. To exemplify the process, we implement a visitor to count the total number of cards in the source. This version assumes that the abstract visitor class defined above is available:

```
public class CountingVisitor extends AbstractCardSourceVisitor {
  private int aCount = 0;

  public void visitDeck(Deck pDeck) {
    for( Card card : pDeck) {
      aCount++;
    }
  }

  public void visitCardSequence(CardSequence pCardSequence) {
    aCount += pCardSequence.size();
  }
```

---

[10] Using generic types, it is also possible to design a solution that does not necessarily require this accumulation of state for output values. In this solution, the `accept` and `visit` methods return a value of a generic type. Design with generic types is outside the scope of this book, so I do not present the solution here. However, a sample implementation is available on the companion website.

```
public int getCount() {
    return aCount;
  }
}
```

To use this operation, it would be necessary to store a reference to the constructed visitor in a variable so that that the count can later be retrieved:

```
CountingVisitor visitor = new CountingVisitor();
root.accept(visitor);
int result = visitor.getCount();
```

As our final example, we define a visitor that implements an operation to check whether a card source structure contains a certain card. Such an operation requires both input and output.

```
public class ChecksContainmentVisitor
    extends AbstractCardSourceVisitor {
    private final Card aCard;
    private boolean aResult = false;

    public ChecksContainmentVisitor(Card pCard) {
        aCard = pCard;
    }

    public void visitDeck(Deck pDeck) {
        for( Card card : pDeck) {
            if( card.equals(aCard)) {
                aResult = true;
                break;
            }
        }
    }

    public void visitCardSequence(CardSequence pCardSequence) {
        for( int i = 0; i < pCardSequence.size(); i++ ) {
            if( pCardSequence.get(i).equals(aCard)) {
                aResult = true;
                break;
            }
        }
    }

    public boolean contains() {
        return aResult;
    }
}
```

Although this implementation works, it is not as efficient as it should be because aggregate nodes are traversed even when a card has already been found. Fortunately, the structure of the VISITOR allows us to eliminate this source of inefficiency with very little impact on the overall design: all we need to do is to provide an implementation for `visitCompositeCardSource` that only triggers the traversal if the card has not already been found.

```
public void visitCompositeCardSource(
  CompositeCardSource pCompositeCardSource) {
  if( !aResult ) {
    super.visitCompositeCardSource(pCompositeCardSource);
  }
}
```

Insights

This chapter introduced inversion of control as a way to separate the management of stateful information from the viewing of this information. Inversion of control is the principle behind the OBSERVER pattern which, in turn, is the key mechanism that enables the development of graphical user interface frameworks.

- Avoid PAIRWISE DEPENDENCIES† to keep state synchronized between objects;
- Consider separating the code responsible for storing data from the code responsible for viewing this data from the code responsible for changing the data (the Model–View–Controller decomposition);
- To decrease the coupling between views and model, consider using the OBSERVER pattern, which promotes inversion of control for updating views;
- With an application of the OBSERVER, the model class can be used without any observer, and generally does not depend on the specific types of any observer that observes it;
- In the OBSERVER, the model aggregates a number of abstract observers. The abstract observer is an interface that is implemented by the concrete observers;
- The abstract observer interface should define one or more callback methods that map to state-changing events in the model;
- The model needs to notify observers when it changes its state, but when to issue that notification is a design decision;
- There are two strategies for exchanging data between a model and its observers: push or pull. These strategies can be combined;
- Callback methods can be thought of as *events* to support a type of *event-based programming*. In this case, models are the event source and observers are the event handlers;
- An abstract observer can define multiple callbacks. Abstract observer interfaces can also be split up in smaller observer interfaces to afford more flexibility in defining how observers can respond to events;
- If it is often the case that observers implement callbacks by doing nothing, consider using adapter classes or default methods;
- A GUI application is built by instantiating an application skeleton provided by the GUI framework. Application code to extend and customize the framework can be separated into two categories: component graph construction and event handling;

- It can be useful to think of the GUI component graph from three different perspectives: user experience, source code, and run time;
- The component graph must be instantiated before the user interface becomes visible. In JavaFX this instantiation is triggered in the `start` method of the application class;
- You can inherit from component classes of the GUI framework to create custom graphical components that can be added to an application's GUI component graph;
- To make a GUI application interactive, it is necessary to define handlers for GUI events that originate from different objects in the component graph. Handlers are defined as observers of objects in the component graph;
- Handlers can be defined as function objects, or the handling can be delegated to objects of the component graph.
- Consider using the VISITOR pattern to allow extending an object structure with an open-ended set of operations, without requiring modification to the interface of the classes that define this object structure.

Further Reading

As for the other patterns, the Gang of Four book [6] has the original treatment of the OBSERVER and VISITOR patterns.

In the book *Patterns of Enterprise Application Architecture* [4], Fowler provides a description of the Model–View–Controller as a web presentation pattern. The book *Pattern-Oriented Software Architecture Volume 4: A Pattern Language for Distributed Computing* [2] presents it as a pattern for software architecture, and integrates it into a general system of patterns for designing distributed applications.

It is possible to find extensive additional information on the JavaFX framework on the websites of Java technology providers, and in particular Oracle and Open-JDK.

Chapter 9
Functional Design

Concepts and Principles: Behavior parameterization, first-class function, higher-order function, functional programming, functional interface, lambda expression, method reference, stream, map–reduce;
Patterns and Antipatterns: STRATEGY, COMMAND.

Object-oriented design offers valuable principles and techniques for structuring data and computation. However, alternative ways to structure software can also be leveraged when designing applications. This chapter provides an introduction to a style of design that uses the function as its primary building block. With functional-style design, structuring the code is achieved through the use of higher-order functions, that is, functions that take other functions as argument. To use higher-order functions requires the programming language to provide support for functions as a first-class program entity. This chapter provides an overview of the Java mechanisms that support functional-style programming and how to use them to integrate elements of functional style into the design of an overall application.

Design Context

The design problems considered in this chapter focus on the processing of collections of objects to represent playing cards. Problems include sorting a collection of cards, comparing cards, filtering cards, and computing various aggregate values about a collection of cards. We will also revisit the implementation of the CardSource interface introduced in Section 3.1.

© Springer Nature Switzerland AG 2022
M. P. Robillard, *Introduction to Software Design with Java*,
https://doi.org/10.1007/978-3-030-97899-0_9

9.1 First-Class Functions

Up to now, we have applied most software design principles by organizing data
and computation in terms of classes and objects, and interactions between them.
This is consistent with the object-oriented programming paradigm. There are, however, situations where the use of objects to realize a design solution seems a bit
contrived. We have already seen an example of such a situation in Section 3.4,
which introduced function objects. For example, to sort a list of cards, the library method `Collections#sort(...)` requires as input an argument of type
`Comparator<Card>` whose sole purpose is to provide an implementation of the
method `compare(Card, Card)`.[1] We can provide this argument by creating a function object that is an instance of an anonymous class:

```
List<Card> cards = ...;
Collections.sort(cards, new Comparator<Card>() {
  public int compare(Card pCard1, Card pCard2) {
    return pCard1.getRank().compareTo(pCard2.getRank());
  }
});
```

The reason the code above is contrived is that, from a software design point
of view, what the `sort` method needs is only the desired comparison behavior for
cards, yet what we actually supply is a reference to an object, something generally
understood as an assembly of data and methods to operate on this data. There is thus
a conceptual mismatch between the design goal and the programming mechanism
employed to fulfill it. The design goal is to *parameterize the behavior* of the `sort`
method, and the mechanism we use to do this is to *pass a reference to an object*.
What would be a better fit, would be for the `sort` method to take in as input the
desired sorting function directly.

Providing functions as input to other functions, however, requires the programming language to allow this by supporting *first-class functions*. This essentially
means treating functions as values that can be passed as argument, stored in variables, and returned by other functions.

Since version 8, Java supports a syntax which, in practice, emulates first-class
functions. For example, we could define a function in class `Card` that compares two
cards by rank:

```
public class Card {
  public static int compareByRank(Card pCard1, Card pCard2) {
    return pCard1.getRank().compareTo(pCard2.getRank());
  }
}
```

and supply a reference to this function as the second argument to method `sort`:

```
Collections.sort(cards, Card::compareByRank);
```

---

[1] In this chapter, the term *function* is used as a general abstraction of computation. In Java, the term
would refer to both static and instance methods.

This code, which compiles and does what we want, is actually syntactic sugar that gives the illusion of first-class functions but actually converts the method reference `Card::compare` into an instance of `Comparator<Card>`. The syntax and detailed behavior of the code above is described in Section 9.2. The implications of being able to design with first-class functions is significant. They are a major design tool which, in some cases, allows us to consider design solutions that make the intent behind the solution clearer, reduce clutter in the code, and help reuse code more effectively.

With first-class functions, it becomes possible to design functions that take other functions as arguments. Such functions are called *higher-order functions*. In a way, when considering the above code from a functional point of view, we can say that `Collections#sort` is a higher-order function. In some contexts, it is possible to build entire applications from the principled use of higher-order functions. In such cases, we would say that the application is designed in the *functional programming paradigm*. Using higher-order functions does not, by itself, mean that an application's entire design becomes *functional*. Functional programming is a much more comprehensive paradigm whereby computation is organized by transforming data, ideally without mutating state.

Functional programming, even in the limited context of the Java language, is a major topic whose detailed treatment is outside the scope of this book. There are good references available for learning about the ins and outs of functional programming features in Java and beyond (see Further Reading). The goal of this chapter is to provide enough of an introduction to basic functional programming features to allow the integration of functional elements into an otherwise object-oriented design. First-class functions support a whole new level of versatility for exploring the design space, realizing design principles, and applying design patterns. For this reason, it is important to know about functional-*style* programming even if we are not building an application strictly in the functional paradigm. This being said, the last part of the chapter introduces the map–reduce programming model, which will take us as close to full-fledged functional programming as we will get in this book.

9.2 Functional Interfaces, Lambda Expressions, and Method References

The three mechanisms that enable first-class functions in Java are functional interfaces, lambda expressions, and method references.

Functional Interfaces

In Java, a *functional interface* is an interface type that declares a single abstract method. For example, we could define an interface to represent *filtering* behavior for a collection of cards:

```
public interface Filter {
  boolean accept(Card pCard);
}
```

Except for the constraint that they must only have one abstract method, there is nothing special about functional interfaces. We can declare classes to implement them as usual. For example, we can use an anonymous class to define a filter that only accepts cards with a black suit (Spades or Clubs);

```
Filter blackCardFilter = new Filter() {
  public boolean accept(Card pCard) {
    return pCard.getSuit().getColor() == Suit.Color.BLACK;
  }
};
```

This example shows how the functional interface `Filter` defines a small slice of behavior, an idea introduced in Section 3.2. In the context of functional-style programming, functional interfaces serve another important purpose, though: they define a *function type*. The idea of a function type basically goes as follows. If we forget about the implicit parameter for a second, we can consider method `accept` of interface `Filter` to be a function that takes as parameter a `Card` instance and returns a `boolean`. Thus, we have a function of type `Card` $\rightarrow$ `boolean`. Now, because our `Filter` interface only defines a single abstract method, implementing this interface amounts to supplying the implementation for this single function. With a bit of imagination, we can consider that obtaining an instance of `Filter` is equivalent to obtaining an implementation of a method that takes as argument a reference to a `Card` instance and returns a `boolean`. Hence, functional interfaces can play the role of function types.

The use of the word *abstract* in the definition of a functional interface is important. Starting with version 8 of the language, interfaces in Java can define static and default methods. Because an implementation for such methods is provided directly in the interface, implementing types are not required to provide one. Static and default methods are thus, by definition, not abstract. This means that an interface can define multiple methods, and still qualify as a functional interface if only one of them is abstract. An example of such an interface is `Comparator<T>` (see Section 3.4). The `Comparator<T>` interface defines numerous static and default methods, whose purpose is going to become clear later in this chapter. However, the interface defines a single abstract method: `compare(T,T):int` (where `T` is a type parameter). For this reason, `Comparator` is a functional interface that defines the function type `(T,T)` $\rightarrow$ `int`. The implication for functional-style programming is that we are able to treat instances of `Comparator<T>` as first-class functions.

With functional-style programming, Java 8 introduced a library of convenient functional interfaces, located in package `java.util.function`. These interfaces provide the most common function types, such as `Function<T,R>`, a generic type that can represent the type of any unary function between reference types.[2] The interface has a single method `apply`.

---

[2] There are equivalent interfaces to represent functions that involve primitive types, such as `IntFunction<R>`.

To use a library type instead of our custom `Filter` interface, we use the functional interface `Predicate<T>`, which represents the type of a function with a single argument of type `T` and returns a `boolean`.[3] The name of the abstract method for `Predicate<T>` is `test(T)`. We can thus rewrite the code above as follows:

```
Predicate<Card> blackCardFilter = new Predicate<Card>() {
   public boolean test(Card pCard) {
      return pCard.getSuit().getColor() == Suit.Color.BLACK;
   }
};
```

Because they define function types, functional interfaces serve as the basis for all functional-style design in Java.

Lambda Expressions

With functional interfaces, we get one step closer to being able to program with first-class functions. However, with anonymous classes, specifying the behavior of our example function still has a definite object-oriented look. If we recall our implementation of the *black cards* predicate, above:

```
Predicate<Card> blackCardFilter = new Predicate<Card>() { ... };
```

The use of the `new` keyword in the definition of the behavior of our predicate betrays the fact that we are still creating an object. To more directly express our design in terms of a first-class function, we can define the implementation of a functional interface as a *lambda expression*. Lambda expressions are a compact form of expression of functional behavior whose name is derived from the term *lambda calculus*, a mathematical system for expressing computation. In Java, lambda expressions are basically anonymous functions. They were briefly introduced in Section 3.4. Now we can take a second look at them in the context of functional-style programming. To convert our example to use a lambda expression, we would write:

```
Predicate<Card> blackCardFilter =
   (Card card) > card.getSuit().getColor() == Suit.Color.BLACK;
```

The syntax of lambda expressions is detailed below, but for now it is sufficient to know that the function parameter is declared on the left of the arrow (`->`), and the expression on the right of the arrow represents the body of the function. Although this code has the same effect as using an anonymous class, the syntax no longer makes use of the `new` keyword. In addition to being more compact, the code makes it more obvious that what we are trying to achieve is to initialize `blackCardFilter` with *behavior* (a function) as opposed to *data* (an object). We can also say that the function is *anonymous* because no function name appears in its declaration. From a

---

[3] In contrast to `Function<T,R>`, `Predicate<T>` has a single type parameter because the return type is implied by the interface. The function type that corresponds to `Predicate<T>` is thus $T \rightarrow boolean$. We could also specify our filter interface as `Function<Card, Boolean>`, but this option is less efficient because it relies on autoboxing.

design point of view, we do not care about the actual name of the function because it will get called polymorphically through the name of the method in the functional interface. Because functional interfaces are intended to be reused, the name of the method they define tends to be very general, and so it carries little information about what the method does. In our example, the method in the `Predicate<T>` functional interface is `test(T)`: this says nothing about the actual behavior of our lambda expression (which is to return `true` if the suit of the card is black). Information about the behavior of the lambda expression is typically the code of the lambda expression itself or, at best, an informative variable name (as above). In Java, lambda expressions are not typically documented with a header comment.

The syntax of lambda expressions comprises three parts: a list of parameters, a right arrow (the characters `->`), and a body. In the example above, the list of parameters is `(Card card)`. When the lambda expression requires no parameter, we simply provide an empty set of parentheses `()->`. The body of the lambda expression can take one of two forms:

- a single expression (e.g., `a == 1`).
- a block of one or more statements (e.g., `{return a == 1;}`).

In the `blackCardFilter` example, the definition of the body of the lambda expression uses the first option. Because, given the functional interface, the return type is expected to be `boolean` and the expression evaluates to a Boolean value, the use of the `return` keyword is superfluous and can be assumed to be the result of the evaluation. Using the `return` keyword would turn the expression into a statement, thus breaking the syntax. It is worth noting how expressing the body of a lambda as an expression does not require a semicolon after the expression. In the `blackCardFilter` example, the final semicolon terminates the entire assignment statement, not the lambda expression. Let us rewrite the lambda expression to express the body as a block:

```
Predicate<Card> blackCards =
  (Card card) ->
    { return card.getSuit().getColor() == Suit.Color.BLACK; };
```

This code does exactly the same thing as previously. However, because the body of the lambda expression is no longer a single expression, we need to add curly braces around the block that consists of a single statement, use the `return` keyword to indicate what we are returning, and terminate the statement within the block with a semicolon. As can be seen, the first form (using an expression) is more compact. Normally, when we write lambda expressions, we define them as expressions whenever possible and, when the computation is complex and we need multiple statements, fall back on defining them as a block.

Behind the scenes, lambda expressions are checked by the compiler and turned into function objects through a process of inference. Essentially, when the Java compiler sees a lambda expression, it tries to match it to a functional interface. In the code above, the right-hand side of the assignment is a lambda expression. The compiler will thus look for the type of the variable to which this lambda is assigned to make sure everything matches, namely:

- The type of the variable is a functional interface;
- The parameter types of the lambda expression are compatible with those of the functional interface;
- The type of the value returned by the body of the lambda expression is compatible with that of the abstract method of the functional interface.

The compiler can actually do a bit more than check the code for correctness: it can also *infer* some information about it. Because the types of the parameters of the function implemented by the lambda expression are already encoded in the definition of the abstract method in the corresponding functional interface, it is not necessary to repeat them in the declaration of the lambda expression. To make our code more compact, we could also omit the optional declaration of parameter type `Card`:

```
Predicate<Card> blackCardFilter =
  (card) -> card.getSuit().getColor() == Suit.Color.BLACK;
```

In fact, if the function type takes a single parameter, we can even omit the parentheses around the parameter:

```
Predicate<Card> blackCardFilter =
  card -> card.getSuit().getColor() == Suit.Color.BLACK;
```

Whether or not to include parameter types in the declaration of a lambda expression is a matter of style. However, it is good to keep in mind that they can help make the code more readable. When types are provided, a compact variable name becomes more acceptable. For example, we could rewrite the above as:

```
Predicate<Card> blackCardFilter =
  (Card c) -> c.getSuit().getColor() == Suit.Color.BLACK;
```

Essentially, lambda expressions are an idiom used to instantiate functional interfaces, just like anonymous classes. As such, the single method implemented through a lambda expression is called like any other method. For example, to count the number of black cards in an instance of `Deck`, we could do (assuming the `Deck` is iterable):

```
Deck deck = ...
Predicate<Card> blackCardFilter =
  card -> card.getSuit().getColor() == Suit.Color.BLACK;
int total = 0;
for( Card card : deck ) {
  if( blackCardFilter.test(card) ) {
    total++;
  }
}
```

Lambda expressions are also a good match for providing behavior in-place when required by library or application functions. For example, the method `removeIf` of class `ArrayList` takes a single argument of type `Predicate<T>` and removes all elements in the `ArrayList` for which the predicate is true. Given an `ArrayList` of `Card`, we can remove all black cards from the list with a single call:

```
ArrayList<Card> cards = ...
cards.removeIf(
  card -> card.getSuit().getColor() == Suit.Color.BLACK);
```

Method References

Lambda expressions are especially useful when we need to supply custom behavior not defined anywhere else. However, it is also common that one part of the code requires behavior that is already implemented. Let us consider a slight variant of the design of the `Card` class where the class includes the definition of the helper method:

```
public final class Card {
  public boolean hasBlackSuit() {
    return aSuit.getColor() == Color.BLACK;
  }
}
```

If, as above, we are writing some code to delete all back cards from an `ArrayList`:

```
ArrayList<Card> cards = ...
cards.removeIf(
  card -> card.getSuit().getColor() == Suit.Color.BLACK);
```

then we are essentially rewriting the code of method `Card.hasBlackSuit`. This does not look so bad here because the code is tiny. However, the reasoning would become more compelling for a larger piece of code (for example, code with a compound condition). In any case, writing a solution we have already coded is an example of DUPLICATED CODE†, which it is a good idea to avoid whenever possible. One solution is to call the helper method within the lambda:

```
cards.removeIf(card -> card.hasBlackSuit());
```

This is better, but what we really want in the present scenario is to reuse our method `hasBlackSuit` as a first-class function. In other words, we want to pass a reference to `hasBlackSuit` as an argument to method `removeIf`. We can do just that with *method references*. In Java, method references are indicated with a double colon expression `P::m` where `m` refers to the name of the method of interest and `P` is a prefix that can take different forms. In our case, `P` refers to the class in which the method is defined. Thus, `Card::hasBlackSuit` refers to method `hasBlackSuit` of class `Card`. With this method reference, we can rewrite our code as:

```
cards.removeIf(Card::hasBlackSuit);
```

It hardly gets more compact and explicit than that: the code almost reads like plain English.

Using method references in Java is not trivial, though, because there are different ways to refer to a method. In the code above, we have used a *reference to an instance method of an arbitrary object of a particular type*. In this scenario, the argument of the call to the method of the functional interface is bound to the implicit parameter of the method reference. This can be seen from the lambda equivalent `card -> card.hasBlackSuit()`. There are other ways in which the compiler can match method references to functional interfaces.

Another way is to use a *reference to a static method*. For example, we could also have the following static method in some utility class:

```
public final class CardUtils {
  public static boolean hasBlackSuit(Card pCard) {
    return pCard.getSuit().getColor() != Color.BLACK;
  }
}
```

and use a reference to that method instead:

```
cards.removeIf(CardUtils::hasBlackSuit);
```

Although the method reference looks exactly the same as the instance method, the compiler uses the reference in a different way. In this case, the method reference is interpreted as:

```
cards.removeIf( card -> CardUtils.hasBlackSuit(card));
```

As we see, in this case, the argument is bound to the explicit parameter of the method reference.

Java also supports supplying a *reference to an instance method of a particular object*, using the notation `o::m` where `o` is an expression that evaluates to a reference to an object and `m` is the method. For example, let us assume that our `Deck` class has a method `topSameColorAs(Card)` which returns `true` if the argument is of the same color as the card at the top of the deck. To remove all cards in the list whose color is the same as the card at the top of the deck, we would do:

```
Deck deck = new Deck();
...
cards.removeIf(deck::topSameColorAs);
```

In this case, the `Card` argument would be matched to the *explicit* argument of the instance method of `Deck` that is called on a *specified* instance of deck. The equivalent lambda expression is:

```
cards.removeIf(card -> deck.topSameColorAs(card));
```

Finally, an important aspect of method references is that they do not have to match their corresponding functional interface *exactly*. Technically, a method reference only needs to be *compatible* with its required assignment, invocation, or casting context (see Section 9.4 for an example). How the compiler correctly determines what to do is outside the scope of this book. However, it is important to know that method references support using both static and instance methods as first-class functions, and that the mapping between the reference and the interface method is based on the parameter and return types.[4] In our case, both `Card::hasBlackSuit`, `CardUtils::hasBlackSuit`, and `deck::topSameColorAs` return a `boolean` and

---

[4] It is also possible to use method references to refer to constructors and array initializers: see Further Reading.

take as input a single parameter of type Card. In the case of the *instance method of a given type* (Card::hasBlackSuit), the parameter is the implicit parameter of the method; In the case of the *static method* (CardUtils::hasBlackSuit), the parameter is the explicit parameter of the method; In the case of the *instance method of a particular object*, the parameter is also the explicit parameter of the method, whose implicit object is specified in the method reference. In all cases, the function type is Card → boolean and the reference can thus be assigned to a variable of type Predicate<Card>.

9.3 Using Functions to Compose Behavior

First-class functions make it possible to define small pieces of behavior, such as to filter or compare objects. Taking this idea further, we can use the principle of divide and conquer to express more complex behavior in terms of simpler behavior. Let us consider the problem of comparing two cards, introduced in Section 3.4. Using a lambda expression, we can define the behavior of the comparison using the Comparator<Card> interface as follows:

```
public class Card {
  public static Comparator<Card> bySuitComparator() {
    return (card1, card2) ->
      card1.getSuit().compareTo(card2.getSuit());
  }
}
```

This design uses a static factory method to return a comparator object that compares two cards in terms of their suit, as defined by the declaration order in the enumerated type Suit. Because we use a lambda expression, the code expresses the solution more in terms of a first-class function than a function object.

This solution is incomplete because if two cards have the same suit, their relative order is undefined, which is not ideal for many card sorting contexts. To complete the solution, we need to specify a secondary comparison order by rank. One way to do this would be to extend the code of the lambda expression:

```
public static Comparator<Card> bySuitThenRankComparator() {
  return (card1, card2) -> {
    if( card1.getSuit() == card2.getSuit() ) {
      return card1.getRank().compareTo(card2.getRank());
    }
    else {
      return card1.getSuit().compareTo(card2.getSuit());
    }
  };
}
```

This code supports a well-defined total order for cards, at the cost of a more complex lambda expression for which we need to resort to the less compact block form. This code is also less flexible, because if we wish to sort by rank, then suit instead, we

need to write an entirely new comparator that repeats most of the code, but with
the order of comparison switched. Moreover, if we want to sort in descending order
instead of ascending order for either rank or suit, we need to yet again rewrite the
code. Ultimately, we have eight options for a basic card comparator: by rank then
suit or suit then rank (two options), where either rank or suit can be ascending or
descending (times four options). To cover all possibilities with factory methods, we
would thus need eight factory methods, and plenty of DUPLICATED CODE†.

To work with finer abstractions, we could start by offering comparison in both
relative levels (suit, then rank, and rank, then suit) by creating two factories for
single-level comparison (rank or suit) and two additional factories for complete
comparisons, where the two complete orders are composed of the single-level comparisons by suit and rank.

```java
public static Comparator<Card> byRankComparator() {
  return (card1, card2) ->
    card1.getRank().compareTo(card2.getRank());
}

public static Comparator<Card> bySuitComparator() {
  return (card1, card2) ->
    card1.getSuit().compareTo(card2.getSuit());
}

public static Comparator<Card> byRankThenSuitComparator() {
  return (card1, card2) -> {
    if( byRankComparator().compare(card1, card2) == 0 ) {
      return bySuitComparator().compare(card1, card2 );
    }
    else {
      return byRankComparator().compare(card1, card2 );
    }
  };
}

public static Comparator<Card> bySuitThenRankComparator() {
  return (card1, card2) -> {
    if( bySuitComparator().compare(card1, card2) == 0 ) {
      return byRankComparator().compare(card1, card2 );
    }
    else {
      return bySuitComparator().compare(card1, card2 );
    }
  };
}
```

Unfortunately, without extra help, this idea does not mitigate the complexity of
the composite function (and does not even cover the option to reverse the order of
either suit- or rank-based ordering). The way out of this situation is the insight that
if we want to express a solution in terms of first-class functions, we can also use
functions to do the composition. In the case of functions to express comparisons,
the Comparator interface provides many static and default methods intended to

compose comparison functions out of smaller abstractions. Let us try to rewrite our solution to the problem of supporting the comparison of cards by either rank, then suit, or suit, then rank, in ascending or descending order, using these helper methods. We will proceed bottom up, from the smaller abstractions to the more complex ones.

A first key method is comparing(...). The signature of this method is a bit complex but, essentially, comparing(...) creates a comparator by building on a function that extracts a comparable from its input argument. For example, we could rewrite byRankComparator() as:

```
public static Comparator<Card> byRankComparator() {
   return Comparator.comparing(card -> card.getRank());
}
```

and similarly for bySuitComparator. How exactly the method comparing works is explained in the next section. For now, it is sufficient to understand the behavior intuitively: the argument to the method is itself a function that extracts the value we want to compare on, and the return value is a comparator structure. The resulting behavior is identical to the original solution using the direct comparison between Rank instances.

The second major service available in class Comparator is a method to cascade comparisons (for example to compare by suit if the rank is the same, or vice versa). This functionality is provided by the method thenComparing. This method is a default method called on a comparator that takes as input another comparator for the same type.[5] With thenComparing, we can express our cascaded comparison more directly:

```
public static Comparator<Card> byRankThenSuitComparator() {
   return byRankComparator().thenComparing(bySuitComparator());
}
```

We can observe how this code is already much more explicit about the intent of the computation than the version above, which explicitly does the cascading of comparisons. Inversing the comparison levels then becomes a question of inversing the order of the comparators in the call chain:

```
public static Comparator<Card> bySuitThenRankComparator() {
   return bySuitComparator().thenComparing(byRankComparator());
}
```

The final step required to complete our solution is to provide a way to reverse the comparison order, from ascending to descending and vice-versa. For example, this would mean going from either ace to king or from king to ace for the rank comparison (assuming ace is the first card in the sequence, called an ace-low sequence). To accomplish this without helper methods, we would need to go back to our basic implementation of comparators and switch the order of the arguments:

```
public static Comparator<Card> byRankComparatorReversed() {
   return (card1, card2) ->
     card2.getRank().compareTo(card1.getRank());
}
```

---

[5] Or a super type, although this eventuality is not covered here.

In the code above, the order of the two parameters in the body of the lambda expression are reversed. Expressing this difference requires a different factory. Fortunately, it is possible to avoid this DUPLICATED CODE† thanks to the helper method reversed(), which creates a new comparator that orders elements using the reverse of the order used by the implicit argument of reversed(). We can then use reversed() to reverse either or both of the comparison levels. For example, to sort by descending suit, then ascending rank, we create a comparator factory as follows

```
public static Comparator<Card>
  bySuitReversedThenRankComparator() {
    return bySuitComparator()
      .reversed()
      .thenComparing(byRankComparator());
}
```

Similarly, to sort by descending suit, then descending rank:

```
public static Comparator<Card>
  bySuitReversedThenRankReversedComparator() {
    return bySuitComparator()
      .reversed()
      .thenComparing(byRankComparator()
        .reversed());
}
```

At this point, we can express all eight possible comparison orders simply by combining functions with the help of other functions. The resulting code is so straightforward to understand that the abstraction benefit gained by encapsulating comparators in a factory method becomes marginal. In the last code fragment above, the name of the factory method is basically the list of steps directly visible in the function call chain in the body of the method. For this reason, here it would make sense to get rid of the factory methods for the comparators.

Because the only part of the Card interface needed to define the comparison behavior is already available through the getter methods getSuit() and getRank(), the factory methods are not strictly necessary. Removing the comparator factories from the interface of class Card helps mitigate the threats of SPECULATIVE GENERALITY†, namely to provide services that are never used. With the helper methods of Comparator, developers will be able to provide compact and explicit definitions of the desired comparison behavior directly where needed. For example, if a code location requires sorting cards by descending order of suit, then rank, the following code could be used:[6]

```
List<Card> cards = ...
cards.sort(Comparator.comparing((Card card) -> card.getSuit())
    .reversed()
    .thenComparing(Comparator.comparing(
      (Card card) -> card.getRank())
        .reversed()));
```

---

[6] In this context the parameter types must be supplied as part of the lambda expression because the compiler does not have enough information to infer them.

Although this code is already explicit, there are three significant ways in which we can further improve it. First, we can use Java's static import feature to eliminate the need to qualify the static methods:

```
import static java.util.Comparator.comparing;
```

This allows us to remove the qualification of the static method `comparing`:

```
cards.sort(comparing((Card card) -> card.getSuit())
    .reversed()
    .thenComparing(comparing((Card card) -> card.getRank())
      .reversed()));
```

Second, as explained in Section 9.2, we can use method references to refer to `getSuit()` and `getRank()` instead of redefining a lambda expression that simply calls them.

```
cards.sort(comparing(Card::getSuit)
    .reversed()
    .thenComparing(comparing(Card::getRank)
      .reversed()));
```

Finally, we can observe that class `Comparator` has an overloaded version of `then-Comparing` that combines the behavior of `comparing` and `thenComparing` by directly taking a function that returns the value of the key we wish to use for comparison. In this case we can move the reversal of the comparison to the final comparator. Our code can thus be reduced to:

```
cards.sort(comparing(Card::getSuit)
  .thenComparing(Card::getRank)
  .reversed());
```

This general principle of leveraging library functions to compose first-class functions can be used in a variety of contexts, so before writing Java code that uses first-class functions as abstractions, it is worthwhile to study the options possible. Most of the functional interfaces provided in package `java.util.function` include some static or default helper methods that can be used to compose other functions. For example, returning to our definition of a `Predicate` for filtering black cards (see Section 9.2):

```
Predicate<Card> blackCardFilter =
  card -> card.getSuit().getColor() == Suit.Color.BLACK;
```

If we want only red cards, we can do:[7]

```
Predicate<Card> redCardFilter = blackCardFilter.negate();
```

---

[7] This assumes there are only two colors, which is true in this case and for a standard deck of cards.

9.4 Using Functions to Supply, Consume, and Map Objects

In Section 9.1, I presented how first-class functions can be used to parameterize the behavior of a higher-order function. Another way to think about this design feature is that first-class functions allow us to specify some processing behavior but to *defer* its execution to the point where it is required. In this section I discuss examples of three common types of deferred processing: *supplying* an object, *consuming* an object, and *mapping* an object to another object.

Let us start with the problem of defining an implementation of `CardSource` (introduced in Section 3.1) that can provide an *infinite* number of cards:

```java
public class InfiniteCardSource implements CardSource {
  public Card draw() {
    // Return a card.
  }

  public boolean isEmpty() {
    return false;
  }
}
```

How can we return an infinite number of cards? Clearly, it will not be possible to initialize the card source with all of the different cards to return, because there will be an infinity of them. One potential solution is to initialize `InfiniteCardSource` with a STRATEGY that is a *card factory*. In our context, a card factory is any function that can return a `Card` object. In Section 3.7 we saw how to implement this idiom in pure object-oriented style. I now present a variant of the solution that uses the concepts seen in this chapter. The Java class library conveniently provides a functional interface to capture the behavior of a method responsible for returning an object: `Supplier<T>`. Its method `get` takes no argument and returns a value of type `T`, the type argument of the `Supplier<T>` interface. In our case we replace the type parameter with the concrete type `Card` to yield the function type $() \rightarrow Card$. A basic supplier-based solution would look like this:

```java
public class InfiniteCardSource implements CardSource {
  private final Supplier<Card> aCardSupplier;

  public InfiniteCardSource(Supplier<Card> pCardSupplier) {
    aCardSupplier = pCardSupplier;
  }

  public Card draw() {
    return aCardSupplier.get();
  }

  public boolean isEmpty() {
    return false;
  }
}
```

With this class, we can now easily create various kinds of infinite card sources. For example, we could define a static method `random()` on class `Card`, which returns a random card, and do:

```
InfiniteCardSource randomCardSource =
  new InfiniteCardSource(Card::random);
```

As another example, we could also create an infinite source of Ace of Hearts cards:

```
InfiniteCardSource aceOfHearts =
  new InfiniteCardSource(()-> Card.get(Rank.ACE, Suit.HEARTS));
```

The key insight to observe from this demonstration is that, conceptually, what we are handling are functions to *obtain* objects, as opposed to the required objects themselves. This allows us to *defer* the execution of the factory method until the very point where the object is required.

A similar idea can be used to create designs where we wish to parameterize how a certain object is used, or *consumed*. As an example, we will design a `ConsumingDecorator` which executes some parameterized behavior whenever a card is drawn from a `CardSource` (see Section 6.4 to review the design of a DECORATOR). In this case, we need to parameterize what will happen to the card being drawn. This requires a function type $Card \rightarrow void$, which can be realized by invoking the generic functional interface `Consumer<T>`, which has the abstract function `accept(T)` which returns `void`.

```
public class ConsumingDecorator implements CardSource {
  private final CardSource aSource;
  private final Consumer<Card> aCardConsumer;

  public ConsumingDecorator(CardSource pSource,
    Consumer<Card> pCardConsumer) {
    aSource = pSource;
    aCardConsumer = pCardConsumer;
  }

  public Card draw() {
    Card card = aSource.draw();
    aCardConsumer.accept(card);
    return card;
  }

  public boolean isEmpty() {
    return aSource.isEmpty();
  }
}
```

As can be seen from the implementation of `draw`, we are parameterizing our class with behavior that is executed only at the specific point where it is needed, namely when a card is drawn. The following code shows how we can use a `ConsumingDecorator` to create a `Deck` that prints every card drawn to the console:

```
CardSource source = new ConsumingDecorator(new Deck(),
  System.out::println);
```

In this example, the first argument is an instance of `Deck` (a concrete subtype of `CardSource`), and the second argument is our consumer of `Card` objects. The argument is a *reference to an instance method of a particular object*, namely the method `println(Object)` of the library static field `System.out` (of class `Printstream`), which is the standard mechanism for printing to the console. The code thus provides an example of a case where a method reference is matched to a functional interface with a compatible, but not identical, function type (see Section 9.2). In our case, we are supplying a method of type `Object` $\rightarrow$ `void` to a context that requires `Card` $\rightarrow$ `void`. This assignment is compatible because, according to the rules of the type system, it is safe for the type of a method argument to be *more specific* that the type of the formal parameter.[8]

Supplier and consumer functions support one-way deferred data flow. Naturally, there can also be situations where we need to both consume and supply a value. The generic function type that captures this requirement is $T \rightarrow R$, and it is supported by the functional interface `Function<T,R>` (introduced in Section 9.2). Another way to understand this behavior is that we need a function that *maps* an object of type `T` into an object of type `R`. As it turns out, we have already used this mechanism.

The static method `Comparator#comparing`, presented in the previous section, requires as input a `Function` called a *key extractor*. If we want to build a comparator that compares `Card` objects based on their suit, we do:

```
Comparator<Card> bySuit = Comparator.comparing(Card::getSuit);
```

The argument to `comparing` is an instance of `Function<Card,Suit>`, an invocation of the functional interface `Function<T,R>` whose method `apply` takes an argument of type `Card` and returns a reference to an object of type `Suit`. This means that the code that implements method `comparing` will have a way to *map* an instance of `Suit` from an instance of `Card` whenever necessary in the logic of the method's implementation. Let us explore how the method works. The code below is a slightly simplified version of the actual implementation of `comparing` as instantiated for the `Card` and `Suit` type parameters:

```
public static Comparator<Card> comparing(
  Function<Card, Suit> keyExtractor) {
    return (card1, card2) -> keyExtractor.apply(card1)
      .compareTo(keyExtractor.apply(card2));
}
```

A sample use of this code is as follows:

```
Comparator<Card> comparator =
  Comparator.comparing(Card::getSuit());
comparator.compare(card1,card2);
```

When `comparing` is called, it creates a new function object that binds `Card::getSuit` to `keyExtractor`, but without calling either `apply` or its delegate `getSuit`.

---

[8] In consequence, a reference to `println` can be used when a `Consumer` is expected. For example, the default library interface method `Iterable#forEach` takes a `Consumer` as input. Hence, to print all elements in an iterable, we can simply call `forEach(System.out::println)` on that iterable.

That is, `comparing` uses the function as a building block when creating a new function. Similarly to how we used suppliers and consumers, above, this indirection is necessary because the comparison behavior needs to be executed on-demand *within* the `compare` method. Hence, when method `compare` is called, only then is `apply` called, this time twice, once for each card. Because `apply` delegates to `getSuit`, at that point the suit value is obtained from the card and used in the comparison. Figure 9.1 illustrates the complete sequence.

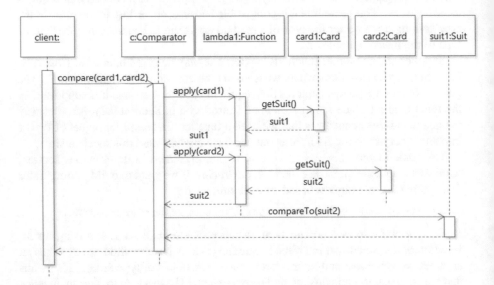

Fig. 9.1 Sequence of calls for comparing two cards using a comparator created with `Comparator#comparing`

Code Exploration: JetUML · Property

Using suppliers and consumers to define general properties.

In JetUML, diagram elements have different *properties*. For example, a class node in a class diagram has *name*, *attributes*, and *methods* properties. A `Property` object represents a property value, but does not *store* the value. Instead, an instance of `Property` acts as *proxy* for obtaining and supplying a value stored in a different object (typically, a `DiagramElement` object). A `Property` object thus has a field of type `Supplier<Object>` that it uses to *get* the value from the host object, and a field of type `Consumer<Object>` to *set* the value within the host object. Properties are created in method `buildProperties()` of the different `DiagramElement` subtypes, and used by class `PropertySheet`.

9.5 First-Class Functions and Design Patterns

Many design patterns rely on polymorphism to enable variation points in the solution. For example, the STRATEGY pattern relies on polymorphism to allow client code to dispatch the execution of an algorithm to a dynamically selected variant (see Section 3.7). Similarly, the OBSERVER pattern relies on polymorphism to allow a subject to notify observers whose exact nature is also determined at run time (see Section 8.3). In the original object-oriented description of the design patterns, this polymorphism is enabled by extending classes and implementing interfaces.

In functional-style design, first-class functions provide a different perspective on behavior parameterization. Instead of creating objects of different classes and enabling polymorphism through a common supertype, we can define families of functions whose type is compatible and invoke them interchangeably. This is possible in any context, but it is interesting to note that first-class functions allow a re-thinking of the implementation of design patterns. By way of illustration, in this section I revisit the implementation of the STRATEGY and OBSERVER patterns using a functional style.

Functional-Style STRATEGY

In simple cases where strategies are stateless and their interface boils down to a single method, we can express the abstract strategy as a functional interface. I have already illustrated this scenario in Section 9.4, by using the `Supplier<T>` interface as an abstract strategy for card factories.

As a different illustration, let us consider a context where client code can use diffcrent strategies for selecting a card in a list. Here, concrete strategies are implementations of method `apply` of interface `Function<List<Card>, Card>`, which becomes the abstract strategy. In our case, method `apply` takes as input a list of cards and returns a single card. As an example of a client class for the strategy, we could have:

```java
public class AutoPlayer {
  private Function<List<Card>, Card> aSelectionStrategy;

  public AutoPlayer(Function<List<Card>, Card> pSelectionStrategy)
  { aSelectionStrategy = pSelectionStrategy; }

  public void play() {
    Card selected = aSelectionStrategy.apply(getCards());
    ...
  }

  // Gets the cards to supply to the strategy
  private List<Card> getCards() {...}
}
```

In this design, the card selection strategy is provided as an argument to the constructor when the client `AutoPlayer` object is created. Because the strategy is a first-class function, defining it involves defining the behavior of this function at any convenient point in the code. One option could be to define it on the fly at the location where the instance of `AutoPlayer` is created. For example, a strategy to always select the first card would be:

```
AutoPlayer player = new AutoPlayer(cards -> cards.get(0));
```

For more elaborate strategies, another option could be to define a collection of common strategies in a utility class:

```
public final class CardSelection {
  private CardSelection() {}

  public static Card lowestBlackCard(List<Card> pCards) { ... }
  public static Card highestFaceCard(List<Card> pCards) { ... }
  ...
}
```

and use method references to select a strategy:

```
AutoPlayer player =
  new AutoPlayer(CardSelection::lowestBlackCard);
```

This implementation style is very compact, and even perhaps too much so. The use of the general `Function` functional interface in this context has two potential limitations. First, it has low documentation effectiveness. Looking at the type `Function<List<Card>, Card>`, all we know is that it can return a `Card` given a list of cards. For this reason, any reference to the card selection strategy needs to be done through well-named variables for the code to remain readable. Here, field `aSelectionStrategy` fulfills the requirement. A second problem is that the single method in the `Function` interface is also general-purpose, and for this reason cannot include any context-specific information. In our context, we need to determine how to handle the case where the list is empty. One possibility would be to redefine the strategy as `Function<List<Card>, Optional<Card>`, and somehow remember that by convention passing an empty list results in an empty optional object. Another possibility would be to state that the input list must not be empty is a precondition for the strategy. In both cases, it is not clear where one would document this critical piece of information.

For these reasons, defining an additional functional interface to represent the strategy will lead to clearer code and a more self-explicit design. The new interface can also be used to hold some standard strategies. The following code shows an implementation of a STRATEGY application for selecting cards that uses design by contract to guard against the case of selecting from an empty list and uses the `Optional` type to guard against the case where a strategy yields no card. Although in this case it would make sense to return `Optional.empty()` if the input list is also empty, both options are included for sake of illustration.

```
public interface CardSelectionStrategy {
  /**
   * Select an instance of Card from pCards.
   * @param A list of cards to choose from.
   * @pre pCards != null && !pCards.isEmpty()
   * @post If RETURN.isPresent(), pCards.contains(RETURN.get())
   */
  Optional<Card> select(List<Card> pCards);

  public static Optional<Card> first(List<Card> pCards) {
    return Optional.of(pCards.get(0));
  }

  public static Optional<Card> lowestBlackCard(List<Card> pCards)
  {...}

  public static Optional<Card> highestFaceCard(List<Card> pCards)
  {...}
}
```

Code Exploration: Solitaire · GreedyPlayingStrategy

Using method references to build a main strategy out of sub-strategies.

The Solitaire application provides an example of behavior composition using first-class functions in the definition of automatic playing strategies. One of the features of the application is to automatically play a move based on some heuristic when a user types the *Enter* key. However, in a game of Solitaire, there are often situations where multiple legal moves are possible. Class `GreedyPlayingStrategy` provides an implementation of the `PlayingStrategy` interface by defining a number of sub-strategies as static methods, where each sub-strategy is one type of move (e.g., to select a card from the deck, to move a card to a foundation pile, etc.). The overall strategy can then be reduced to the order in which substrategies are attempted. The meta-heuristic (high-level operation) implemented by the actual strategy method is to cycle through a collection of first-class functions that represent sub-strategies, apply them, and stop as soon as one strategy is successful (as determined by a non-empty value in the `Optional` return value).

Functional-Style OBSERVER

In the OBSERVER pattern, an *observable* object notifies its observer objects by calling their callback method(s). In contexts where we can define an abstract observer with a single callback, we can use functional-style design to create a compact application of the pattern.

As an example, we will create an `ObservableDeck` class that is essentially a version of `Deck` whose calls to method `draw()` can be observed. Using the push data-flow strategy, we want to notify observers every time a card is drawn from the deck, letting them know which card was drawn. The functional type for the callback is thus `Card` → `void`. This is exactly the functional type of `Consumer<Card>`, so we can use `Consumer<Card>` as our abstract observer interface:

```
public class ObservableDeck extends Deck {
  private Consumer<Card> aDrawHandler;

  public ObservableDeck(Consumer<Card> pDrawHandler) {
    aDrawHandler = pDrawHandler;
  }

  public Card draw() {
    Card card = super.draw();
    aDrawHandler.accept(card);
    return card;
  }
}
```

To create an observable deck, we instantiate the class with a function that implements the callback. For a basic logging feature, we could just use `println`:

```
ObservableDeck deck = new ObservableDeck(System.out::println);
```

With this code in place, extending the class to support observer to `shuffle()` events would simply be a matter of duplicating the design to support a second observer.

It is interesting to contrast the design of `ObservableDeck` with the design of the `ConsumingDecorator`, presented in Section 9.4. In light of the current discussion, it should become apparent that the `ConsumingDecorator` is essentially an observable `CardSource`. While the `ConsumingDecorator` used aggregation to attach an observer, the `ObservableDeck` used inheritance. The use of the `Consumer<Card>` interface, however, fulfills exactly the same role in both designs: to inject additional behavior that executes in response to an event in the life-cycle of the observable object.

Code Exploration: JetUML · EditorFrame

Using lambda expressions to define event handlers.

In JavaFX, the interface used to represent handlers of different GUI events is a functional interface. This decision enables using lambda expression to define concrete observers (that is, event handlers). JetUML makes extensive use of lambda expressions to define event handlers in classes of package `...gui`. Class `EditorFrame` contains the code that implements the menu actions. The creation of menu item objects is done with the help of method `createMenuItem` of class `MenuFactory`. This method takes, as one of its argument, an object of the functional interface type `EventHandler<ActionEvent>`. Most calls to method `createMenuItem` specify the event handler for a menu item using a lambda expression.

9.6 Functional-Style Data Processing

Up to now, the design ideas presented in this chapter involve introducing functional elements into an otherwise object-oriented design. In some cases, the design context motivates solutions that have a much stronger flavor of functional-style programming. One scenario where functional-style programming shines is to structure code responsible for processing a collection of data. In a way, most of what software does is to process data, so here we can tighten the definition and consider that functional-style programming provides good support for design problems that involve applying transformations to sequences of data elements. An example of data processing that meets this definition is counting the number of acronyms in a body of text. In this case, the input is a sequence of words, and the transformations are to filter the input for acronyms, and then to compute the total number of instances found.

Functional-style design is a good match for this type of data processing because it naturally calls for the use of behavior parameterization and higher-order functions. Higher-order functions implement the general data-processing strategies, which are then parameterized for a particular context with first-class functions. In the text-processing example above, the general strategy is to check whether each input element (a word) matches a certain predicate (acronym or not). Although the general strategy of filtering over a predicate is likely to apply to many different problems, the predicate itself (acronym detection) is specific to the particular design context. In other cases we might want to write code that detects short words, proper nouns, etc. This idiom can be illustrated by the statement:

```
data.higherOrderFunction(firstClassFunction);
```

Applied to our current example, this would mean:

```
listOfWords.filter(isAcronym);
```

Functional-style data processing is a major topic in software design. This section provides a basic overview of the main concepts and techniques that underlie this design style, and how to realize them in Java.

Data as a Stream

The main concept that enables functional-style data processing in Java and similar technologies is that of a *stream*. Simply stated, a stream is a sequence of data elements, a bit like a collection. However, the major conceptual difference between a stream and a collection is that a collection represents a *store* of data whereas a stream represents a *flow* of data. This distinction is similar to the difference between storing music as a file vs. playing music via an on-line streaming service. For software design, the distinction between collections and streams has many practical implications:

- Elements in a collection have to exist before they are added to the collection, but elements in a stream can be computed on-demand.

- Although collections can only store a finite number of elements, streams can technically be infinite. For example, although it is not possible to define a list that contains all the even numbers, it is possible to create a stream that produces this data.
- Collections can be traversed multiple times, but the traversal code is located outside the collection, for example in a `for` loop or iterator class. In contrast, streams can only be traversed once: their elements are *consumed* as part of the traversal. However, the traversal code is hidden within the higher-order functions provided by the stream's interface.
- Streams are amenable to being parallelized, mainly because the traversal of their elements is hidden as part of the stream abstraction.

An additional, more pragmatic, difference relates to the evolution of the Java language. Collection classes (`List`, `Set`, etc.) were released before the language had explicit support for first-class functions, so collections provide almost no support for higher-order functions.[9] In contrast, Java 8 provides support for first-class functions (in the form of method references and lambda expressions) and includes a powerful `Stream` API designed to support functional-style design. The remainder of this section shows how to design functional-style data processing in Java using the `Stream` API.

In Java, a simple way to obtain a stream is to call the `stream()` method on an instance of a collection class. For example, if we have a method to return the list of cards in an instance of the `Deck` class, we can also stream this data. Figure 9.2 shows the structures involved.

Fig. 9.2 Version of the `Deck` and `CardStack` classes with methods for returning the cards they contain

Obtaining a stream of cards from the deck is then just a matter of calling `stream()` or the output of `cards()`:

```
new Deck().cards().stream();
```

By themselves, streams already support many useful (non-higher-order) functions. For example, we can count the elements in the stream:

```
Stream<Card> cards = new Deck().cards().stream();
long total = cards.count();
```

Streams also support operations that take a stream as their implicit argument and output a different stream. This process is called *pipelining*. For example, the `sorted`

---

[9] The notable exception is the default method `forEach` available on the `Iterable<T>` interface since Java 8.

method returns the elements of the original stream in sorted order. Because method `sorted()` requires the instances in the stream to be subtypes of `Comparable`, the code below assumes the version of class `Card` used implements `Comparable`:

```
Stream<Card> sortedCards = cards.stream().sorted();
```

Pipelining also makes it possible to combine operations on streams. For example, method `limit(int max)` returns up to `max` elements from the stream. To obtain the first ten cards in sorted order, we can thus write:

```
Stream<Card> sortedCards = cards.stream().sorted().limit(10);
```

It is also possible to combine multiple streams. For example, to assemble all the cards from two decks and sort them, we can do:

```
Stream<Card> cards =
  Stream.concat(new Deck().cards().stream(),
    new Deck().cards().stream());
```

To revert to a single deck, one option is to remove the duplicates using `distinct()`:

```
Stream<Card> withDuplicates =
  Stream.concat(new Deck().cards().stream(),
    new Deck().cards().stream());
Stream<Card> withoutDuplicates = withDuplicates.distinct();
```

Applying Higher-Order Functions to Streams

The main way that streams support functional-style programming is that they define a number of higher-order functions. A basic higher-order function for streams is `forEach`, which applies an input *consumer* function to all elements of the stream. For example, to print all cards in a stream in a functional way, we could do the following:

```
new Deck().cards().stream()
  .forEach(card -> System.out.println(card));
```

The method `forEach` takes an argument of type `Consumer<? super T>`, which means we can supply it a reference to a function that defines a single parameter of type `Card` (or any supertype of `Card`). In the example above this reference is supplied in the form of a lambda expression, but we could also use a method reference `System.out::println` (see Section 9.4). Because `forEach` is not guaranteed to respect the order in which elements are encountered in the stream, a second version, `forEachOrdered`, can be used if ordering is important. Because it does not return a stream, the outcome of the `forEach` function (either variant) cannot be further transformed as part of a pipeline. Generally speaking, stream functions that do not produce a stream of results that can be further processed as part of a pipeline are called *terminal* operations. Another example of a terminal operation on streams is the `count` function seen above.

Other types of terminal higher-order functions that can be applied to streams include searching functions such as `allMatch`, `anyMatch`, and `noneMatch`, which take as argument a predicate on the stream element type and return a Boolean value that indicates respectively whether all, any, or none of the elements in the stream evaluate the predicate to `true`. For example, to determine whether all cards in a list are in the Clubs suit, we would do:

```
List<Card> cards = ...;
boolean allClubs = cards.stream()
  .allMatch(card -> card.getSuit() == Suit.CLUBS );
```

Filtering Streams

The `sorted()` stream function, mentioned above, shows how we can define *intermediate* operations to create a pipeline of transformations on a stream. An intermediate operation thus has a stream as an implicit argument, and returns a stream. An important function in this pipelining process is the `filter` method, which takes a `Predicate` and returns a stream that consists of all the elements of the original stream for which the predicate evaluates to true. For example, assuming we want to count the face cards in a list of cards:

```
long numberOfFaceCards = cards.stream()
  .filter(card -> card.getRank().ordinal() >=
    Rank.JACK.ordinal()).count();
```

To leverage the benefits of both object-orientation and functional-style programming, predicates such as the one above are best captured as instance methods:

```
public final class Card {
  public boolean isFaceCard() {
    return getRank().ordinal() >= Rank.JACK.ordinal();
  }
}
```

This allows us to use method references and make the functional code self-explanatory:

```
long numberOfFaceCards = cards.stream()
  .filter(Card::isFaceCard)
  .count();
```

At first glance, capturing predicates in dedicated methods may seem like an obstacle to the creation of compound predicates. For example, what if we want to count only face cards in the Clubs suit? Do we have to revert to our original lambda expression?

```
long result = cards.stream()
  .filter(card -> card.getRank().ordinal() >= Rank.JACK.ordinal()
    && card.getSuit()==Suit.CLUBS).count();
```

A key insight to avoid ugly code like this is to observe that filters, being an intermediate operation, can also be pipelined:

```
long result = cards.stream()
    .filter(Card::isFaceCard)
    .filter(card -> card.getSuit() == Suit.CLUBS)
    .count();
```

At this point, it should become apparent that our functional-style code is starting to look much more like a set of high-level rules for processing data than a set of instructions telling a program how to operate on inputs. Indeed, one major advantage of writing data-processing code in a functional style is that the result is more declarative than imperative, and thus better conveys the intent behind the code. Here, for example, a single glance at the statement shows that we wish to only consider face cards, then further restrict the data to only consider cards in the Clubs suit, and then finally count the data elements. It is also worth noting how the code is formatted, with each stream operation indented and prefixed with its period starting the visible part of a line. This coding style is a usual convention for formatting stream operations in Java. Its benefit is that it emphasizes the declarative nature of the code.

Mapping Data Elements

There are often situations in data processing where we need to transform all data elements in a stream into a derived value. In this case, we leverage the idea of *mapping* objects to their desired value, already introduced in Section 9.4. In functional-style programming, the word *mapping* is employed in the mathematical sense synonymous to a function. For example, consider how the function that computes the square of a number x, usually denoted x^2, actually *maps* a number x to its square $x \cdot x$.

Many programming languages that support some form of functional-style processing provide a mechanism to apply a map (that is, a function) to every element in a data collection. In Java the `Stream` class defines a `map` method that takes as input a parameter of type `Function<? super T, ? extends R>`. In other words, the argument to the `map` function is another function that takes as input an object of type `T` and returns an object of type `R`.[10] This means that the `map` function will transform a stream of objects into another stream where every object is obtained by applying a function to an object in the first stream.

As an example, we can consider a function that maps an instance of `Card` to an instance of an enumerated type `Color` that represents the color of the card's suit. We can apply this function systematically to all elements in a stream using the `map` method:

```
cards.stream().map(card -> card.getSuit().getColor() );
```

If this expression is evaluated on a shuffled deck, the resulting stream will be a random interleaving of the values `Color.BLACK` and `Color.RED`. Because the result is also a stream, we can pipeline the result of a mapping operation as for any other

---

[10] Technically, T or one of its supertypes, and R or one of its subtypes. The same type can be used to instantiate both type parameters T and R.

stream. For example, to count the number of black cards in a collection, we could write:

```
long result = cards.stream()
  .map(card -> card.getSuit().getColor() )
  .filter( color -> color == Color.BLACK )
  .count();
```

Although the same result can be achieved more directly by using `filter` with a lambda expression that retrieves the card's color, the example above illustrates how we can use `map` to unpack an object and use only the part of the object that is of interest for a given computation.

Mapping, however, can accomplish much more than extracting data from an input element. Let us consider a second example, where we want to compute the score that a card represents. In some games, cards are assigned a point value that corresponds to their rank (for instance, Three of Clubs is worth three points), except for face cards which are all worth ten points. With a mapping process, we can convert a stream of card objects into a stream of integers that correspond to the score of each card in the original stream:

```
cards.stream()
  .map(card -> Math.min(10, card.getRank().ordinal() + 1));
```

The result of this expression will be a stream of `Integer` objects that represent the score of each card. As usual, whether to encapsulate the score computation in an instance method of class `Card` is a context-sensitive design decision. If the score value is used in multiple calling contexts, then it would make sense to add a method `getScore()` to the interface of class `Card`. Otherwise, the lambda expression will suffice.

When mapping to numerical values, as in this case, it is useful to know that the language provides specialized support for streams of numbers in the form of classes such as `IntStream` and `DoubleStream`. These types of streams work like other streams, but they define additional operations that only make sense when processing numbers, such as summing the elements in the stream. To adapt our scoring example to get the total score, the code needs to explicitly map to an `IntStream`, and then call the `sum` terminal operation:

```
int total = cards.stream()
  .mapToInt(card -> Math.min(10, card.getRank().ordinal() + 1))
  .sum();
```

As an alternative and more declarative way to specify this computation, we could also do:

```
int total = cards.stream()
  .map(Card::getRank)
  .mapToInt(Rank::ordinal)
  .map(ordinal -> Math.min(10, ordinal + 1))
  .sum();
```

In the examples above, we mapped values one-to-one: `Card` to `Color`, `Card` to `Integer`, `int` to `int`, etc. It some cases, however, we want to be able to operate on a stream created from a structure that involves a one-to-many relation between objects. For example, let us say we have a list of `Deck` instances:

```
List<Deck> listOfDecks = Arrays.asList(new Deck(), new Deck());
```

How can we operate on all the cards reachable through the list? Streaming the list with `deck.stream()` will produce a stream of instances of `Deck`, not `Card`. We need an additional operation to unpack the decks into a stream of cards. We could try mapping using `Deck#cards()`:

```
listOfDecks.stream()
  .map(deck -> deck.cards().stream())
  .forEach(System.out::println);
```

This, however, will not work because the `map` function returns a *stream* of the return type of its argument function. Because the function type of the argument is `Deck → Stream<Card>`, `map` will return an instance of `Stream<Stream<Card>>` when what we want is just `Stream<Card>`. The requirement to map an object to multiple (zero or more) objects can instead be handled using a special kind of mapping function called a *flat map*. Conceptually, a flat map operation maps each input object to a stream, but *merges* the resulting streams into a single one instead of collecting the streams as individual elements of another stream. In Java, this service is provided by method `flatMap`. In our scenario, we would thus use `flatMap` as follows:

```
listOfDecks.stream()
    .flatMap(deck -> deck.cards().stream())
    .forEach(System.out::println);
```

Reducing Streams

When working with streams of data, a common scenario is that we want to not only process each data element, but also do something with the data as a whole. Typically, this means either:

- Aggregating the effect of the operations into a single result. Terminal operations such as `count()` and `sum()` are good examples of data aggregation in that sense;
- Collecting the individual results of the operations into a stored data structure. In Java this would typically mean a `List` or other collection type.

Although they seem different, these alternatives actually have in common that, conceptually, they represent *reducing* a stream to a single entity. In the second case, the entity may be a collection of many elements, but conceptually it is nevertheless a single, stored structure as opposed to a stream. The advantage of generalizing all types of data aggregation as a single high-level operation, reduction, is that it introduces a clear distinction between intermediate operations, namely mapping,[11] and

---

[11] We can consider that filtering is a type of mapping without loss of generality.

terminal operations, namely reducing. In fact programming systems where computation is expressed as a series of mapping operations followed by a reduction operation are commonly known as the *map–reduce programming model*. Although the term *map–reduce* is mostly used in the context of cluster computing, the basic model itself is directly applicable to functional-style programming with streams.

In Java, reduction is supported through various overloaded versions of the `reduce` method available in `Stream` classes. Implementing a reduction from scratch can be tricky, and the complete details are outside the scope of this book. However, the general idea is to provide the `reduce` function with an *accumulator* object that can incrementally update the reduced version of the input every time an element is encountered. For example, to implement the `sum` operation on an `IntStream` using the `reduce` method, the following code is used:

```
IntStream numbers = ...;
int sum = numbers.reduce(0, (a, b) -> a+b);
```

In practice, a summing reduction uses 0 as the base case and accumulates results by iteratively adding elements. The code below shows a simplified mock-up implementation of the `reduce` method for `IntStream`:

```
public int reduce(int pBase, IntBinaryOperator operator) {
    int result = pBase;
    Iterator<Integer> iterator = this.iterator();
    while( iterator.hasNext() ) {
        int number = iterator.next();
        result = operator.applyAsInt(result, number);
    }
    return result;
}
```

Initially, the result of the reduction operation is set to the base provided, in our case 0. Then, for each element in the stream, the binary operator provided as input to `reduce` is applied, using as arguments the current result and the next element in the stream. In our case the binary operator was specified using the lambda expression `(a,b) -> a+b`. Thus, for each element in the stream, the value of the current reduction will be assigned to itself plus the value of the next element.

This being said, because most common reduction operations (`min`, `max`, `count`, `sum`, etc.) are directly supported by the stream classes, it is possible to get started with streams and actually get quite far without mastering the art of writing reductions.

Reductions that serve to accumulate data in a structure are a special case. Let us say we wish to collect all face cards in a list of cards in a separate list. One quick solution would be to use the `forEach` method to store the elements of the stream in the target list:

```
List<Card> result = new ArrayList<>();
cards.stream()
    .filter(Card::isFaceCard)
    .forEach(card -> result.add(card));
```

Although workable, this design loses some of the properties of declarative, functional-style expressions of a computation, because the first-class function that simulates the reduction is implemented using explicit list manipulation operations. As an alternative that supports a more functional style, the Java libraries provide helper methods to create a type of reduction called a *collector*. A collector is a reduction that accumulates elements into a collection. With a collector, the code above can be rewritten as:

```
List<Card> result = cards.stream()
  .filter(Card::isFaceCard)
  .collect(Collectors.toList());
```

In this last example, the details of the implementation of the accumulation of elements into a list remain hidden, and the code directly expresses the desired intent: to collect the elements of the stream into a list.

Code Exploration: JetUML · EditorFrame

Streaming operations on GUI components.

JetUML makes targeted use of the streaming API to streamline some algorithms within methods. Among others, class `EditorFrame` provides two examples. In method `getNumberOfUnsavedDiagrams`, I use stream operations to filter and count the number of graphical user interface *tabs* that contain an unsaved diagram. In method `setMenuVisibility`, I use a flat map to *flatten* top-level menu items and their sub-items into a single stream, which I then filter for some property, and then disable. Searching the project for the string `".stream()"` will reveal numerous other examples of streaming within the code base.

Insights

This chapter introduced functional-style design and the programming language mechanisms that support it, and showed how to employ these mechanisms to embed functional elements into an object-oriented design.

- Consider a solution in the functional style for parts of a design that involve parameterizing behavior;
- Lambda expressions should be short and self-documenting: consider reorganizing your code to make them so;
- Favor short lambda expressions where the body is also an expression (as opposed to a sequence of statements);
- To emphasize flexibility and extensibility in your design, use library functional interfaces to define function types; to emphasize design constraints and intent, use application-defined functional interfaces;

- When designing methods, keep in mind how they could be used through references: ensure they are a good match for likely functional interfaces;
- Compose functions using functions, as opposed to imperative statements;
- Use the helper methods of library types to compose functionality in intuitive ways;
- Consider using supplier, consumer, and mapping function types to parameterize behavior;
- Consider defining strategies in the STRATEGY pattern as functional interfaces;
- Consider the possibility of composing strategies;
- Consider using first-class functions to define abstract observers in the OBSERVER pattern;
- Structure data-processing code so that it is more declarative than imperative in style;
- Use the mapping abstract operation to convert data elements into the values that are directly used by a computation;
- Use collector objects to accumulate the result of stream operations.

Further Reading

An excellent resource for diving more deeply into functional-style programming in Java is the book *Java 8 in Action* by Urma et al. [16]. The book is for experienced programmers, but it provides an accessible introduction to the topic and a progressive treatment, which allows the reader to go as far as they are comfortable with. In terms of code style, *Effective Java* by Bloch [1] includes a chapter *Lambdas and Streams* which provides additional coaching on using these mechanisms in practice. The advice therein is consistent with the recommendations provided in this chapter, but includes additional discussions and examples.

For a more pragmatic review of the topic, the Java Tutorial [10] has a section on *Lambda Expressions* which also covers method references. The section of the tutorial on collections also covers streams, in a subsection titled *Aggregate Operations*.

Appendix A
Important Java Programming Concepts

This appendix provides a brief orientation through the concepts of object-oriented programming in Java that are critical for understanding the material in this book and that are not specifically introduced as part of the main content. It is not intended as a general Java programming primer, but rather as a refresher and orientation through the features of the language that play a major role in the design of software in Java. If necessary, this overview should be complemented by an introductory book on Java programming, or by the relevant sections in the Java Tutorial [10].

A.1 Variables and Types

Variables store values. In Java, variables are typed and the type of the variable must be declared before the name of the variable. Java distinguishes between two major categories of types: *primitive* types and *reference* types. Primitive types are used to represent numbers and Boolean values. Variables of a primitive type store the actual data that represents the value. When the content of a variable of a primitive type is assigned to another variable, a copy of the data stored in the initial variable is created and stored in the destination variable. For example:

```
int original = 10;
int copy = original;
```

In this case variable `original` of the primitive type `int` (short for *integer*) is assigned the integer literal value `10`. In the second assignment, a copy of the value 10 is used to initialize the new variable `copy`.

Reference types represent more complex arrangements of data as defined by classes (see Section A.2). The important thing to know about references types is that a variable of a reference type T stores a *reference* to an object of type T. Hence, values of reference types are not the data itself, but a reference to this data. The main implication is that copying a value means sharing a reference. Arrays are also reference types. For example:

```
int[] original = new int[] {1,2};
int[] copy = original;
copy[0] = 3;
int result = original[0]; // result == 3
```

In this case, `copy` is assigned the value stored in `original`. However, because the value stored in `original` is a reference to an object of an array type, the copy also refers to the object created in the first statement. Because, in effect, `copy` is only a different name (or *alias*) for `original`, modifying an element in `copy` also modifies that element in `original`.

A.2 Objects and Classes

Essentially, an *object* is a cohesive group of variables that store pieces of data that correspond to a given abstraction, and methods that apply to this abstraction. For example, an object to represent the abstraction *book* could include, among others, the book's title, author name, and publication year. In Java, the *class* is the compile-time entity that defines how to build objects. For example, the class:

```
class Book {
  String title;
  String author;
  int year;
}
```

states that objects intended to represent a book will have three *instance variables* named `title`, `author`, and `year` of type `String`, `String`, and `int`, respectively. In addition to serving as a template for creating objects, classes also define a corresponding reference type. Objects are created from classes through a process of instantiation with the `new` keyword:

```
Book book = new Book();
```

The statement above creates a new *instance* (object) of class `Book` and stores a *reference* to this object in variable `book` declared to be of reference type `Book`. Instance variables, also known as *fields*, can be accessed by *dereferencing* a variable that stores a reference to the object. The dereferencing operator is the period (`.`). For example, to obtain the title of a book stored in a variable `book`, we do:

```
String title = book.title;
```

When discussing software design, it is good to avoid subconsciously using the terms *class* and *object* interchangeably. Objects and classes are different concepts. A class is a compile-time entity that does not exist in running code. Conversely, objects are run-time entities that do not have any representation in program source code. Mixing them up can lead to ambiguity and confusion.

A.3 Static Fields

Java allows the declaration of *static fields*:

```
class Book {
   static int MIN_PAGES = 50;
   String title;
   String author;
   int year;
}
```

The effect of declaring a field `static` means that the field is not associated with any object. Rather, a single copy of the field is created when the corresponding class is loaded by the Java virtual machine, and the field exists for the duration of the program's execution. Access to static fields can be restricted to only the code of the class in which it is declared using the access modifier `private`. If declared to be `public`, a static field can be accessed by any code in the application, in which case it effectively constitutes a *global variable*. Because it is generally a bad practice to modify globally-accessible data, global variables are best defined as *constants*, that is, values not meant to be changed. Globally-accessible constants are declared with the modifiers `public`, `static`, and `final`, and typically named using uppercase letters (see Appendix B).

```
class Book {
   public static final int MIN_PAGES = 50;
   ...
}
```

Static fields are accessed in classes other than the class that declares them by prefixing their name with the name of their declaring class, followed by a period. For example:

```
int minNumberOfPages = Book.MIN_PAGES;
```

A.4 Methods

In Java and other object-oriented programming languages, a *method* is the abstraction for a piece of computation. A method definition includes a return type, a name, a (possibly empty) list of parameters, a (possibly empty) list of exceptions that can be thrown by the method, and a method body. The return type can be replaced by the keyword `void` to indicate that the method does not return a value. The method body comprises the statements that form the implementation of the method.

Methods correspond to procedures in procedural languages and functions in functional languages. Java supports two main categories of methods: *static* methods and *instance* methods. Static methods are essentially procedures, or "non-object-oriented" methods. Although they are declared in a class for reasons discussed in Chapter 2, they are not automatically related to any object of the class and must

explicitly list all their parameters in their signature. Method `abs(int)`, declared in
the library class `java.lang.Math`, is a typical example of a static method. It takes
an integer as an input and returns an integer that is the absolute value of the input
number: no object is involved in this computation. Static methods are declared with
the `static` modifier:

```
static int abs(int a) {...}
```

and called by prefixing the name of the method with the name of the class that
declares the method, for example:

```
int absolute = Math.abs(-4);
```

Another example of a static method would be a method `getTitle(Book book)`
that returns the title of a book. Because this is a static method, it requires all necessary data to be provided as input:

```
class Book {
  String title;
  ...
  static String getTitle(Book book) {
    return book.title;
  }
}
```

In contrast, instance methods are methods intended to operate on a specific instance of a class. For this reason, instance methods have an *implicit parameter* of
the same type as the type of the class they are declared in. For example, because
method `getTitle(Book)` operates on an instance of class `Book`, it makes more
sense to declare it as an instance method of class `Book`. In this case, the parameter
`book` becomes *implicit*: it is not declared in the method's list of parameters, and its
corresponding value becomes accessible inside the body of the method in a special
variable called `this`. The code for `getTitle` written as an instance method is thus:

```
class Book {
  String title;
  ...
  String getTitle() {
    return this.title;
  }
}
```

An instance method gets invoked by dereferencing a variable that stores a reference to an object. The result of the process is that the object referenced becomes the
implicit argument to the instance method. In the statement:

```
Book book = ...;
String title = book.getTitle();
```

the object referenced by variable `book` becomes bound to the `this` pseudo-variable
within the body of `getTitle()`.

A.5 Packages and Importing

Compilation units that declare types such as classes are organized into *packages*. Types declared to be in one package can be referenced from code in a different package using their *fully-qualified name*. A fully-qualified name consists of the name of the type in the package prefixed by the package name. For example, class `Random` of package `java.util` is a pseudo-random number generator. Its fully-qualified name is `java.util.Random`. Declaring a variable using a fully-qualified name can be rather verbose:

```
java.util.Random randomNumberGenerator = new java.util.Random();
```

For this reason, it is possible to *import* types from another package using the `import` statement at the top of a Java source code file:

```
import java.util.Random;
```

This makes it possible to refer to the imported type using its simple name (here `Random`) instead of the fully-qualified name. In Java, the import statement is only a mechanism to avoid having to refer to various program elements using fully-qualified names. In contrast to other languages, it does not have the effect of making libraries available that were not already available through their fully-qualified name.

In addition to importing types, Java also makes it possible to import static fields and methods. For example, instead of referring to the `abs` method of class `java.util.Math` as `Math.abs`, we can statically import it:

```
import static java.lang.Math.abs;
```

and then just refer to `abs` in the code:

```
int absolute = abs(-4);
```

In the code fragments in this book, all types referenced in the code are assumed to be imported. When necessary, the surrounding text will clarify the source of the imported type.

A.6 Generic Types

A type definition can depend on another type. For example, we can consider the following type `OptionalString`, which may hold a `String` (the concept of the optional type is covered in more detail in Section 4.5):

```
public class OptionalString {
  String object = null;

  OptionalString(String object) {
    this.object = object;
  }
```

```
boolean isPresent() {
  return object != null;
}

String get() {
  return object;
}
}
```

A class such as this one could, in principle, be used to wrap any other kind of reference type. For this reason, it is useful to be able to *parameterize* some of the types that a class depends on. This concept is supported in Java through *generic types*. Generic types are type declarations that include one or more *type parameters*. Type parameters are specified in angle brackets after the type name. In the declaration of a type, a type parameter acts as a placeholder for an actual type, which will be supplied when the generic type is used. Class OptionalString can be rewritten to work with any reference type by parameterizing the type of the object it holds:

```
class Optional<T> {
  T object = null;

  Optional(T object) {
    this.object = object;
  }

  boolean isPresent() {
    return object != null;
  }

  T get() {
    return object;
  }
}
```

In the above code, the letter T does not represent an actual type, but a parameter (i.e., a placeholder) that is replaced by the actual type when the generic type is used:

```
Optional<String> myString = new Optional<>();
```

The type declaration for variable myString includes a *type instance* String. The effect of this type parameter instantiation is to replace the type parameter T with String everywhere in the declaration of Optional<T>. In the corresponding constructor call, the argument of the type parameter can be inferred, so an empty set of angle brackets (<>) need only be provided. This empty set of angle brackets is also called the *diamond operator*.

Generic types are used extensively in the library implementations of abstract data types (see Section A.7). Other features that involve generic types include generic methods, type bounds, and type wildcards. This book does not delve into the design of generic types because it is a relatively specialized topic. The content occasionally uses generic types to elaborate design solutions, but to the extent possible, these are limited to the basic instantiation of type parameters.

A.7 Collection Classes

Many of the examples in this book use library implementations of abstract data types (list, set, etc.). In Java, this set of classes is commonly referred to as the *Collections framework*, and located in the package `java.util`. Collection classes are generic (see Section A.6). This means that the type of the elements held in a collection, such as an `ArrayList`, is a parameter that is provided when the collection type is used. For example, the following statement declares and instantiates a list of `String` instances:

```
ArrayList<String> myStrings = new ArrayList<>();
```

A comprehensive knowledge of the Collections frameworks is not necessary to appreciate the material in the book. However, at a minimum, readers should be familiar with the interface types `List<T>`, `Set<T>`, and `Map<T>` as well as their commonly used implementations `ArrayList<T>`, `HashSet<T>`, and `HashMap<T>`.

A.8 Exception Handling

Java provides a way for methods to indicate when they cannot complete normally through an *exception-handling* mechanism. In Java, exceptions are objects of a type that is a subtype of `Throwable`. To throw an exception, an exception object must be first created, and then thrown using the `throw` keyword:

```
void setMonth(int month) {
  if( month < 1 || month > 12)
    throw new InvalidDateException();
}
```

Throwing an exception causes the control flow of the executing code to jump to a point in the code where the exception can be handled, unwinding the call stack as it goes. To handle an exception, it is necessary to declare a `try` block with one or more `catch` clauses. A `catch` clauses declares a variable of an exception type. An exception raised in or propagated into a `try` block is *caught* by the block's `catch` clause if the type of the exception can be legally assigned (through subtyping) to the exception variable. In this example:

```
try {
  calendar.setMonth(13);
} catch( InvalidDateException e ) {
  System.out.println(e.getMessage());
}
```

the call to `setMonth` throws an exception of type `InvalidDateException` which is immediately caught by the `catch` clause and bound to the variable `e`, which can then be dereferenced, for example to retrieve the message of the exception. If the type of the `catch` clause had been something else (for example `NumberFormatException`), the exception would not have been caught, and would have propagated to the previous enclosing `try` block in the control flow.

Appendix B
Coding Conventions

Coding conventions are guidelines for organizing the presentation of source code. Aspects that fall under coding conventions include naming conventions, indentation, use of spaces, and line length. Following a set of coding conventions can help improve the readability of the code and prevent some types of errors. Coding conventions can vary from one organization to another because of cultural or practical reasons (each convention has its advantages and disadvantages).

In this appendix, I highlight of the coding conventions used in this book and in the example projects (see Appendix C). For an extensive discussion of coding conventions and why they matter, see Chapters 2, 4, and 5 of the book *Clean Code: A Handbook of Agile Software Craftmanship* by Robert C. Martin [7].

Medial Capitals for Identifier Names

As is usual in Java, the identifier names use medial capitalization, also known as camel case. With medial capitalization, words in a phrase are in lower case and each new word in the phrase starts with an uppercase letter. Type names start with an uppercase letter (e.g., `ArrayList`, `HashMap`) and method names start with a lowercase letter (e.g., `indexOf`, `replaceAll`). Instance variables (i.e., fields), class variables (i.e., static fields), and local variable names also follow medial capitalization, but with a special convention for fields (see below).

All Capitals for Constants

Constants (i.e., fields declared static and final) are named in all uppercase letters, with an underscore separating words (e.g., `WINDOW_SIZE`).

© Springer Nature Switzerland AG 2022
M. P. Robillard, *Introduction to Software Design with Java*,
https://doi.org/10.1007/978-3-030-97899-0

Variable Name Prefixes

Field names are prefixed with a lowercase `a` (for *attribute*, a synonym for field), e.g., `aData`. Method parameter types are camel-cased and prefixed with a lowercase `p` (for *parameter*), e.g., (`pData`). Local variables are camel-cased and start with a lowercase letter, without a prefix (e.g., `data`). The only exception to these guidelines is for the names of the parameters in lambda expressions, which are named like local variables. The advantages of this convention are:

- Within a code block, it is always possible to determine what type of variable a name refers to without having to navigate to the declaration of this variable;
- The convention eliminates the risk of having a local variable hide a field by reusing the same name;
- The convention eliminates the necessity to use the `this` keyword to disambiguate a field that has the same name as a method or constructor parameter (e.g., `this.data = data;`).

The systematic use of prefixes is one of the rare points where I disagree with the advice of Robert C. Martin (referenced above). He states:

> Your classes and functions should be small enough that you don't need [prefixes]. And you should be using an editing environment that highlights or colorizes members to make them distinct. [7, p. 24]

Although desirable, both conditions (small classes and the use of an editor) are not guaranteed to hold. In particular, viewing code hosted on a website such as GitHub or reading it in a book means we cannot always rely on dynamic code highlighting tools. In a book that makes extensive use of partial code fragments, the prefixes are also helpful for providing the necessary context for a name.

Code blocks, braces, and indentation

In Java, code blocks are defined with *braces*. There are two families of conventions for structuring code blocks in Java, based on where the opening brace is located. A first style is to locate the opening brace on the same line as its corresponding declaration or statement:

```
String getTitle() {
   return title;
}
```

An alternative style is to position the braces on their own line such that corresponding braces are vertically aligned:

```
String getTitle()
{
   return title;
}
```

In either case, code statements within a block are indented by one unit (typically four spaces or one tab character) with respect to the statement or declaration that introduces the block. In the book, I use the same-line variant because it is more compact and thus amenable to presentation in a book. In the sample code available on-line, I instead use the vertically-aligned variant because, without the space constraint, it makes the scope of a code block more salient.

Use of the `@Override` Annotation

Methods intended to override an inherited method or implement an interface method are annotated with `@Override`:

```
@Override
public String toString() {
   return String.format("[w=%d x h=%d]", aWidth, aHeight);
}
```

Code Comments

Classes and interfaces should include a Javadoc [9] header comment, along with the methods they declare. In-line comments are kept to a minimum.

Ellipses and Adaptations

Code in the example applications follows these coding conventions strictly. However, for code fragments in the chapter content I make various concessions for conciseness.

In particular, code fragments should not be assumed to constitute complete implementations. In most cases, I silently elide parts of the code not essential to the discussion. When there is a risk of ambiguity, I use an ellipsis (. . .) to indicate elision, either in a block of code or in the parameter list of a method signature or argument list of a method call.

I also use an indentation tighter than four characters. For one-line methods, I may also inline the statement and both curly braces. If necessary to avoid a page break in a code fragment, I place the body of the method on the same line as its signature. I will also typically not include the comments and `@Override` annotation. The code below is a version of the `toString()` method above with the three adaptations discussed:

```
public String toString() { return String.format(...); }
```

Appendix C
Sample Applications

Reading and trying to understand existing code is an essential part of learning software design. The two software projects described below provide sample code in the form of complete working applications.

Both applications were developed following the principles and techniques presented in this book. Throughout the chapters, brief sections titled *Code Exploration* illustrate how some of the material presented in the chapter is applied in practice. To maximally benefit from the sample applications, I recommend downloading a local copy of the code. The *Code Exploration* sections are indexed with the name of the application followed by the class where the relevant code can be found. The intent for this structure is to facilitate diving into code with a minimum of effort by using the *open file* shortcut key combination available in most development environments.

The two applications offer distinct levels of challenge in code understanding. The complete source code and installation and usage instructions can be found on GitHub at the URLs indicated below.

Solitaire

The first application, *Solitaire*, implements the card game of the same name. This application serves as the context for many of the running examples in the book. It realizes some non-trivial requirements while remaining of overall manageable complexity. It should thus be possible to understand the general architecture of this project and many of the detailed design and implementation decisions after a few months of study. For some of the discussions in the chapters, knowledge of the game terminology will be useful. Figure C.1 illustrates the layout of a game of Solitaire in progress and includes overlays to indicate important terms. At the top-left is the *deck* of face-down cards. A user *draws* a card from the deck and places it face up in the *discard pile*. The four piles at the top right of the layout are the *foundation piles* (these can be empty). Finally, the seven piles of cards that fan downwards are jointly called the *tableau* (tableau piles can also be empty). The code discussed in the book is consistent with Release 1.2.

```
https://github.com/prmr/Solitaire
```

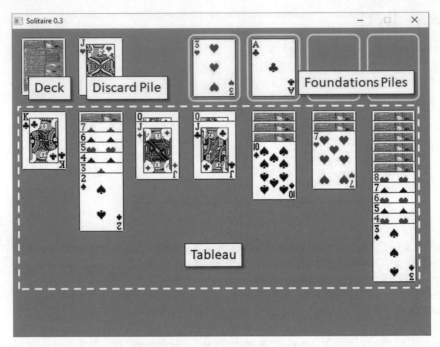

Fig. C.1 Domain terminology for the Solitaire card game

JetUML

The second application, *JetUML*, is the interactive tool used to create all of the UML diagrams in this book. Although still modest in size compared to many software applications, it can be considered real production code and its design involves some decisions that go beyond the material covered in the book. The code discussed is consistent with Release 3.3.

https://github.com/prmr/JetUML

References

1. Joshua Bloch. *Effective Java*. Addison-Wesley, 3rd edition, 2018.
2. Frank Buschmann, Kevin Henney, and Douglas C. Schmidt. *Pattern-Oriented Software Architecture Volume 4: A Pattern Language for Distributed Computing*. Wiley, 2007.
3. Martin Fowler. *Refactoring: Improving the Design of Existing Code*. Addison-Wesley, 1999.
4. Martin Fowler. *Patterns of Enterprise Application Architecture*. Addison-Wesley Professional, 2002.
5. Martin Fowler. *UML Distilled: A Brief Guide to the Standard Object Modeling Language*. Addison-Wesley, 3rd edition, 2004.
6. Erich Gamma, Richard Helm, Ralph Johnson, and John Vlissides. *Design Patterns: Elements of Reusable Object-Oriented Software*. Addison-Wesley Professional, 1994.
7. Robert C. Martin. *Clean Code: A Handbook of Agile Software Craftmanship*. Prentice Hall, 2009.
8. Bertrand Meyer. Applying "design by contract". *Computer*, 25(10):40–51, 1992.
9. Oracle. How to write doc comments for the Javadoc tool. `https://www.oracle.com/technetwork/java/javase/documentation/index-137868.html`. Accessed 21-Oct-2021.
10. Oracle. The Java tutorials. `https://docs.oracle.com/javase/tutorial/`. Accessed 21-Oct-2021.
11. David Lorge Parnas. On the criteria to be used in decomposing systems into modules. *Communications of the ACM*, 15(12):1053–1058, 1972.
12. David Lorge Parnas. Software aging. In *Proceedings of the 16th ACM/IEEE International Conference on Software Engineering*, pages 279–287, 1994.
13. Mauro Pezzè and Michal Young. *Software Testing and Analysis: Process, Principles and Techniques*. Wiley, 2007.
14. Martin P. Robillard. Sustainable software design. In *Proceedings of the 24th ACM SIGSOFT International Symposium on the Foundations of Software Engineering*, pages 920–923, 2016.
15. James Rumbaugh, Ivar Jacobson, and Grady Booch. *The Unified Modeling Language Manual*. Addison-Wesley, 2nd edition, 2004.
16. Raoul-Gabriel Urma, Mario Fusco, and Alan Mycroft. *Java 8 in Action*. Manning, 2015.
17. Oliver Vogel, Ingo Arnold, Arif Chughtai, and Timo Kehrer. *Software Architecture: A Comprehensive Framework and Guide for Practitioners*. Springer, 2011.

© Springer Nature Switzerland AG 2022
M. P. Robillard, *Introduction to Software Design with Java*,
https://doi.org/10.1007/978-3-030-97899-0

Index

Printed in the United States
by Baker & Taylor Publisher Services